RECYCLED LIVES

CHILDREN OF LUCIFER
The Origins of Modern Religious Satanism
Ruben van Luijk

SATANIC FEMINISM
Lucifer as the Liberator of Woman in Nineteenth-Century Culture
Per Faxneld

THE SIBLYS OF LONDON
A Family on the Esoteric Fringes of Gregorian England
Susan Sommers

WHAT IS IT LIKE TO BE DEAD?
Near-Death Experiences, Christianity, and the Occult
Jens Schlieter

AMONG THE SCIENTOLOGISTS
History, Theology, and Praxis
Donald A. Westbrook

RECYCLED LIVES
A History of Reincarnation in Blavatsky's Theosophy
Julie Chajes

RECYCLED LIVES

A HISTORY OF REINCARNATION IN BLAVATSKY'S THEOSOPHY

Julie Chajes

OXFORD
UNIVERSITY PRESS

OXFORD
UNIVERSITY PRESS

Oxford University Press is a department of the University of Oxford. It furthers
the University's objective of excellence in research, scholarship, and education
by publishing worldwide. Oxford is a registered trade mark of Oxford University
Press in the UK and certain other countries.

Published in the United States of America by Oxford University Press
198 Madison Avenue, New York, NY 10016, United States of America.

CIP data is on file at the Library of Congress
ISBN 978-0-19-090913-0

1 3 5 7 9 8 6 4 2

Printed by Sheridan Books, Inc., United States of America

For my father, Tony,
and dedicated to the memory of my mother, Rejane.

CONTENTS

———◆———

ACKNOWLEDGEMENTS

———◆———

In the brief years between the submission of my doctorate and the completion of the book manuscript, what seems an unusually large number of friends and relatives have died. From the seemingly blessed naiveté of youth, I was initiated into a truer appreciation of impermanence, and at an age that was probably younger than average. Meanwhile, I was writing about how people thought about death. I developed empathy for my subjects. They were no strangers to sorrow, and Helena Blavatsky—whose rebirth doctrines are the subject of this book—was no exception. Her mother died when she was only ten, one of her brothers already having died in infancy. Perhaps Blavatsky found solace in an occult doctrine that taught that nothing was insignificant, not the life or death of even the smallest creature. Within the ever-progressing cosmic 'hall of mirrors' she described, the life of every being was an integral part of a process that would find its culmination in God's self-knowledge. Thus ever-connected, all humans, animals, plants, and even minerals were the children of the universe and an intrinsic component of its evolving fabric. Against contemporary Spiritualists, Blavatsky argued we would not meet our loved ones in the form in which we had known them. Nevertheless, they were bound to us forever.

I too have been linked to others in meaningful ways through the production of this book. I am blessed with a wonderful community of friends who are like a large adopted family, and whose members have each, consciously or unconsciously, contributed to my well-being and productivity during the peregrinations that led to this book. Marc Epstein and Ági Veto supported me at the beginning of what was to be a long and difficult journey. Orly and Josh Lauffer hosted me and my family in their beautiful home for several significant life events. David and Sarah Benjamin, among many other remarkable acts of kindness, let me finish the doctoral thesis on which this book was based in their house when I desperately needed a quiet writing space. Elisheva and Barrie Rapoport have kept me sane, each in their own unique way, and Sara and Eliahu Shiffmann are the dearest of friends and substitute grandparents to my son. Many other friends have offered their support, and I can only apologise that there is not enough space to mention any more, other than the four girlfriends with whom I have been especially close in recent years: Lee Hod, Jelena Shapir, Rosella De Jong, and Shifra Goldberg.

Moving on to those who have had the most direct impact on the present volume, the Blavatsky Trust provided me with the grant that enabled me to finish the manuscript. Without them, this book would probably not exist. I thank all the trustees, but particularly the president, Colin Price. Clare Goodrick-Clarke, widow of my PhD adviser, Professor Nicholas Goodrick-Clarke, played an indispensable role in getting me the grant. Clare believed that a good way to continue Nicholas's legacy was through his students. I hope I would have made him proud and it is my belief that a part of him lives on in this book. My debt to him (whose suggestion it was that I even work on Blavatsky in the first place) is the greatest.

Having lost my PhD adviser just months after I was awarded my doctorate, it fell to others to offer a helping hand to a young scholar. Extra special thanks go to Professor Karl Baier for his continuing support and generosity of spirit. I owe too a debt of gratitude to Professor Boaz Huss, my postdoctoral supervisor at Ben-Gurion University of the Negev; Professor Yossi ben Artzi, who gave me my first postdoctoral fellowship, at the University of Haifa; and Professor Yossi Schwartz, who hosted me at Tel Aviv University. Thanks to Professor Christian

Wiese and the team at the *Forschungskolleg* in Bad Homburg, I spent a blissful month in academic paradise. Professor Steven Weitzman, Dr. Natalie Dohrman, and all the staff at the Herbert D. Katz Center for Advanced Judaic Studies at the University of Pennsylvania made my stay in Philadelphia a particularly enjoyable and fruitful one. Finally, my thanks to the donors who keep the Katz Center afloat (especially Eloise Wood, who funded my fellowship) and to Professor David Ruderman, the former director, who has the rare and wonderful talent of encouraging me to be at the top of my game.

If there is a place in heaven reserved for teachers and mentors, there is a special corner of it reserved for people like Professors Jim Moore and Joy Dixon, both of whom offered me their expert feedback without ever having met me, after I had the bare-faced cheek of contacting them by email. In this age of overburden, I consider these acts of extraordinary generosity. My thanks too to Projit Mukhariji, Mriganka Mukhopadhyay, Vadim Putzu, Erin Prophet, Jake Poller, Joseph Tyson, and James Santucci for reading and commenting on material that is included in this book, as well as to Cathy Gutierrez, Christine Ferguson, Jean-Pierre Brach, Olav Hammer, Maria Carlson, Aren Roukema, and Jimmy Elwing for their various kindnesses. Erica Georgiades and Massimo Introvigne were generous with their help when it came to the tricky question of what to put on the cover. John Patrick Deveney, Marc Demarest, John Buescher, Robert Gilbert, and Leslie Price are, all five of them, living, breathing libraries of Theosophical, Spiritualist, and occultist history. They have helped me locate sources and read and commented on my work. Marc, Pat, and John have also amused me with their irreverent banter and ironic take on the period we study, a contribution I value tremendously. Marc Demarest and colleagues' database of Spiritualist, occultist, and Theosophical periodicals, iapsop. com, is a phenomenal achievement that will serve many future generations of scholars. It has opened up research vistas I could not have dreamt of when I began my doctorate.

Thanks go to my parents, Anthony Hall and Rejane Gomes de Mattos Hall; my grandparents, Edith and Murilo Gomes de Mattos and Giuliana and Leslie Hall; as well as my brother Joseph. My husband, Yossi Chajes, has supported me in many ways over what is now the best part of a decade, and has provided much inspiration. His children from his first marriage, Ktoret, Levana, Yoel, and Nehora, are the best siblings my son Yishai could have hoped for. Yishai has contributed to the production of this book by forcing me to keep to a strict schedule. He has also revealed to me a type of love I was unaware of before he came into the world, and taught me the unique joy of being bathed in a child's laughter, the perfect antidote to the types of malaise that sometimes arise from spending long hours at a desk.

Finally, I thank Helena Blavatsky herself, without whom this book could never have been written. Independent, intelligent, and unconventional, Blavatsky was certainly a very interesting person, if, at times, also a difficult one. These are precisely the qualities I would usually enjoy in a friend.

Introduction

AN INFORMAL SURVEY OF your friends and relatives may reveal that many of them believe in reincarnation and karma in some form, or at least do not dismiss them out of hand. Research shows this to be the case for a sizeable minority (around 20 per cent) of people in the Western world who have no particular connection with Eastern religions.[1] In Asian countries, reincarnation as an animal may be considered an undesirable possibility, but in Europe and America, reincarnation is usually thought of as a return to life in a human body for the purpose of spiritual advancement or self-improvement.[2] After two millennia of the virtual absence of any such doctrine in the Christian world, how has this particular belief suddenly become so unremarkable?

This study explores the seminal contribution of one woman: the notorious Russian occultist and 'great-grandmother' of the New Age

---

[1] Perry Schmidt-Leukel, *Transformation by Integration: How Inter-Faith Encounter Changes Christianity* (London: SCM Press, 2009), 68. The 'West' is a problematic category that I use here only for the sake of convenience. For a summary of problems relating to its use, see Kennet Granholm, 'Locating the West: Problematizing the *Western* in Western Esotericism and Occultism', in *Occultism in a Global Perspective*, ed. Henrik Bogdan and Gordan Djurdjevic (Durham: Acumen, 2013).

[2] Tony Walter and Helen Waterhouse, 'Lives-Long Learning: The Effects of Reincarnation Belief on Everyday Life in England', *Nova Religio* 5, no. 1 (October 2001). For a recent exploration of reincarnation belief, see Lee Irwin, *Reincarnation in America: An Esoteric History* (Lantam, MD, and London: Lexington Books, 2017). For a shorter treatment, see Lee Irwin, 'Reincarnation in America: A Brief Historical Overview', *Religions* 8, no. 10 (October 2017).

Movement, Helena Petrovna Blavatsky (1831–1891). Blavatsky was one of the leading figures of the nineteenth-century 'occult revival', a period during which there was a relative surge in popular interest in all things esoteric, mystical, and magical.[3] Occultism found distinctive expressions in Britain, mainland Europe, and America, where it interconnected with currents such as Spiritualism, Mesmerism, and Freemasonry, all of which reached a peak more or less around the middle decades of the century. Blavatsky was the matriarch and primary theorist of the most influential occultist organisation of the late-nineteenth and early-twentieth centuries, the Theosophical Society, founded in New York in 1875. In addition to fourteen volumes of collected writings and several other books, Blavatsky was the author of two Theosophical treatises: *Isis Unveiled* (1877) and *The Secret Doctrine* (1888). These works had a lasting impact on the occult revival, related twentieth-century developments, and ultimately on the development of the New Age Movement, that loosely organised and diffuse spiritual and political movement that arose from the counterculture of the 1960s and 1970s, initially in America.[4] The New Age was one of the most far-reaching cultural and religious developments of the late twentieth century, and Blavatsky's ideas are fundamental to understanding its emergence, as well as the emergence of modern and postmodern forms of religion more generally.

Blavatsky instructed her followers in what she claimed was an ancient wisdom tradition, the true, esoteric teachings underlying all religion, philosophy, and science. Sages throughout history had supposedly taught the principles of this doctrine, which had been brought

[3] The term 'revival' is problematic, as it implies the *reappearance* of an occult that existed previously. I use the term here without this implication.
[4] On the connection between reincarnation belief in present-day America, New Age, and Theosophy, see Courtney Bender, 'American Reincarnations: What the Many Lives of Past Lives Tell Us about Contemporary Spiritual Practice', *Journal of the American Academy of Religion* 75, no. 3 (September 2007). On the New Age Movement in general, see Paul Heelas's pioneering study, *The New Age Movement: The Celebration of the Self and the Sacralization of Modernity* (Oxford: Blackwell, 1996). On the definition of New Age, see George D. Chrysiddes, 'Defining the New Age', in *Handbook of the New Age*, ed. Daren Kemp and James R. Lewis (Leiden: Brill, 2007). See also James R. Lewis, 'Science and the New Age', in *Handbook of the New Age*.

from the continent of Atlantis before its submersion. Its tenets had been handed down from master to pupil, with initiates taking responsibility for transmitting them from one generation to the next. Blavatsky claimed aspects of the ancient wisdom were still discernible within the world's religions and mythologies, but only when interpreted correctly. This was because throughout the centuries, they had been corrupted through misunderstanding and deliberate falsification. Reincarnation had been part of the secret tradition, and the ancient Greeks, Egyptians, Jews, Hindus, and Buddhists had all taught it.

According to Blavatsky, humans have an immortal soul whose origin lies in an impersonal divine absolute, which she simultaneously identified with the highest neo-Platonic hypostasis (the One), the Hindu *parabrahman*, and the Buddhist *Adi Buddha*. This divine absolute was said to emanate all creation from itself in a series of levels. Straightforwardly put, emanation is a concept reminiscent of a champagne fountain in which the champagne cascades from the bottle into the glass at the top and thereafter into the glasses beneath. In the religious or philosophical theory, the metaphorical champagne bottle never empties; the Divine continually emanates without diminution into the various levels of the cosmos it produces. Prominent in neo-Platonic, Hermetic, Gnostic, and Kabbalistic thought, many different variants of this basic idea have been proposed throughout the centuries.

In Blavatsky's version, the human spirit originated in one of the emanated levels of creation, the Universal Soul, from which they were emitted and sent on a journey into matter, reincarnating many times in different bodies and on different planets. They continually evolved, until they eventually became fully 'spiritualised', reuniting with the divine source from which they had come. Each time the spirit incarnated, it was 'dressed' in various garments that allowed it to function. These vestments were said to account for the physical, emotional, intellectual, and spiritual attributes experienced during a particular lifetime. Through accumulating the experiences of more and more lives, human evolution would be inevitable, although it could be faster or slower depending on individual will and effort.

This was the reincarnation doctrine Blavatsky taught from around 1882 onwards. It is fairly well known. However, the presence in her first major work, *Isis Unveiled*, of statements that seem to deny reincarnation have confused Blavatsky's readers from her lifetime to the present day. As this study will demonstrate, this is because Blavatsky actually taught two distinct theories of rebirth. In *The Secret Doctrine*, she taught reincarnation, but in *Isis Unveiled*, she taught a theory of post-mortem ascent to higher worlds, which she called metempsychosis.

Madame Controversy

Helena Petrovna von Hahn was of aristocratic Russian and German ancestry. With her stout frame, piercing blue eyes, and wiry blonde hair, she cut a curious figure and made a range of impressions on her contemporaries. At one extreme were those who considered her an initiate, the agent of spiritual masters who had sent her on a mission to save the West from its materialism and nihilism. Alternately, there were those who considered her a dangerous fraud intent on nothing but self-aggrandisement through the deceit of others. Without question, Blavatsky was a complex woman with many facets. Eccentric, opinionated, and out of the ordinary, she did not suffer fools lightly. She was capable of fits of temper and the use of foul language, which, together with her smoking of tobacco and hashish could be quite a shock to polite society.[5] Yet she could also be perceived as refined, courteous, and even sensitive, and without a doubt she was intelligent, creative, and extremely well read. Blavatsky's friend the physician and Platonist Alexander Wilder was among her admirers:

> She did not resemble in manner or figure what I had been led to expect. She was tall, but not strapping; her countenance bore the marks and exhibited the characteristics of one who had seen much, thought much, travelled much, and experienced much. [. . .] Her appearance was certainly impressive, but in no respect was she coarse, awkward, or ill-bred. On the other hand, she exhibited culture, familiarity with the manners of the most courtly society and genuine courtesy itself. [. . .] [She] made no affectation of superiority. Nor did I ever see or

---

[5] On Blavatsky's defiance of the norms of nineteenth-century femininity, see Catherine Tumber, *American Feminism and the Birth of New Age Spirituality: Searching for the Higher Self 1875–1915* (Lanham, MD: Rowman, 2002), 142f.

know of any such thing occurring with anyone else. She professed, however, to have communicated with personages whom she called 'the Brothers', and intimated that this, at times, was by the agency, or some means analogous to what is termed 'telepathy'. [. . .] She indulged freely in the smoking of cigarettes, which she made as she had occasion. I never saw any evidence that these things disturbed, or in any way interfered with her mental acuteness or activity.[6]

The 'brothers' Wilder referred to were one the most controversial aspects of Blavatsky's life and work. She claimed they were advanced spiritual masters whose initiative it had been to establish the Theosophical Society. She asserted she had travelled to Tibet, where she studied for around two years with the masters Morya and Koot Hoomi, who ran a school for adepts there.[7] Blavatsky also received letters from these masters, and so did other Theosophists, notably, Alfred Percy Sinnett (1840–1921) and Allan Octavian Hume (1829–1912), both of whom wrote important Theosophical works based on these correspondences. Like Blavatsky herself, the masters received a mixed response from the public. Theosophists saw them as advanced spiritual guides, others as a figment of Blavatsky's imagination. They remain unidentified to this day.[8]

In 1885, a report was issued by a society established to investigate the claims of Spiritualism, the Society for Psychical Research. It was based on the investigations of Richard Hodgson (1855–1905), who concluded Blavatsky was neither 'the mouthpiece of hidden seers, nor [. . .] a mere vulgar adventuress; we think that she has achieved a title to permanent remembrance as one of the most accomplished, ingenious,

[6] Alexander Wilder, 'How *Isis Unveiled* Was Written', *The Word* 7 (April–September 1908), 80–82.
[7] Nicholas Goodrick-Clarke, *Helena Blavatsky* (Berkeley: North Atlantic Books, 2004), 4–5.
[8] K. Paul Johnson has argued that Blavatsky's masters were mythical constructs based on real people whom she knew, such as the Maharaja Ranbir Singh of Jammu and Kashmir, whom Johnson proposes was the template for Morya. K. Paul Johnson, *In Search of the Masters* (South Boston: Self Published, 1990), and *The Masters Revealed: Madame Blavatsky and the Myth of the Great White Lodge* (Albany: State University of New York Press, 1994).

and interesting imposters in history.'[9] The report severely damaged Blavatsky's reputation. Her standing was further weakened by accusations of plagiarism made by a Spiritualist and opponent of Theosophy, William Emmette Coleman, who claimed Blavatsky had copied passages from the works of others without attribution. Coleman's accusations and Blavatsky's response will be discussed further in the following chapter.

This study sets aside the issue of Blavatsky's writing vis-à-vis the category 'plagiarism' to focus instead on what her sources were, how she used them, and what this can tell us about nineteenth-century history and culture. Blavatsky engaged with a comprehensive spectrum of writings when discussing her rebirth doctrines. This study will not provide an exhaustive treatment but an illustrative one, one that reveals the most pertinent historical contexts of her work as well as the principles of her hermeneutics. We will concentrate on four areas in particular: Spiritualism, science, Platonism, and Orientalism, showing how Blavatsky's interpretations of each had a formative influence on her rebirth doctrines.

Kabbalah, Egyptology, and Rebirth

Although the limitations of space require us to restrict the historical contextualisation to these four main subjects, two omissions deserve special mention, namely, Kabbalah and Egyptology, both of which Blavatsky discussed in relation to her rebirth theories. Kabbalistic sources present diverse and complex theories of reincarnation, the earliest source being the *Sefer ha-Bahir* (Book of Light) first published around 1176, in which no special term for reincarnation was given.[10] With the publication of the *Sefer ha-Zohar* (Book of Splendour) in early fourteenth-century Spain, the term *gilgul* came to be used.[11] In the sixteenth century, Isaac

---

[9] On the Hodgson Report, see J. Barton Scott, 'Miracle Publics: Theosophy, Christianity, and the Coulomb Affair', *History of Religions* 49, no. 2 (November 2009).
[10] For an English translation, see *The Bahir*, trans. Aryeh Kaplan (New York: Samuel Weiser, 1979).
[11] For an English translation, see *The Zohar: Pritzker Edition*, 12 vols. (Stanford: Stanford University Press, 2003–2017).

Luria (1534–1572), the leading member of the Kabbalistic school of Safed in present-day northern Israel, put forward a theory of reincarnation. His most important student, Chayim Vital (1543–1620), was the author of *Sefer ha-gilgulim* (Book of Re-Incarnations), a systematic description of Luria's teachings. This text became known to the Christian world through the Latin translation in the *Kabbalah Denudata* (1677–1684), a three-volume anthology of Kabbalistic texts translated by the seventeenth-century Christian Hebraist Christian Knorr von Rosenroth (1631–1689).[12] Blavatsky complained about Rosenroth's 'distorted Latin translations' and quoted a brief Latin passage from him.[13] But she did not read Rosenroth in the Latin original. Rather, as I have argued elsewhere, she drew on the works of the American lawyer Samuel Fales Dunlap (1825–1905).[14] Another possible source was the abridgement and translation of Rosenroth's compilation, *The Kabbalah Unveiled* (1887) by the British occultist Samuel Liddell MacGregor Mathers (1854–1918).[15] Blavatsky referred to 'the Hebrew book, The Revolution of the Souls', certainly a reference to Vital's text, but she read about it in the writing of the French occultist Eliphas Lévi, which she was translating.[16]

Blavatsky's approach to Kabbalah was an occultist one that was indebted to the Christian Kabbalah of the Renaissance and early-modern periods.[17] Kabbalists in this Renaissance tradition tended to assert

[12] Christian Knorr von Rosenroth, *Kabbala Denudata* (Hildesheim and New York: George Olms Verlag, 1974).

[13] H. P. Blavatsky, *The Secret Doctrine: The Synthesis of Science, Religion, and Philosophy*, 2 vols. (London: The Theosophical Publishing Company, 1888), vol. I, 215 and 391.

[14] Julie Chajes, 'Construction through Appropriation: Kabbalah in Blavatsky's Early Works', in *Theosophical Appropriations: Esotericism, Kabbalah, and the Transformation of Traditions*, ed. Julie Chajes and Boaz Huss (Beer Sheva: Ben-Gurion University Press, 2016).

[15] Samuel Liddell MacGregor Mathers, *The Kabbalah Unveiled* (London: George Redway, 1887).

[16] See her translation: H. P. Blavatsky, 'The Magical Evocation of Apollonius of Tyana: A Chapter from Eliphas Lévi', *Spiritual Scientist* 3, no. 9 (4 November 1875), 104–105.

[17] This tradition was represented by such figures as the Italian nobleman Giovanni Pico della Mirandola (1463–1494) and the humanist priest Marsilio Ficino (1433–1499). Other significant figures were the German humanist Johannes Reuchlin (1455–1522), the French linguist Guillaume Postel (1510–1581), and the German polymath and magician Heinrich Cornelius Agrippa (1486–1535).

the existence of a perennial philosophy and read Christian doctrines into Jewish Kabbalistic texts.[18] Occultists like Mathers and Lévi interpreted Christian Kabbalist ideas in a nineteenth-century occultist context. Blavatsky did the same, drawing on authors like Lévi and Mathers as well as the studies of Kabbalah that were available in languages she could read, notably, *La Kabbale ou la philosophie religieuse des Hébreux* by the French-Jewish scholar Adolphe Franck (1809–1893) and *The Kabbalah: Its Doctrine, Development, and Literature* (1865) by the Jewish-born Christian scholar Christian David Ginsburg (1831–1914).[19] These works were indebted to the academic study of Kabbalah that had emerged at the beginning of the nineteenth century in the context of the German-Jewish 'science of Judaism', the *Wissenschaft des Judentums*.[20] Blavatsky also consulted works that dealt with Kabbalah as part of a broader consideration of the history of religion or mythology, such as *The Gnostics and Their Remains* (1865) by the British classicist, writer, and expert on gemstones Charles William King (1818–1888), and

---

[18] On Renaissance and early-modern Christian Kabbalah, see Wilhelm Schmidt-Biggemann, *Geschichte der christlichen Kabbala*, 4 vols. (Stuttgart-Bad Cannstatt: Frommann Holzboog, 2015). For an English-language introduction, see Peter J. Forshaw, 'Kabbalah', in *The Occult World*, ed. Christopher Partridge (Abingdon: Routledge, 2015). For a longer treatment, see Joseph Dan, *The Christian Kabbalah: Jewish Mystical Books & Their Christian Interpreters: A Symposium* (Cambridge, MA: Harvard College Library, 1997). On perennialism, see Charles Schmidt, 'Perennial Philosophy from Agostino Steuco to Leibniz', *Journal of the History of Ideas* 27 (1966). On the Jewish adoption of the notion of 'perennial philosophy', see Moshe Idel, 'Kabbalah, Platonism, and Prisca Theologia: The Case of R. Menasseh ben Israel', in *Menasseh ben Israel and His World*, ed. Y. Kaplan, H. Méchoulan, and Richard H. Popkin (Leiden: Brill, 1989).

[19] Adolphe Franck, *La Kabbale ou la philosophie religieuse des Hébreux* (Paris: Librairie de L. Hachette, 1843) and David Ginsburg, *The Kabbalah: Its Doctrines, Development, and Literature. An Essay* (London: Longmans, Green, Reader, and Dyer, 1865).

[20] On the *Wissenschaft des Judentums*, see George Kohler, 'Judaism Buried or Revitalised? *Wissenschaft des Judentums* in Nineteenth-Century Germany—Impact, Actuality, and Applicability Today', in *Jewish Thought and Jewish Belief*, ed. Daniel J. Lasker (Beer Sheva: Ben-Gurion University Press, 2012). On the relationship between occultist and scholarly approaches to Kabbalah in the nineteenth century, see Wouter J. Hanegraaff, 'The Beginnings of Occultist Kabbalah: Adolphe Franck and Eliphas Lévi', in *Kabbalah and Modernity: Interpretations, Transformations, Adaptations*, ed. Boaz Huss, Marco Pasi, and Kocku von Stuckrad (Leiden and Boston: Brill, 2010). See also Chajes, 'Construction through Appropriation'.

Sōd: The Son of the Man (1861) by Samuel Fales Dunlap, among many others.[21]

Blavatsky presented Kabbalah as a universal tradition originally transmitted from Egypt and Chaldea (Babylonia).[22] She argued that the Kabbalistic notion of *Ain Soph* represented the divine absolute and equated the Kabbalistic concept of *Adam Kadmon* with the Second Logos of the Platonists or the Universal Soul, which was the source of all reincarnating spirits.[23] Blavatsky referred to Kabbalistic texts in corroboration first of metempsychosis, and later of reincarnation. Thus, in her first major work, *Isis Unveiled*, she referred to the central Kabbalistic text, the *Zohar*, to *disprove* the commonly understood notion of reincarnation.[24] However, in a later text, *The Key to Theosophy* (1889), Blavatsky referred to the *Zohar* to argue *for* reincarnation on Earth in keeping with her new convictions.[25]

Egypt, supposedly an ancient homeland of Kabbalah, also had its own place in Blavatsky's writings on rebirth. In the early-modern esoteric currents that were so influential in her thought, Egypt had typically been perceived as a mysterious and exotic source of perennial wisdom.[26] One of the figures Blavatsky mentioned from this period was the Jesuit polymath Athanasius Kircher (1602–1680), whose most famous work, *Oedipus Aegyptiacus* (1652–1654), was an account of ancient Egyptian

[21] C. W. King, *The Gnostics and Their Remains, Ancient and Medieval* (London: David Nutt, 1887) and S. F. Dunlap, *Sōd: The Son of the Man* (London and Edinburgh: Williams and Norgate, 1861).
[22] H. P. Blavatsky, 'Kabalah and Kabalists at the Close of the Nineteenth Century', *Lucifer* 10, no. 57 (May 1882), 268. Blavatsky, *Secret Doctrine I*, 352–353.
[23] Blavatsky, *Secret Doctrine I*, 16, 179, 214, and 573. The association between the souls of humanity and *Adam Kadmon* was not an innovation of Blavatsky's; it was present in Jewish Kabbalistic sources. Gershom Scholem, *On the Mystical Shape of the Godhead* (New York: Schocken 1991), 229.
[24] H. P. Blavatsky, *Isis Unveiled: A Master-Key to the Mysteries of Ancient and Modern Science and Theology*, 2 vols. (New York: J. W. Bouton, 1877), vol. I, 259.
[25] H. P. Blavatsky, *The Key to Theosophy* (London and New York: The Theosophical Publishing Company, 1889), 110–113.
[26] See Antoine Faivre, 'Egyptomany', in *Dictionary of Gnosis and Western Esotericism*, ed. Wouter Hanegraaff in collaboration with Antoine Faivre, Roelof van den Broek, and Jean-Pierre Brach (Leiden and Boston: Brill, 2006), 328.

life, culture, and religion.[27] From the eighteenth century through the nineteenth, ancient Egypt was depicted in diverse literary and artistic contexts. Notably, Freemasonry was full of Egyptian iconography.[28] The development of Egyptology from the early nineteenth century considerably intensified the public's interest in Egypt. Many discoveries were made in a short period of time, especially during the 1870s and 1880s, when Egyptology came to be a major cultural force.[29] It is therefore unsurprising that Blavatsky used Egyptological findings to corroborate her Theosophical teachings, even though she denounced scholarly 'misunderstanding' of Egyptian religion and magic.[30]

The association between ancient Egypt and reincarnation is longstanding, but early Egyptologists expressed differing opinions on the matter. In 1705, Thomas Greenhill published a seminal treatise on Egyptian civilisation and mummification in which he claimed the Egyptians mummified their dead because they believed in a type of reincarnation into the same body.[31] On the other hand, in 1836, John Davidson conducted a surgical exploration of mummification and rejected the idea that the Egyptians embalmed mummies because of a belief in reincarnation. Instead, he concluded they did it as a re-enactment of the myth of Osiris.[32] In *The Secret Doctrine*, Blavatsky affirmed the Egyptians' reincarnationism. Referring to *The Book of the Dead*, she argued against those who denied the Egyptian belief, which she described in terms of the emergence of the solar boat from the realm of *Tiaou* (the realm of the cause of life).[33] As part of her discussion, she provided a

---

[27] Athanasius Kircher, *Oedipus Aegyptiacus* (Rome: 1652–1654). Blavatsky mentions Kircher's work, for example, in *Secret Doctrine II*, 207.

[28] See James Stevens Curl, *The Egyptian Revival: Ancient Egypt as the Inspiration for Design Motifs in the West* (London and New York: Routledge, 2005), 132 and Frances Yates, *The Rosicrucian Enlightenment* (London and New York: Ark Paperbacks, 1986), 212–213.

[29] David Gange, *Dialogues with the Dead: Egyptology in British Culture and Religion, 1822–1922* (Oxford: Oxford University Press, 2013).

[30] Blavatsky, *Secret Doctrine I*, xix, xxix.

[31] John David Wortham, *British Egyptology: 1549–1906* (Newton Abbot: David and Charles, 1971), 10 and 45.

[32] Wortham, *British Egyptology*, 93–94.

[33] Initially believed to be the 'Egyptian Bible', *The Book of the Dead* refers to an Egyptian funerary text called 'The Spells of Coming or Going Forth by Day' intended

concise statement of her reincarnation doctrine, in which each of the stages was equated with Egyptian terms.[34]

Blavatsky brought these interpretations of Kabbalistic and Egyptian teachings together with the Spiritualistic, scientific, Platonic, Buddhist, and Hindu themes that will be explored in greater detail in the chapters that follow. Their confluence resulted in a global and uniquely hybridic reincarnationism, in which the idea of a repeated return to life on Earth after death was entwined with the literature and concerns of the nineteenth century. The theory was then bequeathed to Blavatsky's successors, undergoing various 'reincarnations' of its own as it passed through the doctrinal systems of the many Theosophically inspired spokespersons of heterodox thought in the twentieth century. Eventually, Blavatskyan elements found their way into the New Age.[35] Today, the New Age is extremely pervasive, its concepts permeating even the world of business and the realms of supposedly traditional religions.[36] It is characterised by elements central to Blavatsky's thinking, such as syncretism, an emphasis on Eastern, 'esoteric', 'mystical', and pagan traditions,[37] the channelling of entities, and the compatibility

---

to assist the dead in their journey to the afterlife. Samuel Birch published the first English translation in 1867. Wortham, *British Egyptology*, 97. This was the translation Blavatsky used, and it could be found at the end of a book she is known to have consulted, volume 5 of C. C. J. Baron Bunsen's *Egypt's Place in Universal History* (London: Longmans, Green, and Co., 1867). On Blavatsky's use of this source, see Michael Gomes, *Theosophy in the Nineteenth Century: An Annotated Bibliography* (New York and London: Garland Publishing, 1994), 150.

[34] Blavatsky, *Secret Doctrine I*, 226–227.

[35] On the debt of the New Age Movement to Theosophy, see Wouter Hanegraaff, *New Age Religion and Western Culture: Western Esotericism in the Mirror of Secular Thought* (Leiden: Brill, 1996). See also Wouter Hanegraaff, 'The New Age Movement and Western Esotericism', in *Handbook of the New Age*, 25–50; Olav Hammer, *Claiming Knowledge: Strategies of Epistemology from Theosophy to the New Age* (Leiden: Brill, 2004), and Olav Hammer, 'Jewish Mysticism Meets the Age of Aquarius: Elizabeth Clare Prophet on the Kabbalah', in *Theosophical Appropriations*, ed. Julie Chajes and Boaz Huss.

[36] See Martin Ramstedt, 'New Age and Business', in *Handbook of the New Age*. On the overlap between New Age ideas and more 'traditional' Jewish ideas, see Boaz Huss, 'The New Age of Kabbalah', *Journal of Modern Jewish Studies* 6, no. 2 (2007), 107–125.

[37] On the connection between Theosophy and neo-Paganism see Ronald Hutton, *Triumph of the Moon: A History of Modern Pagan Witchcraft* (Oxford: Oxford University

of spirituality and science.[38] Karma and reincarnation are, of course, prominent.[39] Blavatsky's writings are fundamental in understanding how that came to be.

Chapter Outline

This study approaches a wide variety of issues in the history of the nineteenth century through a detailed reading of two closely related doctrines, metempsychosis and reincarnation. Blavatsky's works are generally considered quite difficult, and this has sometimes led to their dismissal as obscurantist and contradictory. As I will show throughout this book, passages in Blavatsky that may seem convoluted and non-sensical are often comprehensible once understood in the context of the development of her thought. Understanding Blavatsky, however, can be difficult, because rather than providing straightforward expositions, she usually scattered her ideas piecemeal throughout her writing. This can be frustrating, and it is one reason why a clear guide is needed. In fact, it is high time for a detailed analysis of Blavatsky's thought as a whole, and this study is a contribution to that larger project. It is hoped that by making Blavatsky more accessible and highlighting her historical importance, it will contribute to a growing appreciation of this significant and influential thinker of the nineteenth century.

Following an introduction to Blavatsky and the development of her theories of rebirth in chapter 1, chapters 2 and 3 are internalist in orientation, that is, they focus on elements internal to Blavatsky's thought. Theosophical principles have usually been treated quite briefly in academic studies to date. Taking a different approach, this study affirms the importance of a detailed reading of Blavatsky's tenets, demonstrating

Press, 1999). See also Melissa Harrington, 'Paganism and the New Age' and Daren Kemp, 'Christians and New Age', both in *Handbook of the New Age*.

[38] On 'spirituality' as a category, see Boaz Huss, 'Spirituality: The Emergence of a New Cultural Category and Its Challenge to the Religious and the Secular', *Journal of Contemporary Religion* 29, no. 1 (2014). On the notion of 'spiritual but not religious' see Robert C. Fuller, *Spiritual, but Not Religious: Understanding Unchurched America* (Oxford: Oxford University Press, 2011), especially 4–7.

[39] On reincarnation in the New Age Movement, see Hanegraaff, *New Age Religion*, chapter 9.

that the ideas themselves must be understood clearly before they can be situated in the intellectual, social, religious, and political concerns of the times.

Due to Blavatsky's seeming contradictions, there has been no little confusion among scholars about her teachings on rebirth in her first major work, *Isis Unveiled* (1877). In chapter 2, on the basis of a systematic examination of the text alongside some early letters, I demonstrate that during the first period of her career as an occultist, Blavatsky taught that living humans are composed of three parts: body, soul, and spirit, and that immortality can be achieved by joining the soul with the spirit during life on Earth through occult practice. Blavatsky argued that once immortality had been achieved, after death, the conjoined soul-spirit entity would begin a journey of metempsychosis through higher spheres. If immortality had not been achieved, then annihilation followed. In exceptional circumstances, such as the death of an infant, reincarnation of the spirit together with the same soul provided a 'second chance' for the spirit to live on Earth and achieve immortality. Chapter 2 considers these doctrines in detail, including aspects not yet discussed in the scholarly literature. These include the acquisition of a new 'astral body' in each sphere during metempsychosis and unusual circumstances involving 'terrestrial larvae' and the 'transfer of a spiritual entity'. The discussion clarifies Blavatsky's teachings about metempsychosis through mineral, plant, and animal forms, and how these stages are 'relived' in utero, a Theosophical interpretation of the contemporary scientific theory of recapitulation.

Around 1882, Blavatsky began teaching something different to metempsychosis: the normative, repeated, and karmic return of the human spirit to life on Earth. She called this new doctrine 'reincarnation' but denied she had changed her mind. To admit this would be to admit the masters had changed their minds, and this was unacceptable. Blavatsky tried to harmonise her accounts, but contemporaries noted the presence of a new perspective and its difference to the previous one. Indeed, the divergence is exposed from a close reading of the texts.

To understand reincarnation as presented in Blavatsky's magnum opus *The Secret Doctrine* (1888) and writings of the same period, it is necessary first of all to understand the unique and complex cosmology that forms its basis; indeed, reincarnation is inseparable from this wider doctrinal context. Chapter 3 examines this 'macrocosmic' aspect of Blavatsky's reincarnationism in detail, charting the spirit's 'pilgrimage' from its emission from the 'Universal Soul' through its journey into matter and back again to its divine source. This spirit was said to travel together with many others through incarnation on six invisible planets, evolving on Earth by passing through seven 'root races', of which present humanity was the fifth.

Chapter 3 also considers the 'microcosmic' aspects of the reincarnation doctrine: Blavatsky's teachings about birth, death, and the revival of life on Earth. These processes mirrored the macrocosmic ones, a fact not coincidental in the writings of a thinker influenced by the Hermetic axiom 'as above, so below'. It describes the death and rebirth process and analyses Blavatsky's reinterpretation of the 'second chance' she believed would be given to those who died in childhood and other exceptional occurrences. Finally, I consider Blavatsky's claim in *The Secret Doctrine* that despite the usual acquisition of a new personality in each lifetime, it was possible for an adept to preserve their personal identity throughout repeated incarnations.

With the details of Blavatsky's theories established, the remaining chapters take an externalist approach, that is, they consider elements external to the theories in order to situate them more broadly. Chapters 4 through 7 contextualise Blavatsky's theory in four dimensions of nineteenth-century intellectual and cultural life. They draw insights from diverse fields of nineteenth-century cultural and intellectual history, consolidating and sometimes challenging previous conclusions.[40]

Chapter 4 frames Blavatsky's rebirth doctrines in the development of Spiritualism from the mid-nineteenth century. A central cultural force in America and Europe at the time, Spiritualism tried to mediate between

---

[40] For the foundation of present debates on the category 'Western esotericism', see Antoine Faivre, *Western Esotericism* (Albany: State University of New York Press, 2010). For a concise discussion of the meaning of the term 'esotericism' and the category 'Western esotericism', see Wouter J. Hanegraaff, 'Esotericism', in *Dictionary of Gnosis and Western Esotericism* (Leiden, Brill, 2006). On problems relating to the definition of Western esotericism and a cultural-studies argument for the category as an 'empty signifier', see Michael Bergunder, 'What Is Esotericism? Cultural Studies Approaches and the Problems of Definition in Religious Studies', *Method and Theory in the Study of Religions* 22, no. 1 (2010).

science and religion at the same time as it attempted to establish contact with the dead. In general, British and American Spiritualists denied reincarnation and affirmed progress on higher worlds whereas French Spiritists—the followers of Allan Kardec (1804–1869)—believed in the repeated reincarnation of the same personality. Through reference to books and Spiritualist periodicals, the chapter situates Blavatsky's early theory of metempsychosis in relation to anti-reincarnationist currents in Anglo-American Spiritualism, especially as represented by the British medium Emma Hardinge Britten (1823–1899), the American magician Paschal Beverly Randolph (1825–1875), and the Hermetic Brotherhood of Luxor, an occultist organisation beginning its public work in 1884. Joscelyn Godwin, Christian Chanel, and John Patrick Deveney were the first to highlight the similarity between Blavatsky's early ideas and those of Britten, Randolph, and the H. B. of L., but I delve further, revealing some of the differences, as well as the similarities, between the rebirth theories of these individuals.[41] I also broaden the scope of the discussion, considering the nineteenth-century Spiritualist reincarnation debate more widely. Central issues involved whether humans were intrinsically immortal or had to win immortality during Earth life, and whether the personality would be retained from life to life.

As much as it is impossible to understand Blavatsky's doctrines without understanding their Spiritualist heritage, it is equally impossible to understand them without reference to her continuous and vociferous rejection of the French variant: Spiritism. Already during the 1870s, Blavatsky's statements about Spiritualism were ambivalent: she sometimes described herself as a Spiritualist and sometimes criticised the movement. Although some of her best friends were French Spiritists, she was particularly critical of their beliefs about reincarnation. Blavatsky found Kardec's conception of the repeated return of the *same person* to life on Earth to be unacceptable. As I will show, her eventual embrace of reincarnation during her later period did not indicate acceptance of Kardec's theory.

---

[41] Joscelyn Godwin, Christian Chanel, and John Patrick Deveney, *The Hermetic Brotherhood of Luxor: Initiatic and Historical Documents of an Order of Practical Occultism* (York Beach: Samuel Weiser, 1995).

Chapter 5 considers the relationship between Blavatsky's rebirth teachings and her constructions of the ancient Greeks. Indeed, her works are an important—and hitherto unacknowledged—site for the intersection of occultist thought with nineteenth-century Classicism. The chapter situates Blavatsky's engagement with the Classical world in the context of her discussions of rebirth within a far-ranging nineteenth-century fascination with the Greeks. This cultural interest is evident in Blavatsky's source texts as well as more widely. Nineteenth-century authors constructed the Greeks according to their needs, their depictions falling into the broadly defined categories of the more conservative and the more transgressive. Blavatsky's interpretations had substantial anti-establishment elements. They were influenced by her friend, the American physician Alexander Wilder (1823–1908), himself a member of an American Platonic tradition with roots in Transcendentalism and the thought of the English neo-Platonist Thomas Taylor (1758–1835). Interpreting these influences, Blavatsky construed the Greeks according to her occultist exegesis to argue that Greek ideas had parallels in Hebraic, Gnostic, and Indian thought and that Hellenism had an Oriental source. First, she argued Pythagoras and Plato were advocates of metempsychosis. Later, she maintained the taught reincarnation.

Blavatsky's conceptualisations of rebirth also owe a considerable debt to the scientific theories under discussion at her time of writing. Chapter 6 demonstrates that she referred to numerous contemporary scientists in justifying aspects of her thought, basically dividing them into two camps, those whose ideas could be interpreted as supporting Theosophy (at least in some way) and those whom she believed understood nothing, usually because of their supposed materialism. Blavatsky framed her theses in opposition to the latter. At the same time, she selectively appropriated elements from the writings of scientists she approved of in a 'scientism' that was an essential feature of her thought. In this way, Blavatsky contributed to spreading the ideas of leading scientists, an active agent in the construction of science-related knowledge and of science itself, as a category. Blavatsky's activities occurred within a cultural world in which the boundaries of 'legitimate' science were more contested than they are today. Some believed science should exclude all metaphysical speculation, but others believed some sort of reconciliation might still be found. Among the latter were professional scientists as well as occultists and Spiritualists. The chapter explores Blavatsky's debt to two Scottish physicists, Balfour Stewart (1828–1887) and Peter Guthrie Tait (1831–1909), who were criticised for 'pseudo science' in their day but on whom Blavatsky drew in her construction of metempsychosis as a sort of 'recycling' of spiritual and physical elements. Citing Stewart and Tait, she positioned Theosophy between the perceived extremes of materialism and dogmatic religion, proposing continuity between the natural and the 'supernatural', as well as the possibility of transferring from one 'grade of being' to another.

One of Blavatsky's chief polemical targets in her discussions of science was the materialist monism of Ernst Haeckel (1834–1919), which, despite having much in common with Theosophy, she deemed incomplete and misleading. Another was Darwinism. Blavatsky perceived natural selection as materialistic, chance-driven, and anti-spiritual, and offered her depiction of a reincarnationary, teleological ascent through a vitalist 'great chain of being' as an alternative. Her concepts were indebted to some of the theories of evolution popularised during the 1880s, such as the idea that higher intelligences assist in evolutionary processes and the notion that the cosmos has an intrinsic tendency to evolve. The latter hypothesis was termed orthogenesis, and Blavatsky quoted teleological versions of it proposed by the Swiss botanist Carl Wilhelm von Nägeli (1817–1891), the Estonian scientist Karl Ernst von Baer (1792–1876), and the British biologist Richard Owen (1804–1892). German Romantic themes were significant here, especially concepts of progress and becoming, as well as Aristotelian and Platonic notions of a hierarchy of fixed types.

Chapter 7 describes Blavatsky's arrival in India and Ceylon, the establishment of branches of the Society there, and her contact with numerous locals, including monks, university scholars, and pandits, many of whom came from the upper echelons of Indian society. Some wrote articles for *The Theosophist* on topics closely related to reincarnation, such as the nature of the soul, *moksha*, and nirvana. Blavatsky's close friend, Henry Olcott, claimed it was in India where she first 'became absorbed in the problems of the soul's cyclic progressions and reincarnations', and it seems reasonable to assume, on the basis of this and other primary sources, that Indian influences contributed to Blavatsky's eventual acceptance of reincarnation.

Blavatsky's metaphysics had a neo-Platonic basis, but she framed her ideas in Vedantic terms provided, in part, by notable early Indian Theosophists such as Mohini M. Chatterji (1858–1936) and Tallapragada Subba Row (1856–1890). In his discussions of *Vedanta*, Subba Row drew on the social Darwinist Herbert Spencer (1820–1903), on whom Blavatsky also drew (and sometimes criticised). She also assimilated material from Orientalist scholarship, especially the translation of the *Vishnu Purana* prepared by H. H. Wilson (1786–1860), although she found fault with that too. The outcome of all these selective borrowings was a modernising depiction of Theosophy as the esoteric essence of Hinduism and Buddhism, in which the neo-Platonic One was equated with *parabrahman* and *Adi Buddha* and offered as an alternative to Ernst Haeckel's monism. The chapter thus reveals Blavatsky's reincarnationism as involving an entanglement of Western philosophies with the interpretations of *Vedanta* of Western-educated Hindu elites alongside academic Orientalism.

The result of the interplay of Blavatsky's Platonism, scientism, Spiritualism, and Orientalism were modern perspectives on rebirth that were inseparable from the interrelated nineteenth-century constructions among which they evolved. Appreciation of the embeddedness of Blavatsky's rebirth theories in these contexts allows us to better understand Blavatsky and her period. In addition, it reveals some consequential, perhaps unexpected, and evidently under-acknowledged historical roots of the reincarnationism that is so popular in today's postmodern world.

I

Blavatsky and Reincarnation

HELENA PETROVNA VON HAHN was born in Ekaterinoslav, Ukraine, on 12 August 1831 (31 July in the O.S.). She was of Russian, German, and French ancestry. Her father, Peter Alexeyevitch von Hahn (1799–1875), was an army colonel descended from the German minor nobility. Her mother, Helena Adreyevna de Fadeev (1814–1842), was a novelist descended from the Russian aristocracy. She died when Helena was eleven years old. Helena had a sister, Vera, and a brother, Leonid.[1] From the age of nine, she lived mostly with her mother's parents, Privy Councillor Andrei de Fadeev (1789–1867) and Princess Helena Dolgorukii (1789–1860). During her childhood, Andrei de Fadeev acted as trustee for the nomadic Kalmuck people in their local Province of Astrakhan (in the south-west of Russia). The Kalmuck tribes had embraced Gelugpa Tibetan Buddhism during the seventeenth century. Blavatsky's mother, Helena Adreyevna, even wrote a novel about Kalmuck life.[2] Claiming to have had considerable contact with the Kalmucks in her youth,

---

[1] On Blavatsky's early life, see Maria Carlson, *No Religion Higher than the Truth* (Princeton: Princeton University Press, 1993), 38–42.

[2] Letter to P. C. Mittra on 10 April 1878 and letter to H. Chintamon on 4 May 1878, in H. P. Blavatsky, *The Letters of H. P. Blavatsky 1861–1879*, ed. John Algeo (Wheaton, IL, and Chennai: Quest Books, Theosophical Publishing House, 2003), 410 and 427. H. P. Blavatsky, 'Mr Arthur Lillie', in *Blavatsky Collected Writings*, ed. Boris de Zirkoff (Wheaton, IL: Theosophical Publishing House, 1991), 15 vols, vol. 6, 293 (originally published in *Light* 4, no. 197 (11 October 1884), 418–419. See also Blavatsky, *Isis II*, 551 and 553.

Blavatsky seems to have been inspired by this early exposure to what she must have experienced as an exotic, Oriental religion.[3]

Her mother tongue was Russian, and like most educated Russians of her day, she spoke French well. Blavatsky's ancestry suggests she would have known German but she denied this.[4] Blavatsky initially learned English from a Yorkshire governess. She always claimed her knowledge of the language was limited, but even though her major works were heavily edited, her letters and other writings attest to an excellent command of it.[5] Her friend Alexander Wilder wrote, 'She spoke the English language with the fluency of one perfectly familiar with it, and who thought in it.'[6] Contemporaries credited Blavatsky with knowing Sanskrit, Hebrew, Tibetan, and even Hindi. She does not seem to have objected, although unequivocal evidence for her knowledge is lacking.[7]

Blavatsky was raised in the Russian Orthodox Church.[8] Her statements indicate she was deeply respectful of it, despite her famed aversion

[3] Letter to P. C. Mittra on 10 April 1878 Blavatsky and letter to H. Chintamon on 4 May 1878, in *The Letters of H. P. Blavatsky 1861–1879*, 410 and 427. See also Blavatsky, 'Mr Arthur Lillie', 293 and Blavatsky, *Isis II*, 551 and 553.

[4] In a letter to the Dutch Theosophist Adelberth de Bourbon, Blavatsky stated, 'though my father was a German, a Finlander—Baron Hahn, I do not know German'. 'Letter of H.P.B. to Adelberth de Bourbon', *The Theosophist* 73 (December 1951), 154.

[5] She asked her critics to take into account that she 'had never studied the English language, and after learning it in her childhood colloquially had not spoken it before coming to America half a dozen times during as many years'. H. P. Blavatsky, 'The Claims of Occultism', *The Theosophist* 2, no. 12 (September 1881), 258–260. 'She had been taught to speak English by her first governess, Miss Jeffries.' A. P. Sinnet, *Incidents in the Life of Madame Blavatsky* (New York: J. W. Bouton, 1886), 52. See also 24 and 28.

[6] Wilder, 'How "Isis Unveiled" Was Written', 83.

[7] For example, Joy Dixon notes: 'she claimed to be able to read a fair amount of Sanskrit.' Joy Dixon, *Divine Feminine: Theosophy and Feminism in England* (Baltimore and London: Johns Hopkins University Press, 2001), 24. A contemporary reporter for the *New York Times* wrote, 'Mme. Blavatsky is [. . .] the animated leader of conversation, speaking with equal ease in English, French, Italian, and Russian, or dropping into Sanskrit or Hindoostanee as occasion requires'. 'Blavatsky Still Lives'. *The New York Times* (6 January 1889), 10. The article is an interview with William Quan Judge. No author is given.

[8] Richard Hutch argued that the Russian Orthodox wandering holy men, the *staretsi*, and the folk shamans, the *volkhv*, influenced Blavatsky. Richard A. Hutch, 'Helena Blavatsky Unveiled', *The Journal of Religious History* 11, no. 2 (December 1980). Michael Gomes dismissed Hutch's conclusions. Gomes, *Bibliography*, 264. Brendan French congratulated Hutch for being the first to draw attention to the importance

to Christianity in general and to Protestantism and Catholicism in particular. She wrote to her sister Vera:

> I simply can't listen to people talking about the wretched Hindus or Buddhists being converted to Anglican Phariseeism or the Pope's Christianity; it simply gives me the shivers. But when I read about the spread of Russian orthodoxy in Japan, my heart rejoices. [. . .] I do not believe in any dogmas, I dislike every ritual, but my feelings towards our own church-service are quite different. [. . .] A thousand times rather Buddhism, a pure moral teaching, in perfect harmony with the teachings of Christ, than modern Catholicism or Protestantism. But with the faith of the Russian Church I will not even compare Buddhism. I can't help it. Such is my silly inconsistent nature.[9]

Although Blavatsky received an education at home, she didn't go to university, and in matters beyond the expertise of governesses was largely an autodidact. An early source for the knowledge that would later enable her to write her Theosophical works was the library of her great-grandfather, Prince Pavel Dolgorukii (1755–1837), the father of her grandmother, Princess Helena. Prince Pavel had been a Freemason of the kind who took an interest in occult subjects. Blavatsky claimed to have read the contents of his library in its entirety by age fifteen, and that it had introduced her to the subjects of alchemy, magic, and the

of Blavatsky's native religion but argued that although Blavatsky may not have modelled herself on the *staretsi* and the *volkhv*, she may have modelled the Masters on them. Brendan French, 'Blavatsky, Dostoevski, and Occult *Starchestvo*', *Aries* 7, no. 2 (2007), 167.

[9] Letter to Vera Jelihovsky, cited in *Personal Memoires of H. P. Blavatsky*, compiled by Mary K. Neff (London: Rider, 1937—Kessinger photographic reprint). Blavatsky's statement led Ronald Hutton to conclude that 'the multi-cultural, supranational Blavatsky remained at heart what she had been as a girl: a Russian Orthodox Christian'. Hutton, *Triumph of the Moon*, 19. For more statements of Blavatsky's on the Russian Orthodox Church, *The Letters of H. P. Blavatsky 1861–1879*, 289 and H. P. Blavatsky, 'Our Cycle and the Next', *Lucifer* 4 no. 21 (May 1889), 177–178.

occult sciences, topics that would come to be among the mainstays of Theosophy.[10]

Blavatsky's outspoken, opinionated, and unconventional nature was evident from an early age:

> I hate dress, finery, and civilized society, I despise a ball room, and how much I despise it will be proved to you by the following fact. When hardly sixteen, I was being forced one day to go to a dancing party, a great ball at the Viceroy's. My protests were not listened to, and my parents told me that they would have me dressed up, or rather according to fashion, undressed for the ball by the servants by force if I did not go willingly. I then deliberately plunged my foot and leg into a kettle of boiling water, and held it there till nearly boiled raw. Of course I scalded it horribly, and remained lame for six months. But I was never forced to go to a ball again. I tell you, that there is nothing of the woman in me. When I was young if a man had dared to speak to me of love, I would have shot him like a dog who bit me.[11]

Despite her protestations, on 7 July 1849, at the age of seventeen, Helena married the forty-year-old Nikifor Blavatsky (1809–after 1877), vice-governor of Yerevan province in Armenia. She soon regretted it, however, leaving him just months afterwards in an act in many ways representative of her rejection of the noblewoman's life expected of her. After abandoning her husband, she began her travels.[12] No reliable account of her life for the next twenty-five years exists. They are known as her 'veiled years', and it was during this period she claimed to have met and studied with her mysterious masters in the Far East.

[10] Nicholas Goodrick-Clarke, 'Western Esoteric Traditions and Theosophy', in *Handbook of the Theosophical Current*, ed. Olav Hammer and Michael Rothstein (Leiden and Boston: Brill, 2013), 264.

[11] H. P. Blavatsky, 'On Hibernation, the Ârya Samâj, etc.', in *Blavatsky Collected Writings*, vol. 6, 314.

[12] The name 'Blavatsky' always appeared in English in its masculine form, although Helena's surname was *Blavatskaya* in Russian.

Blavatsky in America and *Isis Unveiled*

Blavatsky was in Paris in 1873, travelling there via Odessa and Eastern Europe. She arrived in New York the same year, around the time of her forty-second birthday.[13] There, she met the American lawyer and journalist Colonel Henry Steel Olcott (1832–1907) who was investigating Spiritualistic phenomena in Chittenden, Vermont, in 1874. They were to become lifelong friends. Olcott was of Presbyterian origin and was educated at Columbia University. He belonged to a social class his biographer, Stephen Prothero, termed the 'metropolitan gentility', a cultural elite that tended to display a 'genteel yearning for cohesion, unity, and order and a didactic conviction the way to achieve harmony was by civilising the masses'.[14] Olcott had worked as an agricultural correspondent for the *New York Tribune,* served in the Union Army during the Civil War, and was later promoted to colonel. He had become a lawyer in 1868 and was married but estranged from his wife.[15] The relationship he developed with Blavatsky was very close (he nicknamed her 'Jack' and she dubbed him 'Maloney'), but it was clearly Platonic.

Fourteen individuals joined Maloney and Jack in establishing the Theosophical Society in New York City two years later, over the course

[13] Many histories of the Theosophical Society and biographies of Blavatsky have been published. Some are listed in Gomes, *Bibliography,* 19–141. Works on Blavatsky include Charles J. Ryan, *H. P. Blavatsky and the Theosophical Movement* (Pasadena, CA: Theosophical University Press, 1975); Marion Mead, *Madame Blavatsky: The Woman Behind the Myth* (New York: G. P. Putnam's Sons, 1980); Sylvia Cranston, *H. P. B. The Extraordinary Life and Influence of Helena Blavatsky, Founder of the Theosophical Movement* (New York: G. P. Putnam's Sons, 1993); Peter Washington, *Madame Blavatsky's Baboon* (New York: Schocken Books, 1995); Joseph Howard Tyson, *Madame Blavatsky Revisited* (Lincoln: iUniverse, 2007); and Gary Lachman, *Madame Blavatsky: The Mother of Modern Spirituality* (New York: Penguin, 2012). For a digest of Blavatsky's writings and a reliable introduction, see Goodrick-Clarke, *Helena Blavatsky.* For a concise history of the Theosophical Society, see James A. Santucci, 'Blavatsky, Helena Petrovna', in *Dictionary of Gnosis and Western Esotericism,* 177–185.
[14] Stephen Prothero, 'Henry Steel Olcott and "Protestant Buddhism"', *Journal of the American Academy of Religion* 63, no. 2 (Summer 1995), 290. See also Stephen Prothero, *The White Buddhist: The Asian Odyssey of Henry Steel Olcott* (Bloomington: Indiana University Press, 1996).
[15] Bruce F. Campbell, *Ancient Wisdom Revived: A History of the Theosophical Movement* (Berkeley: University of California Press, 1980), 7.

of six meetings from September to November. The sixteen formers (as
Olcott called them) were the journalist and bookseller Charles Sotheran
(1847–1902); the New York physician Dr. Charles E. Simmons (1841–
1917); the journalist and army officer of Italian origin H. D. Monachesi
(1854–1900); the barrister and Spiritualist Charles Carlton Massey
(1838–1905); William Livingstone Alden (1837–1908, a writer for the
New York Times who soon left the Society); the engineer and amateur
Egyptologist George Henry Felt (1831–1906), the British Reform Jew
and Freemason David Etienne de Lara (1796–1879); the Spiritualists
Dr. William Goodwin Britten (1822–1894) and his wife, Emma
Hardinge Britten (1823–1899); John Storer Cobb (1838–1904), who was
a non-Jewish editor of the short-lived Reform Jewish periodical *The New
Era*; the Spiritualist Henry J. Newton (1823–1895); the Irish-American
lawyer William Quan Judge (1851–1896); James H. Hyslop (1854–1920);
and H. M. Stevens (on whom we don't have any further information).[16]
At first, the stated objectives of the Theosophical Society included
studying 'the esoteric philosophy of ancient times' and 'collecting and
diffusing knowledge of the laws which govern the universe'.[17] As John
Patrick Deveney has demonstrated, the early Theosophical Society had
a practical orientation. It included a system of three degrees and encouraged temperance and fasting, as well as some form of sexual ab-
stinence. The Society was initially devoted to occult work such as the
projection of the astral double as a means of achieving immortality, the
practice of Indian yoga, and the conjuration of elemental spirits.[18]

[16] Henry Steel Olcott, *Old Diary Leaves First Series* (New York and London: G.
P. Putnam's Sons, 1895), 121–122. On de Lara, see Boaz Huss, 'Qabbalah, the Theos-
Sophia of the Jews: Jewish Theosophists and their Perceptions of Kabbalah', in
Theosophical Appropriations. On de Lara and Cobb, see John Patrick Deveney, 'D. E. de
Lara, John Storer Cobb, and The New Era', *Theosophical History* 15, no. 4 (2011). For
summaries on each of the founders, see Josephine Ransom, *A Short History of the
Theosophical Society* (Adyar: Theosophical Publishing House, 1938), 109–114. It was
not possible to ascertain the life dates for all the formers of the Theosophical Society.
[17] In 1896, these were reformulated to what they remain today: to form a nucleus of the
Universal Brotherhood of Humanity, without distinction of race, creed, sex, caste, or
colour; to encourage the study of comparative religion, philosophy and science; and to
investigate unexplained laws of Nature and the powers latent in man.
[18] On the occult practices pursued by early Theosophists, see John Patrick Deveney,
'The Two Theosophical Societies: Prolonged Life, Conditional Immortality, and the

The Theosophical Society was born into a unique American context. The 'Second Great Awakening' of the early nineteenth century had brought membership of Catholic and Protestant churches to a peak by the 1850s and religious renewal had been so fervent in the western section of New York State it was nicknamed the 'burned-over district' because of the successive waves of revival that had swept it. Numerous new religious groups arose there, and these included the direct forerunner of Theosophy, Spiritualism. When Blavatsky arrived in the New World in the late 1870s, she was already familiar with the French version of Spiritualism—Spiritism. The Spiritualist 'craze' had started in America around the middle of the century and it developed there in a somewhat different direction to that of its continental counterpart. It was a crucial component of what Catherine Albanese termed American 'metaphysical religion', which included currents that had emerged in the eighteenth century, such as Mesmerism and Swedenborgianism, as well as American Transcendentalism, which developed from the 1820s.[19] Later in the nineteenth century, Christian Science, New Thought, and Theosophy were added to the mix, and Albanese characterised these as 'mature forms of metaphysical religion'.[20] She noted four themes within this type of religiosity: a preoccupation with the mind and its powers, a

Individualized Immortal Monad', in *Theosophical Appropriations* and 'Astral Projection or Liberation of the Double and the Work of the Early Theosophical Society', *Theosophical History Occasional Papers* 6 (1997). See also Wouter Hanegraaff, 'Western Esotericism and the Orient in the First Theosophical Society', in *Theosophy Across Boundaries*, ed. Hans-Martin Krämer and Julian Strube, forthcoming. On the practice of yoga in early Theosophy, see Karl Baier, *Meditation und Moderne: Zur Genese eines Kernbereichs moderner Spiritualität in der Wechselwirkung zwischen Westeuropa, Nordamerika, und Asien* (Würzburg: Königshausen & Neumann Verlag, 2009).

[19] For an introduction to Spiritualism, see Cathy Gutierrez, *Plato's Ghost* (Oxford: Oxford University Press, 2009). On Mesmerism in general, see Alan Gauld, *A History of Hypnotism* (Cambridge: Cambridge University Press, 1992). On American Mesmerism, see Robert C. Fuller, *Mesmerism and the American Cure of Souls* (Philadelphia: University of Pennsylvania Press, 1982). On Swedenborg, see Ernst Benz, *Emanuel Swedenborg* (West Chester, PA: Swedenborg Foundation, 2002). On Transcendentalism, see Arthur Versluis, *American Transcendentalism and Asian Religions* (New York: Oxford University Press, 1993) and Joel Myerson, ed., *A Historical Guide to Ralph Waldo Emerson* (Oxford: Oxford University Press, 2000).

[20] Catherine L. Albanese, *A Republic of Mind and Spirit: A Cultural History of American Metaphysical Religion* (New Haven: Yale University Press, 2007), 16–17. On the history

predisposition towards the cosmological theory of correspondence, an understanding of the mind and its correspondences in terms of movement and energy, and a yearning for salvation understood as solace, comfort, therapy, and healing.[21] American metaphysical religion was one of the direct forerunners of the New Age Movement.

Blavatsky was occupied with the writing of her first major work from 1875 and the New York publisher J. W. Bouton published it in 1877, suggesting the title *Isis Unveiled*. According to Henry Olcott, in writing the book, Blavatsky 'copied' extracts from works that were not physically present, seeing them 'astrally'. As mentioned previously, in a series of articles published in the 1890s, the Spiritualist and opponent of Theosophy William Emmette Coleman (1843–1909) accused Blavatsky of plagiarising from unacknowledged sources, which he listed.[22] Coleman wrote, 'About 1400 books are quoted from and referred to in this work; but, from the 100 books which its author possessed, she copied everything in *Isis* taken from and relating to the other 1300.'[23] Here, Coleman highlighted what we might call 'second-hand' or indirect quotations, in which Blavatsky would claim to be citing one work while actually using a later work that quoted to the older one. In previous publications, I identified some of Blavatsky's source texts and explored how she used them, revealing this second-hand quotation to indeed have taken place, at least in some instances.[24]

Blavatsky's response to Coleman's accusation was rather equivocal. On the one hand, she denied the charge of plagiarism, yet on the other,

---

of New Thought and Christian Science, see John S. Haller Jr., *The History of New Thought* (West Chester, PA: Swedenborg Foundation Press, 2012).

[21] Albanese, *Republic*, 13–15.

[22] Notably, Coleman listed around eighty works from which he said Blavatsky had copied. See William Emmett Coleman, 'The Sources of Madame Blavatsky's Writings', in *A Modern Priestess of Isis*, ed. Vsevolod Solovyoff (London: Longmans, Green and Co., 1895). A more complete bibliography of Blavatsky's literary sources than Coleman's can be found in Gomes, *Bibliography*.

[23] Coleman (1895), 354.

[24] See Julie Chajes, 'Construction through Appropriation', and Julie Chajes, 'Blavatsky and Monotheism: Towards the Historicisation of a Critical Category', *Journal of Religion in Europe 9* (2016). Some similar conclusions were reached in Jake B. Winchester, 'Roots of the Oriental Gnosis: W. E. Coleman, H. P. Blavatsky, S. F. Dunlap' (Unpublished M.A. Thesis, University of Amsterdam, 2015).

admitted she had made 'a nosegay of culled flowers', bringing 'nothing of my own but the string that ties them'.[25] It is worth pointing out here that some of Blavatsky's major literary sources made similar statements to this, each acknowledging, defending, or even celebrating what would today be considered plagiarism.[26] These seeming admissions of plagiarism in Blavatsky and the authors to whom she was indebted point to the complexity and ambivalence of contemporary attitudes towards literary originality, Coleman's protestations notwithstanding. As Robert MacFarlane has convincingly argued, it was the early to mid-nineteenth century that had seem the evolution of the '"plagiarism hunter"; a species of literary journalist which specialised in tracking down allusions, borrowings, and derivations, and then listing these examples in an article as an arraignment of an author's originality'.[27] Towards the end of the century, however, a literary trend developed in Britain according to which it was not necessarily considered a bad thing to borrow from, or imitate, other writings.[28] In sum, Coleman was a

---

[25] Blavatsky, *Secret Doctrine I*, xlvi. For Blavatsky's denial of plagiarism, see H. P. Blavatsky, 'My Books', *Lucifer* 8, no. 45 (15 May 1891).

[26] For example, in one of the works Blavatsky consulted, the Irish barrister Edward Vaughn Hyde Kenealy (1819–1880) renounced the 'needless task of recasting the language of others'. E. V. H. Kenealy, *The Book of God: A Commentary on the Apocalypse*, 3 vols. (London: Trübner and Co., [1870]), vol. 3, 2. In 1885, in a work Blavatsky is known to have consulted, British writer on science and religion, Samuel Laing (1812–1897), admitted, 'The first part of this book does not pretend to be more than a compendious popular abridgement of [other authors'] works. I prefer, therefore, acknowledging my obligations to them once and for all, rather than encumbering each page by detailed references.' Samuel Laing, *Modern Science and Modern Thought* (London: Chapman and Hall, 1885), vi. In 1879, the British Indologist John Dowson (1820–1881) wrote, 'It is unnecessary to specify all the works which have been used in the compilation of this book.' He mentioned some, but concluded that there were 'many others too numerous to mention'. John Dowson, *A Classical Dictionary of Hindu Mythology and Religion, Geography, History, and Literature* (London: Kegan Paul, Trench, Trübner and Co., 1914), vi.

[27] Robert Macfarlane, *Original Copy: Plagiarism and Originality in Nineteenth-Century Literature* (Oxford: Oxford University Press, 2007), 41.

[28] Macfarlane, *Original Copy*, 6–7. In the American context, as Lara Langer Cohen argued, readers experienced much anxiety over their ability to discern real literature from fraudulent works (that might include plagiarisms, hoaxes, forgeries, or impostures). Lara Langer Cohen, *The Fabrication of American Literature* (Philadelphia: University of Pennsylvania Press, 2012).

plagiarism hunter, and rather a late one at that. By the time he wrote his articles on Blavatsky, not everyone shared his notions of acceptable literary practice. As if to prove this, and in a rather ironic fashion, Coleman was himself accused of plagiarism in his lifetime.[29] Be that as it may, my concern in the present work is not whether Blavatsky (or Coleman) did or did not plagiarise. Rather, I am interested in what Blavatsky's literary sources were, how she used and interpreted them, and, importantly, how we may historicise and contextualise this usage.

In a recent article, Wouter Hanegraaff highlighted some important contextualisations for the production of *Isis Unveiled*. Olcott and others portrayed Blavatsky's literary borrowings as a type of 'clairvoyance', in which she read books on the astral plane. This practice, Hanegraaff argued, was influenced by ideas deriving from mesmeric and spiritualistic currents that valorised what was basically a form of creative imagination. This imagination was stimulated, at least in Blavatsky's case, by the consumption of hashish, which, at the time, was legal.[30] Handed the enormous and unruly manuscript that resulted, Blavatsky's friend the Platonist Dr. Alexander Wilder (who will be discussed further in chapter 5) set about editing it.[31] The means of production and editorship of others probably goes some way to explaining the sometimes confusing, fragmentary nature of the text. Despite its literary shortcomings, in seven years, the book sold four thousand copies in America.[32] In this first publication, Blavatsky presented immortality as achievable during this lifetime through the unification of two inner spiritual elements, the spirit (a fragment of the Divine) and the soul (the seat of the personality). This unification was to be attained through occult practice such as astral travel and the development of one's moral faculties.

---

[29] See John Patrick Deveney, 'Sauce for the Goose: William Emmette Coleman's Defence to a Charge of Plagiarism', *Theosophical History* 8, no. 10 (October 2002).

[30] Wouter Hanegraaff, 'The Theosophical Imagination', *Correspondences* 5 (2017).

[31] In a 1908 article on 'How Isis Unveiled Was Written', he denied he was the author of the book, as some had claimed, or even that he has edited it substantially, although he acknowledged that he condensed it significantly. Wilder, 'How Isis Unveiled Was Written', 83.

[32] It was less successful in England. Robert Gilbert, *The Great Chain of Unreason: The Publication and Distribution of the Literature of Rejected Knowledge in England during the Victorian Era* (PhD diss., University of London, 2009), 213.

At death, the immortalised spirit-soul entity would undergo metem-psychosis, which, in *Isis Unveiled*, meant successive rebirth on higher worlds or planets until the highest realm was reached. *Isis Unveiled* and contemporaneous writings also taught a doctrine of 'exceptional re-incarnation', meaning the occasional return to Earth life of a spirit who had failed to achieve immortality together with the same soul. These teachings of Blavatsky's early period strongly resonated with a branch of Anglo-American Spiritualism that denied the normative repeated re-turn to Earth life and instead emphasised post-mortem ascent through higher spheres while allowing for occasional 'reincarnation'.

While still in America, Blavatsky and Olcott corresponded with Swami Dayananda Saraswati (1824–1883), a Gujarati Vedic scholar who founded the *Arya Samaj* (Aryan Society) in 1875. Their discussions led to a proposed merger between the two societies, but the relationship with Dayananda fi-nally ended in April 1882 when Olcott realised the *Arya Samaj* had little in common with Theosophy.[33] As Karl Baier has demonstrated, Blavatsky and Olcott had initially hoped Dayananda would teach Indian yogic prac-tices to members of the Society. This enterprise failed, however, and the disillusioned Theosophists thereafter downplayed yogic pursuits such as this.[34] Blavatsky also downplayed other practices initially promoted in the Society, such as astral travel, and increasingly framed Theosophy as an intellectual-spiritual pursuit.[35]

Blavatsky and Olcott arrived in Bombay in February 1879. In October, Blavatsky founded the periodical *The Theosophist*, which would come to play a crucial role in the dissemination and development of Theosophical ideas. She edited most of the issues and within months, it had acquired hundreds of subscribers and become profitable.[36] On 25 May 1880,

[33] Dayananda wished *The Theosophist* to be an exclusively *Arya Samaj* publication, excluding Buddhists and Parsis. Olcott and Blavatsky refused to accept this and Dayananda subsequently became hostile to the Theosophists. See Henry Steel Olcott, *Old Diary Leaves Second Series 1878–83* (Adyar: Theosophical Publishing House, 1974), 150–151 and 363.
[34] See Baier, *Meditation und Moderne*, esp. 329–335.
[35] Deveney, 'Two Theosophical Societies'.
[36] Olcott, *Old Diary Leaves Second Series*, 92–93 and 137. See also Carl T. Jackson, *The Oriental Religions and American Thought: Nineteenth Century Explorations* (Westport, CT, and London: Greenwood Press, 1981), 36. See also Scott, 'Miracle Publics' and

Blavatsky and Olcott took *pansil* in Ceylon, publicly declaring themselves Buddhists. By 1882, they had established the headquarters of the Theosophical Society in Adyar, a neighbourhood in Madras, in the state of Tamil Nadu, India. The Theosophical Society as it developed during this Indian period had a very different character to the one founded in New York four years previously, and it increasingly emphasised Hindu and Buddhist thought in Theosophical interpretation.

In 1880, Blavatsky had met Alfred Percy Sinnett, an English civil servant and journalist with an interest in Spiritualism who would later play a major role in the debates surrounding reincarnation.[37] Between 1880 and 1885, Sinnett exchanged letters with Blavatsky's masters Koot Hoomi and Morya, whose communications often arrived mysteriously, such as falling from the ceiling.[38] Sinnett's correspondence with the masters formed the basis of his work *Esoteric Buddhism* (1883), one of the earliest statements of Theosophical beliefs, and which paralleled the doctrines of Blavatsky's later period.[39] Following an earlier work of Sinnett's, *The Occult World* (1881)—which had not discussed reincarnation[40]—*Esoteric Buddhism* was the first book to lay out the new Theosophical theory of a normative, karmic return to Earth. *The Occult World* and *Esoteric Buddhism* were bestsellers and brought wide publicity to the Theosophical movement in India as well as internationally.[41]

When Did Blavatsky Start Teaching Reincarnation?

Blavatsky had started teaching reincarnation before Sinnett published *Esoteric Buddhism* in 1883, although it is not evident precisely when

Mark S. Morrisson, 'The Periodical Culture of the Occult Revival: Esoteric Wisdom, Modernity, and Counter-Public Spheres', *Journal of Modern Literature* 31, no. 2 (2008).

[37] Sinnett was the editor of the influential Anglo-Indian daily, *The Pioneer.* Janet Oppenheim, *The Other World: Spiritualism and Psychical Research in England, 1850–1914* (Cambridge: Cambridge University Press, 1985), 180.

[38] The originals are in the British Library. Most of the letters Sinnett received between 1880 and 1884 were published in A. Trevor Barker, ed., *The Mahatma Letters to A. P. Sinnett* (London: Unwin, 1923).

[39] Alfred Percy Sinnett, *Esoteric Buddhism* (London: Trübner and Co., 1883).

[40] Alfred Percy Sinnett, *The Occult World* (London: Trübner and Co., 1881).

[41] Goodrick-Clarke, ed., *Helena Blavatsky*, 12.

or how this came about. From the beginning of its publication, *The Theosophist* contained scattered references to reincarnation and karma in the articles of the various European, American, Indian, and Ceylonese contributors, although these represented the views of the authors and didn't prove Blavatsky's endorsement.[42] On the contrary, it is apparent that the importance of reincarnation in her thought between 1870 and 1881 was minimal, at least if *The Theosophist* is anything to go by. For example, in December 1881, she published an article on Hindu thought called 'The Popular Idea of Soul Survival' and barely mentioned reincarnation.[43] Therefore, although according to Olcott, Blavatsky said she had been taught the doctrine of reincarnation in India as early as in 1879, there's no unequivocal evidence in *The Theosophist* for the accuracy of this date.[44]

Olcott claimed reincarnation had been taught in the series of (anonymous) articles published in *The Theosophist* as *Fragments of Occult Truth*, the first of which appeared in October 1881.[45] The author was Allan Octavian Hume, an early political reformer and Theosophist who worked as secretary to the Indian government from 1870 to 1879 and who was one of the founders of the Indian National Congress. Hume was also a crucial early disseminator of teachings received from

[42] For example, the first volume contained an article on *Vedanta* philosophy that stated that those who are wise break free from the transmigrations of the soul and attain *moksha*. It also outlined a doctrine of karma. 'The Vedanta Philosophy Expounded by the Society of Benares Pandits and Translated for *The Theosophist* by Pandit Surya Narayen Sec'y', *The Theosophist* 1, no. 8 (May 1880), 202. See also Rao Bahadar Janardhan Sakharam Gadgil, 'Hindu Ideas about Communion with the Dead', *The Theosophist* 1, no. 3 (Dec 1879).

[43] In Blavatsky's estimation, according to Hindu belief, bad people have to 'linger upon earth until either their next transmigration or complete annihilation'. H. P. Blavatsky, 'The Popular Idea of Soul Survival', *The Theosophist* 1, no. 3 (Dec 1879), 62.

[44] Olcott also claimed reincarnation had been taught in Theosophical circles when he wrote *The Buddhist Catechism* (1881), although he admitted the 'exposition of the Re-incarnation theory was rather meagre in the first edition' but was 'given at much greater length in the revised edition of 1882'. Olcott, *Old Diary Leaves First Series*, 284.

[45] Olcott, *Old Diary Leaves First Series*, 284. [A. O. Hume], 'Fragments of Occult Truth', *The Theosophist* 3, no. 25 (October 1881), 17–22; *The Theosophist* 3, no. 30 (March 1882), 157–160; *The Theosophist* 3, no. 36 (September 1882), 307–314. Olcott discussed these articles, and incorrectly attributed them to Sinnett. Olcott, *Old Diary Leaves First Series*, 286.

Blavatsky's masters. Based on letters he received from the mahatmas, in *Fragments of Occult Truth*, he claimed that to understand the course of man after death, it was necessary to subdivide the three human principles Blavatsky had given in *Isis Unveiled* into seven. At death, if the 'spiritual ego' had possessed 'material tendencies',

> Then at death, it continues to cling blindly to the lower elements of its late combination, and the true spirit severs itself from these and passes away elsewhere. [. . .] (taking with it no fragment of the individual consciousness of the man with which it was temporarily associated) [. . .] But if, on the other hand, the tendencies of the EGO have been towards things spiritual, [. . .] then will it cling to the spirit, and with this pass into the adjoining so-called world of effects, (in reality, a state, and not a place), and there purified of much of its still remaining material taints, evolve out of itself by the spirit's aid a new Ego, to be reborn (after a brief period of freedom and enjoyment) in the next higher world of causes, an objective world similar to this present globe of ours, but higher in the spiritual scale, where matter and material tendencies and desires play a far less important part than here. [. . .] In either case, it is not a matter of Judgment, of Salvation and Damnation, of Heaven and Hell, but solely the operation of the Universal Law of Affinity or Attraction.[46]

This passage didn't state a person was typically reborn on Earth after death, but rather on 'the next higher world', as in metempsychosis. Nevertheless, the ideas discussed by Hume also displayed some marked similarities to Blavatsky's later theory of reincarnation, which would refer to seven principles (unlike the three of metempsychosis), affirm a period of rest between lives, and uphold an impersonal and universal law of karma, emphasising human choice of the material or spiritual. It is notable that in Hume's teaching, if the spirit were to rise, it would take 'no fragment of the individual consciousness of the man with which it was temporarily associated'. This was different to Blavatsky's doctrine of metempsychosis, in which ascent only occurred after the

[46] Hume *Fragments* (Oct 1881), 19.

spirit and soul (personality or 'individual consciousness') were conjoined. Instead, despite not teaching reincarnation, Hume again resonated with Blavatsky's later perspective, in which the spirit was said to repeatedly acquire new souls (personalities).[47] In short, the ideas Hume outlined had elements in common with those of both Blavatsky's earlier and later periods.

In 1882, there were a greater number of references to reincarnation in pages of *The Theosophist*.[48] A clear endorsement of the type of reincarnation characteristic of Blavatsky's later period came from a contributor going by the name of 'an Adept Brother' in June:

> The new *personal* Ego gets re-incarnated into a *personality* when the remembrance of his previous Egoship, of course, fades out, and he can 'communicate' no longer with his fellow-men on the planet he has left forever, as the individual he was there known to be. After numberless re-incarnations, and on numerous planets and in various spheres, a time will come, at the end of the Maha-Yug or great cycle, when each individuality will have become so spiritualised that, before its final absorption into the *One All*, its series of past *personal* existences will marshal themselves before him in a retrospective order like the many days of some one period of a man's existence.[49]

In May and June of the same year, a book review in *The Theosophist* by Sinnett also affirmed a reincarnation doctrine very similar to that of Blavatsky's later period. The work under consideration was *The Perfect Way; Or; The Finding of Christ* (1882) by Dr. Anna Bonus Kingsford (1846–1888), a Spiritualist, convert to Catholicism, and animal rights activist with ties to Theosophy.[50] As a medium, Kingsford worked closely with Edward Maitland (1824–1897) to teach 'a new dispensation'

---

[47] This theme had already been present in Blavatsky's earlier doctrine of metempsychosis, in which the soul and spirit struggled to conjoin and ascend, rather than be annihilated.

[48] For example, see Babu Jwala Prasad Sankhadar, 'Aeen-I-Hoshang', *The Theosophist* 3, no. 8 (May 1882), 210.

[49] 'The Adept Brothers', 'Editor's Note', *The Theosophist* 3, no. 9 (June 1882), 226.

[50] Anna Bonus Kingsford and Edward Maitland, *The Perfect Way; or, The Finding of Christ* (London: Field and Tuer, 1882).

comprising an ahistorical, allegorical interpretation of Christianity. In May, June, and July 1881, Kingsford and Maitland had given a series of lectures outlining their teachings and these were published early in 1882 as *The Perfect Way*. Although there were differences, it was significant that they taught a theory of reincarnation that resonated with Blavatsky's later point of view in its affirmation that the immortal spirit returned with a new soul each time it reincarnated (as affirmed by the 'Adept Bother' above).[51] Kingsford's lectures were backed financially by Marie (née de Mariategue), the Countess of Caithness, a well-connected promoter of Theosophy in France, whose book, published six years before Kingsford's, *Old Truths in a New Light* (1876), anticipated many of the tenets of Blavatsky's *Isis Unveiled*.[52] In that work, Caithness had advocated reincarnation in the style of Allan Kardec, in which the same personality returned repeatedly to life on Earth.[53] Olav Hammer argued that both Caithness and Kingsford were prominent spokespersons for reincarnation in the 1870s, with Kingsford probably learning of reincarnation through Caithness.[54] He affirmed Blavatsky inherited at least some of her tenets from these two women, observing that the '*Secret*

---

[51] Differences between Kingsford's and Blavatsky's reincarnation theories included that Kingsford didn't teach a doctrine of *devachan*, and although she upheld the possibility of reincarnation on other planets, it was a different conception to that outlined by Blavatsky in *The Secret Doctrine*. Kingsford also taught the possibility of reincarnation as an animal following human incarnation, an idea Blavatsky rejected vehemently.

[52] See Marco Pasi, 'Exégèse et Sexualité: L'occultisme oublié de Lady Caithness', *Politica Hermetica* 20 (2006), 76–77; Joscelyn Godwin, *The Theosophical Enlightenment* (Albany: State University of New York Press, 1994), 304–305 and 338; and Joscelyn Godwin, 'Lady Caithness and Her Connection with Theosophy', *Theosophical History* 8, no. 4 (October 2000), 128.

[53] Like Blavatsky, Caithness maintained that a person evolves through mineral, vegetable, and animal stages of development. She described this as a 'law of progress' and asserted retrogression was impossible. She taught that following numerous incarnations on Earth, one would 'rise magnetically to purer spheres'. She offered numerous scriptural proofs for reincarnation and advanced a doctrine of karma, writing, 'Christ frequently gave us to understand that suffering and infirmity was a punishment for sin, either in this or in some previous life.' Her work had a Christian emphasis Blavatsky did not share. Countess of Caithness, *Old Truths in a New Light, or, An Earnest Endeavour to Reconcile Material Science with Spiritual Science, and with Scripture* (London: Chapman and Hall, 1876), 319–320 and 340–341.

[54] Hammer, *Claiming Knowledge*, 464–465.

Doctrine is an elaborate myth in which a rich tapestry of details fills out the bare-bones account of reincarnation that Blavatsky had inherited from Kardec via Kingsford, Lady Caithness and others.'[55]

Did Blavatsky (and consequently other Theosophists, such as Sinnett and Olcott) adopt reincarnation under the influence of Anna Bonus Kingsford? Edward Maitland seemed to think so. Writing of Kingsford's life, he reminisced about an early encounter with Sinnett:

> We were [. . .] greatly surprised to learn from Mr Sinnett that [reincarnation and karma] formed no part of the doctrine of the Theosophical Society, being neither contained in their chief text-book, the *Isis Unveiled* of its founders, nor communicated to it by its Masters, and on these grounds Mr Sinnett rejected them, sitting up with us until long after midnight arguing against them, and saying, amongst other things, of the doctrine of Reincarnation, that even of the Spiritualists only a few who followed Allan Kardec accepted it. Whereupon we stated our conviction that it would yet be given to his Society by its Eastern teachers, and that, as for Allan Kardec's writings, we knew of them enough to know that they were far from trustworthy, and his presentation of that doctrine especially was un-scientific and erroneous.[56]

Maitland also reflected on how a year later, Sinnett had embraced re-incarnation, much to his surprise:

> Recalling [Sinnett's] persistent denial of Reincarnation on his visit to us in the previous year, we were interested to find him now accepting the doctrine. But even here also he differed from us in certain re-spects. For where we had taught the possibility of a soul's return into a form below the human, by way of penance for grievous faults, he insisted to the contrary on the ground that 'Nature does not go back on her own footsteps.'[57]

[55] Ibid., 468.
[56] Edward Maitland, *Anna Kingsford: Her Life, Letters, Diary, and Work* (London: George Redway, 1896), 19.
[57] Edward Maitland, *Anna Kingsford: Her Life*, 67.

Maitland stated he and Kingsford had derived reincarnation 'directly from a celestial source and wholly independently of human authority and tradition, of spiritualism, and of our own prepossessions' and that they adopted if before the Theosophists did:[58]

> It was clear, both by this fact and by the avowals of the parties con-
> cerned, that up to this time the chiefs of the Theosophical Society
> had been unable to obtain from those whom they claimed as their
> masters more than a very meagre instalment of their doctrine. But
> after the arrival of our book in India this state of things was changed.
> It was then declared on behalf of the 'masters' that we had obtained,
> from original and independent sources, a system of doctrine sub-
> stantially identical with that of which they had for ages been, as they
> supposed, in exclusive possession, but had never been permitted to
> divulge, as it had always been reserved for initiates. The revelation of
> it through us, we were informed, had 'forced the hands of the mas-
> ters', by showing them that the time had come when secrecy was no
> longer possible, and compelling them, if only in vindication of their
> own claims, to relax their rule of silence in regard to their mysteries.
> The coincidence between their doctrine and ours comprised sundry
> particulars the most recondite, including—besides the two great
> tenets already named—the multiplicity of principles in the human
> system, and their separation and respective conditions after death,—
> a subject lying outside the cognisance of 'Spiritualism'.[59]

Whereas Maitland chose to emphasise the similarities between Kingsford's and Blavatsky's new theory of reincarnation, Sinnett emphasised the differences, correcting various particulars in his review of *The Perfect Way*. As Maitland mentioned above, the idea of human to animal reincarnation was a particular bone of contention between Sinnett and the authors. 'Nature does not go back upon her own foot-steps in the awkward way here imagined,' wrote Sinnett. 'The animals

[58] Edward Maitland, *The Story of Anna Kingsford and Edward Maitland and of The New Gospel of Interpretation* (Birmingham: Ruskin Press, 1905), 192.
[59] Maitland, *Story of Anna Kingsford*, 192–193.

around us are not re-incarnations of our sinful predecessors, but fresh fruit of the great tree of life.'[60]

In the July 1882 issue of the Spiritualist periodical *Light,* the Spiritualist, lawyer, and early Theosophist Charles Carlton Massey quoted a section of Sinnett's review that affirmed reincarnation alongside some extracts taken from *Isis Unveiled* that seemed to deny it. Massey asked for clarification.[61] In August 1882, Blavatsky published an article in *The Theosophist* admitting the passage in *Isis* in question was incomplete, chaotic, clumsy, and perhaps vague, but arguing there was no discrepancy: it had always been maintained that the same personality would not return to life on Earth under normal circumstances. Her explanation clarified some aspects of the apparent contradiction but left others unresolved.[62]

In January 1883, a letter from Mahatma Koot Hoomi to Sinnett stated the misunderstanding that Kingsford (and Maitland) had adopted reincarnation *before* the Theosophists was in need of correction. Koot Hoomi implored Sinnett to write to Massey. In addition to denouncing the errors of the Kardecist notion of the repeated rebirth of the same personality, Koot Hoomi was obviously concerned people might think the Theosophists had taken the reincarnation teaching from *The Perfect Way.* He used the term 'Monad' to refer to the reincarnating entity.

---

[60] Alfred Percy Sinnett, 'Review of The Perfect Way', *The Theosophist* 3, no. 9 (June 1882), 234. Kingsford replied in a letter written on 10 July and published in *The Theosophist* in September 1882. She argued it was possible 'to descend, as well as to ascend, upon the manifold steps of the ladder of Incarnation and Re-births. Your critic allows, indeed, that the individual may become "extinct", but he rejects the process of deterioration, by means of which alone extinction becomes possible. And, in thus denying a logical and scientific necessity, he both contradicts the teaching of the Hindu and other sacred mysteries, and also, by implication, "represents man as attaining perfection by means mechanical and compulsory, instead of by the inevitable action of free-will."' Anna Bonus Kingsford and Edward Maitland, 'The Perfect Way', *The Theosophist* 3, no. 12 (September 1882), 296.

[61] Charles Carlton Massey, ' "Isis Unveiled" and the "Theosophist" on Reincarnation', *Light* 79, no. 2 (8 July 1882), 323.

[62] H. P. Blavatsky, ' "Isis Unveiled" and the "Theosophist" on Reincarnation', *The Theosophist* 3, no. 11 (August 1882), 288–289.

An affair now so trivial as to seem but the innocent expression of feminine vanity may, unless at once set aright, produce very evil consequences. In a letter from Mrs. Kingsford to Mr. Massey conditionally accepting the presidentship of the British T.S. she expresses her belief—nay, points it out as an undeniable fact—that before the appearance of 'The Perfect Way' no one 'knew what the Oriental school really held about Reincarnation' [. . .] Write then, good friend, to Mr. Massey the truth. Tell him that you were possessed of the Oriental views of reincarnation several months before the work in question had appeared—since it is in July (18 months ago) that, you began being taught the difference between Reincarnation *à la* Allan Kardec, or personal rebirth—and that of the Spiritual Monad; a difference first pointed out to you on July 5th at Bombay.[63]

Eighteen months prior to this letter gives a date of July 1881, and Sinnett had indeed received a letter from Koot Hoomi on 8 July 1881, while he had been staying with Blavatsky in India. The letter discussed 'the whole ladder of Evolution'. The teaching given was that in ascending the ladder, the person who had died would not miss a rung and would halt at every 'star world', 'to perform in it his own "*life-cycle*" ', 'returning and reincarnating as many times as he fails to complete his round of life in it, as he dies on it before reaching the age of reason as correctly stated in *Isis*'. In other words, in addition to travelling up the rungs of the ladder, that is, from 'star world to star world', one had to complete multiple cycles (regenerations) on each world, until 'the age of reason' was reached and graduation to the next level occurred.[64] Koot Hoomi elaborated:

That is what happens. After *circling*, so to say, along the arc of the cycle, circling along and within it (the daily and yearly rotation of the Earth is as good an illustration as any) when the Spirit-man reaches our planet, which is one of the lowest, having lost at every station

---

[63] Letter 57, 6 January 1883, in Barker, ed., *Mahatma Letters to A. P. Sinnett*, 328–329.
[64] This 'age of reason' can be considered analogous to what in *Isis Unveiled* had been presented as the achievement of immortality, in which 'reason becomes active and discriminative'. It will be discussed in the following chapter. Blavatsky, *Isis I*, 351.

some of the etherial and acquired an increase of material nature, both spirit and matter have become pretty much equilibrized in him. But then, he has the Earth's cycle to perform.[65]

In other words, the spirit-man's cycles around one planet (i.e., his re-incarnations) were comparable to the cycles of day and night that occurred as the Earth revolved. There was also a yearly cycle, in which the Earth moved around the sun. This was comparable to the 'cycle' of the spirit-man from planet to planet. Thus, the reincarnating entity travelled from planet to planet but also completed multiple life cycles on each planet. The spirit-man arrived on the Earth from more spiritual planets. Once he reached the most material planet, the Earth, he would be in a state of spirit-matter equilibrium, and would struggle to regain his spiritual nature due to the 'pull' of matter. If successful, he would continue his evolution on more spiritualised planets. Only the few would achieve this.

At that point the great Law begins its work of selection. Matter found entirely divorced from spirit is thrown over into the still lower worlds—into the *sixth* 'GATE' or 'way of rebirth' of the vegetable and mineral worlds, and of the primitive animal forms. From thence, matter ground over in the workshop of nature proceeds *soulless* back to its Mother Fount; while the *Egos* purified of their dross are enabled to resume their progress once more onward. It is here, then, that the laggard *Egos* perish by the millions. It is the solemn moment of the 'survival of the fittest', the annihilation of those unfit. It is but matter (or material man) which is compelled by its own weight to descend to the very bottom of the 'circle of necessity' to there assume animal form.[66]

Two options were given for those spirit-men who reached the Earth. Either they would purify themselves of matter or they would not. If they did, then this cast-off matter would be recycled and ground over

[65] Letter 9, from Koot Hoomi to Sinnett, received 8 July 1881, in Barker, ed., *Mahatma Letters to A. P. Sinnett*, 46–47.
[66] Letter 9, in *Mahatma Letters*, 47.

in the economy of nature, where it would once again proceed through mineral, vegetable, and primitive animal forms in a type of metempsychosis. Egos who failed to cast of matter in this way would be annihilated. According to Koot Hoomi, successful egos would ascend.

> As to the winner of that race throughout the worlds—the Spiritual Ego, he will ascend from star to star, from one world to another, circling onward to rebecome the once pure planetary Spirit, then higher still, to finally reach its first starting point, and from thence— to merge into MYSTERY.[67]

Overall, like Hume's *Fragments of Occult Truth* (1881–1882), Koot Hoomi's July 1881 discussion incorporated elements consistent both with Blavatsky's earlier and later rebirth doctrines.[68] In that he stated humans customarily returned to life on Earth after death, he agreed with what Blavatsky termed reincarnation during her later period, although his account lacked some of the features of hers in its fully elaborated version. Since we cannot come to any definite conclusions about the identity of Koot Hoomi, all this shows is that *a* theory of reincarnation (with some features in common with Blavatsky's) was taught in Theosophical circles in July 1881.

What may we conclude about the provenance of Blavatsky's ideas? Both Koot Hoomi's teachings of July 1881 and Anna Bonus Kingsford's lectures of June and July 1881 anticipated central elements of Blavatsky's later reincarnation doctrine. Blavatsky claimed to have received her Theosophical principles from the masters, but she (and/or Koot Hoomi) may have been inspired by Kingsford or by a third, unknown source on which Kingsford also drew. It seems plausible that, as Olav Hammer surmised, Blavatsky assimilated *some details* of her reincarnationism in its final form from Kingsford. Koot Hoomi may also have been inspired by Kingsford, although what this means with regard to Blavatsky

---

[67] Ibid.
[68] In Blavatsky's metempsychosis doctrine, the majority of monads would be annihilated due to having failed to achieve immortality. In Blavatsky's later theory of reincarnation, the monad was said to travel around seven spheres repeatedly reincarnating on each one. The 'circle of necessity' referred to the cycle of incarnations.

is open to debate. Be that as it may, neither Koot Hoomi nor Kingsford described in its entirety the fractal cosmos of reincarnating universes, planets, and monads (reincarnating entities) characteristic of Blavatsky's later period. Therefore, whatever debt Blavatsky may have owed to Kingsford or a third source, the complex reincarnationist cosmology she eventually elaborated was influenced by a great deal more besides. Among her influences were Platonic and neo-Platonic accounts, diverse contemporary scientific theories of evolution, and modernising interpretations of Hindu and Buddhist thought. These will be explored in detail presently.

The Secret Doctrine and Theosophy's Legacy

Blavatsky left India once and for all in 1885, travelling to Würzburg, Bavaria, where she began writing her magnum opus, *The Secret Doctrine*. She completed it in England and the Theosophical Publishing Company issued it in 1888.[69] Blavatsky's writing process seems to have been similar to that used in the production of *Isis Unveiled*, and contemporaneous sources refer to some sort of undefined 'esoteric' method. It was initially envisaged as a rewriting of *Isis Unveiled*, but this conception soon changed as the work progressed. A central motivating factor was to show that the earlier and later teachings did not contradict one another, a project that, as we will see, had limited success. Importantly, Blavatsky had the help of the prominent Indian Theosophists Tallapragada Subba Row (1856–1890) and Mohini Mohun Chatterji (1858–1936), who will be discussed in chapter 7. The resulting book manuscript was as disorderly as that of *Isis* had been, but this time the editing fell to the Theosophists Bertram Keightley (1860–1944) and his nephew Archibald Keightley (1859–1930).[70]

Blavatsky claimed *The Secret Doctrine* was based on translations of verses from the secret *Book of Dzyan*, a commentary on the books of *Kiu-Te*, both texts that remain unidentified. Basing her discussions on

[69] It was originally to be published by George Redway, but this didn't work out. Gilbert, *The Great Chain of Unreason*, 214–217.
[70] The nephew was indeed one year older than his uncle. Hanegraaff, 'The Theosophical Imagination', 16.

her translations of stanzas of this unknown esoteric text, in *The Secret Doctrine*, Blavatsky now expanded on the teachings presented in Sinnett's *Esoteric Buddhism*, giving a more fully developed account and sometimes correcting Sinnett. She taught the existence of a single absolute reality, the cyclic and evolutionary nature of the universe, the development of humanity through seven root races, and the septenary constitution of the universe and of man. She now taught reincarnation as the normative, repeated, and karmic return of the spirit to Earth life, taking on new lower principles with each incarnation. Blavatsky repeated her views on reincarnation in works such as *The Key to Theosophy* (1889), a digest of Theosophy in the form of questions and answers, and in the numerous articles she wrote for *The Theosophist* and other periodicals.

Blavatsky died in London in 1891. It was the beginning of Theosophy's heyday, which would last until around 1930.[71] During those years, the Theosophical Society attracted a significant amount of press coverage and drew followers substantially from the professional and upper classes. Aristocratic early members included the Russian princess Ada Troubetzkoy, who was living in Italy; the British countess Muriel De La Warr; Viscountess Verena Maud Churchill; and the Earl of Crawford.[72] Other prominent individuals included the American military officer and inventor Abner Doubleday (1819–1893);[73] the French astronomer Camille Flammarion (1842–1925); the inventor of the light bulb, the American Thomas Edison (1847–1931); and the Irish poet William Butler Yeats (1865–1939). Numerous other literary, artistic, political, and religious figures and movements took their inspiration from Theosophy.[74]

---

[71] W. Michael Ashcraft, *The Dawn of the New Cycle: Point Loma Theosophists and American Culture* (Knoxville: University of Tennessee Press, 2002), 23.
[72] Hermann A. O. de Tollenaere, *The Politics of Divine Wisdom: Theosophy and Labour, National, and Women's Movements in Indonesia and South Asia 1875–1947* (Leiden: Uitgeverij Katholiek Universiteit Nijmegen, 1996), 97.
[73] Robert S. Ellwood, 'The American Theosophical Synthesis', in *The Occult in America: New Historical Perspectives*, ed. Howard Kerr and Charles L. Crow (Urbana and Chicago: University of Illinois Press, 1986).
[74] On Theosophy in Russian literature, see Eugene Kuzmin, 'Maksimilian Voloshin and the Kabbalah', in *Theosophical Appropriations*. On Theosophy and the visual arts, in the same volume, see Victoria Ferentinou, 'Light from Within or Light from Above? Theosophical Appropriations in Early Twentieth Century Greek Culture' and Massimo Introvigne, 'Lawren Harris and the Theosophical Appropriation of Canadian

Not least among them were some of the best-known writers on Asian religions of the twentieth century, such as Alexandra David-Néel (1868–1969), Daisetsu Teitaro Suzuki (1870–1966), Walter Evans-Wentz (1878–1965), and Edward Conze (1904–1979).[75] Theosophy influenced the development of modern forms of Buddhism in Sri Lanka, and globally, and had an impact on Mohandas Gandhi (1869–1948) and the Indian National Congress.[76] The Theosophical Society quickly established branches the world over, inspiring numerous other movements and societies themselves highly influential.[77] The best known of these is Anthroposophy, which has a strong and vocal presence, particularly in Germany.[78] The founder, Rudolf Steiner (1861–1925), was a Theosophist who broke away to form his own society, teaching a doctrine of reincarnation that was a complex elaboration of Blavatsky's.

Nationalism'. See also Tessel Bauduin, 'The Occult and the Visual Arts', in *The Occult World*, 429–445.

[75] Paul Pedersen, 'Tibet, Theosophy, and the Psychologization of Buddhism', in *Imagining Tibet*, ed. Thierry Dodin and Heinz Räther (Boston: Wisdom Publications, 2001), 157.

[76] On the impact of Theosophy on Buddhism, see Prothero, *The White Buddhist* and David McMahan, *The Making of Buddhist Modernism* (Oxford: Oxford University Press, 2009). Michael Bergunder has observed that Gandhi drew on Kingsford and Maitland's teachings on reincarnation to bridge Christianity and Hinduism, noting the increasing number of Christians who believed in the possibility of the soul's return to a new body. Michael Bergunder, 'Experiments with Theosophical Truth: Gandhi, Esotericism, and Global Religious History', *Journal of the American Academy of Religion* 82, no. 2 (1 June 2014). On Theosophy and the Indian National Congress, see W. Travis Hanes Jr., 'On the Origins of the Indian National Congress: A Case Study of Cross-Cultural Synthesis', *Journal of World History* 4, no. 1 (Spring 1993), 69–98. See also Shimon Lev, 'Gandhi and His Jewish Theosophist Supporters in South Africa', in *Theosophical Appropriations*.

[77] On movements deriving from Theosophy, see Kevin Tingay, 'Madame Blavatsky's Children: Theosophy and Its Heirs', in *Beyond New Age: Exploring Alternative Spirituality*, ed. Steven Sutcliffe and Marion Bowman (Edinburgh: Edinburgh University Press, 2000).

[78] On the presence and influence of Anthroposophy in Germany, see Helmut Zander, 'Transformations of Anthroposophy from the Death of Rudolf Steiner to the Present Day', in *Theosophical Appropriations*. On the connection between Anthroposophy and Theosophy, see Helmut Zander, *Anthroposophie in Deutschland. Theosophische Milieus und gesellschaftliche Praxis, 1884 bis 1945* (Göttingen: Vandenhoeck and Ruprecht, 2007).

Other well-known figures heavily influenced by Theosophy include the New Age author Alice A. Bailey (1880–1949) and Jiddhu Krishnamurti (1895–1986).[79] The latter was groomed to become the new 'World Teacher' by Blavatsky's successor, Annie Besant (1847–1933), together with Charles Webster Leadbeater (1854–1934).[80] When Krishnamurti renounced this role in 1929, the Society lost many members and never really recovered, going into a long period of decline.

Nevertheless, the Theosophical Society continues to exist and is represented today by three different organisations. The American Section of the Theosophical Society was created in 1886. Theosophical co-founder William Quan Judge remained the head of this organisation until his death, when the leadership passed to Katherine Tingley (1847–1929). It is based in Pasadena, California. The United Lodge of Theosophists is a breakaway from Judge's group founded in 1909 by Robert Crosbie (1849–1919). Finally, the section originally led by Olcott with Annie Besant, is known as the Theosophical Society Adyar and it has the most members. The Indian headquarters are still in Adyar and the American branch is in Wheaton, Illinois.[81]

The historical importance of Theosophy is almost impossible to over-estimate. The heirs of Blavatsky's thought include not only the individuals and societies mentioned above, but also the multitude of people in the predominantly Christian Western countries who identify as 'spiritual but not religious' and who believe that in some sense, all religions point to the same universal truth. They may affirm the value of Eastern spirituality and be suspicious of monotheistic faiths. Many believe in reincarnation and karma or entertain it as plausible. I am not suggesting Blavatsky was solely responsible for these shifts; Theosophy emerged from a cultural milieu permeated by many other factors that challenged traditional forms of faith. Nevertheless, it is undeniable she was a pivotal figure in the development of modern and postmodern spirituality.

[79] See Ellwood, 'The American Theosophical Synthesis', III. For a fuller discussion of those influenced by Theosophy see Kevin Tingay, 'Theosophy and Its Heirs'.
[80] On Besant and Leadbeater, see Jake Poller, 'Under a Glamour: Annie Besant, Charles Leadbeater and Neo-Theosophy', in *The Occult Imagination in Britain, 1875–1947*, ed. Christine Ferguson and Andrew Radford (London: Routledge, 2018).
[81] See Ashcraft, *Dawn of the New Cycle*, 24–26.

2

Isis Unveiled and Metempsychosis

HELMUT ZANDER CLAIMED BLAVATSKY excluded the concept of reincarnation from *Isis Unveiled* (1877) or only used it metaphorically. He observed she distinguished between reincarnation and metempsychosis, which she gave a non-literal interpretation. He acknowledged there were some passages in which Blavatsky wrote approvingly of reincarnation but maintained it would be impossible to build a theory of reincarnation in *Isis Unveiled* without suppressing the places where she denied it, or which were inconclusive and ambiguous.[1,2]

As a matter of fact, it is possible to elucidate how Blavatsky conceived of reincarnation and metempsychosis in *Isis Unveiled*, and it was as distinct doctrines that were understood literally. *Isis Unveiled* offered two main rebirth possibilities: 'metempsychosis' and 'reincarnation'. Metempsychosis was the primary tenet and referred to the transformations (described as 'transmigrations') of the pre-human entity through existences on other spheres, then through mineral, plant, and animal forms on Earth, leading up to the gestational phases of the human embryo prior to human incarnation. After being born on Earth, humans were composed of a 'trinity' of principles: body, soul, and spirit. Immortality could be achieved during Earth-life by conjoining the

---

[1] A version of this chapter was published as Julie Chajes, 'Metempsychosis and Reincarnation in *Isis* Unveiled', *Theosophical History* 16, nos. 3 and 4 (July–October 2012).
[2] Helmut Zander, *Geschichte der Seelenwanderung in Europa: Alternative religiöse Traditionen von der Antike bis Heute* (Darmstadt: Wissenschaftliche Buchgesellschaft, 1999), 478.

spirit and soul through occult practice, leading to progress on spheres higher than the Earth and eventually to nirvana—envisaged as absorption into the divine—in the seventh and highest sphere. The process was considered 'cyclic' inasmuch as all spirits had originally issued from this divine source and were finding their way home and completing the cycle.

Blavatsky referred to the second post-mortem possibility as 'reincarnation', but in *Isis Unveiled*, this term referred to a different theory to the one taught under that name in Blavatsky's second major work, the *Secret Doctrine* (1888). In *Isis Unveiled*, 'reincarnation' nearly always indicated a spirit's second incarnation on Earth with the same soul. This was said to occur only in exceptional circumstances, such as infant death or congenital idiocy, conferring a 'second chance' in cases where post-mortem annihilation (the result of failure to achieve immortality) would have been unjust. Blavatsky was at pains to contrast this theory of exceptional same-soul reincarnation with the popular Spiritist belief that, as a rule, the same soul or personality repeatedly returned to Earth-life. Rather, according to Blavatsky, atypical circumstances were the only ones in which another life on Earth occurred. That being the case, she avoided the use of the term 'reincarnation' in her early publications, because it was associated with French Spiritism.

Blavatsky taught the most common post-mortem occurrence was in fact that the soul and spirit failed to conjoin. For the few who did succeed in achieving immortality, transmigration through the higher spheres awaited. During this metempsychosis, a new astral body would be acquired on each sphere after the previous one had been discarded. This repeated transmigration of the conjoined soul-spirit into a new astral body maintained a constant tripartite composition. Very confusingly, Blavatsky sometimes portrayed this as yet another type of 'reincarnation', although it didn't take place on Earth. In *The Secret Doctrine*, her teachings on human rebirth were different and she tried to harmonise her divergent accounts with limited success.[3] Although

---

[3] Blavatsky, ' "Isis Unveiled" and The "Theosophist" on Reincarnation' and 'Theories about Reincarnation and Spirits', *The Path* 1, no. 8 (November 1886). She wrote the latter in Ostende, Belgium, in October 1886.

she was being somewhat disingenuous when she claimed she had always taught reincarnation, in a sense, she was telling the truth. She *had* previously taught a *type* of 'reincarnation', it just wasn't the same type of reincarnation she later affirmed.

Most previous scholarly discussions of Blavatsky's views on life after death have overlooked metempsychosis as well as the closely related early Theosophical principle of the achievement of immortality.[4] In what follows, I demonstrate, through the analysis of extracts from *Isis Unveiled* and early letters, that Blavatsky taught the two doctrines outlined above. I examine Blavatsky's early statements closely to reveal further details such the repeated acquisition of astral bodies, the case of 'terrestrial larvae', the 'transfer of a spiritual entity' to a student by an adept, and the theory of 'permutation' or 'revolution'.

Pythagorean Metempsychosis versus Kardecist Reincarnation

In her early work, Blavatsky ascribed belief in metempsychosis (rather than reincarnation) to those she most admired. She cited the English Classicist John Lemprière (1765–1824), suggesting Pythagoras learned of metempsychosis in India, and arguing all ancient philosophers had taught metempsychosis, including the Gnostics and Church Fathers. She suggested Pythagoras learned it from the Brahmans and Buddhists:

> There was not a philosopher of any notoriety who did not hold to this doctrine of metempsychosis, as taught by the Brahmans, Buddhists, and later by the Pythagoreans, in its esoteric sense, whether he expressed it more or less intelligibly. Origen and Clemens Alexandrinus, Synesius and Chalcidius, all believed in it; and the Gnostics, who are unhesitatingly proclaimed by history as a body of the most refined, learned, and enlightened men, were all believers in metempsychosis.[5]

---

[4] John Patrick Deveney did note them, pointing to Randolph's denial of reincarnation and affirmation of metempsychosis, and to parallel arguments in Blavatsky's early writings. John Patrick Deveney, *Paschal Beverly Randolph: A Nineteenth-Century Black American Spiritualist, Rosicrucian, and Sex Magician* (Albany: State University of New York Press, 1997), 278–282.

[5] Blavatsky, *Isis I*, 12.

She also mentioned the Pythagorean metempsychosis belief of Giordano Bruno—the Italian philosopher condemned by the Roman Inquisition for heresy in 1600: 'Perfidious as they are, the above words plainly indicate the belief of Bruno in the Pythagorean metempsychosis, which, misunderstood as it is, still shows a belief in the *survival* of man in one shape or another.'[6] Giving further (and witty) endorsement, she linked Pythagorean metempsychosis and evolution: 'If the Pythagorean metempsychosis should be thoroughly explained and compared with the modern theory of evolution, it would be found to supply every "missing link" in the chain of the latter.'[7]

In a letter to Charles Carlton Massey sent in February 1876 (one year before *Isis Unveiled* was published), Blavatsky equated her understanding of the 'Eastern Kabbalah' with Pythagoreanism. She said Pythagoras (and the neo-Platonists) didn't teach reincarnation, as the Spiritists did, but rather an esoteric doctrine.

> The eastern Kabbalah embraces the Pythagorean philosophy; the western, or Rosicrucian, *did not.* But the metempsychosis of Pythagoras was an exoteric expression to cover the esoteric meaning, and his commentators, who had not the key, have misunderstood him as grossly as they have misunderstood everything else written by those of the Neoplatonics, who, like Porphyry, Iamblichus and Plotinus, have been adopting and elaborating his precepts. The spirits upon whose communications the reincarnationist school base their theory, have simply given back the opinions which they found in the heads or brains of their mediums.[8]

Blavatsky claimed European scholars had distorted metempsychosis and stressed the need to understand it *properly.* 'The doctrine of *Metempsychosis* has been abundantly ridiculed by men of science and rejected by theologians, yet if it had been properly understood in its application to the indestructibility of matter and the immortality of spirit,

---

[6] Ibid., 95.
[7] Ibid., 9.
[8] H. P. Blavatsky, 'Letter 65, to C. C. Massey' [February 1876], in Blavatsky, *Letters*, 248–249.

it would have been perceived that it is a sublime conception.'[9] One can hardly imagine a stronger endorsement for metempsychosis than this.

Blavatsky repeatedly affirmed the existence of a true interpretation of metempsychosis, as opposed to 'popular beliefs' about it (i.e., Spiritism).

> It is again from this sense of highest benevolence and charity toward the weaker, however abject the creature may be, that they honor one of the natural modifications of their own dual nature, and that later the popular belief in metempsychosis arose. No trace of the latter is to be found in the *Vedas*; and the true interpretation of the doctrine, discussed at length in *Manu* and the Buddhistic sacred books, having been confined from the first to the learned and sacerdotal castes, the false and foolish popular ideas concerning it need occasion no surprise.[10]

Here, Blavatsky contrasted popular misunderstandings about metempsychosis (which are not to be found in the Vedas, even though— and we may read between the lines—they may be found in 'exoteric' Hinduism) with the true interpretation of metempsychosis (which, according to Blavatsky, *is* found in the Hindu work *The Laws of Manu*, as well as in Buddhist texts).

Blavatsky equated the teachings of Plato, Pythagoras, the Chaldeans, and the late thirteenth-century Kabbalistic text the *Zohar*, arguing all had taught a progress of the spirit on higher worlds after death (i.e., metempsychosis). The *Zohar* was specifically invoked to *disprove* the commonly held Spiritist notion of reincarnation as the repeated return of the same personality.

> Plato, Anaxagoras, Pythagoras, the Eleatic schools of Greece, as well as the old Chaldean sacerdotal colleges, all taught the doctrine of the dual evolution; the doctrine of transmigration of souls referring *only to the progress of man from world to world*, after death [. . .] a soul which thirsts after a reunion with its spirit, which alone confers upon

---

[9] Blavatsky, *Isis I*, 8.
[10] Ibid., 279.

it immortality, must purify itself through cyclic transmigrations, onward toward the only Land of Bliss and Eternal Rest, called in the
Sohar, 'The Palace of Love' [. . .] The proof that transmigration of
the soul does not relate to man's condition on this earth after death,
is found in the *Sohar*.[11]

In other words, transmigration involved progress from one world to
the next (not a return to Earth) and was cast as purificatory and cyclic.
However, the fact it was cyclic did *not* mean it involved a normative
repeated return to Earth. Blavatsky quite clearly stated that transmigration occurred from world to world and didn't relate to man's condition
on Earth.

Transmigrations before, during, and after One Life on Earth

In *Isis Unveiled*, the pre-human entity was said to begin its journey
into matter after having been 'issued forth' from its divine parent. It
would transmigrate through mineral and animal forms until it reached
a human womb, where it 're-lived' a version of those earlier transmigrations before entering human life on Earth for the first and probably
only time. Blavatsky explained 'reincarnationists' (i.e., of the Spiritist
Allan Kardec school) quoted Apuleius (author of the second-century
Latin work *The Golden Ass*, or *Metamorphoses*) in corroboration of their
theory that man passed through a succession of physical human births
on Earth, but Blavatsky claimed Apuleius corroborated her denial of
reincarnation, not the Spiritist affirmation of it.

Says Apuleius [. . .] 'The soul is born in this world upon leaving *another world* (*anima mundi*), in which her existence precedes the one
we all know (on earth). [. . .]' This language can hardly be called ambiguous, and yet, the Reincarnationists quote Apuleius in corroboration of their theory that man passes through a succession of physical
human births upon this planet, until he is finally purged from the
dross of his nature. But Apuleius distinctly says that we come upon

[11] Ibid., 279–280.

this earth from another one, where we had an existence, the recol-
lection of which has faded away. As the watch passes from hand to
hand and room to room in a factory, one part being added here and
another there, until the delicate machine is perfected, according to
the design conceived in the mind of the master before the work was
begun; so, according to ancient philosophy, the first divine conception of man takes shape little by little, in the several departments of
the universal workshop, and the perfect human being finally appears
on our scene.[12]

In other words, souls didn't arrive on Earth having lived a previous
life on Earth, as the Spiritists claimed, but rather from another planet.
These planets were like the different rooms of a watch factory, where the
watches were perfected. This perfection was not dependent on karma,
which, although mentioned occasionally in *Isis Unveiled*, didn't play a
major role in Blavatsky's thinking at the time. Her cosmos perfected
anyway, without a developed theory of karmic retribution.

Having arrived from another planet, metempsychosis would continue on Earth. Blavatsky discussed the Earth-stage in detail, using the
term 'monad' for the reincarnating entity:

The monad was shot down into the first form of matter and became
encased in stone; then, in course of time, [. . .] the monad crept out
of its prison to sunlight as a lichen. From change to change it went
higher and higher; [. . .] until its physical form became once more
the Adam *of dust*, shaped in the image of the Adam Kadmon. Before
undergoing its last earthly transformation, the external covering of
the monad, from the moment of its conception as an embryo, passes
in turn, once more, through the phases of the several kingdoms. In
its fluidic prison it assumes a vague resemblance at various periods
of the gestation to plant, reptile, bird, and animal, until it becomes
a human embryo.[13]

[12] Ibid., 345.
[13] Ibid., 202–203.

The monad's journey through these forms was an elaboration of Blavatsky's wider belief that there was no such thing as dead matter: everything was infused with spirit. The 'Adam of Dust' represented the human being, and Adam Kadmon was a Kabbalistic term Blavatsky understood as a divine template for humanity. The monad would transmigrate through mineral, vegetable, and animal forms until it reached the last form it would take on Earth: human. In order to take that form, the monad would relive versions of all previous evolutionary phases within the womb (its 'fluidic prison'). This was a Theosophical interpretation of the contemporaneous evolutionary theory of recapitulation, popularised by Ernst Haeckel and others, which stated an embryo would pass through structures corresponding to the previous evolutionary phases of that particular organism. (This evolutionary hypothesis and some of its proponents will be considered in detail in chapter 5.) Blavatsky complained, 'no physiologist or anatomist seems to have had the idea of applying to the development of the human being—from the first instant of its physical appearance as a germ to its ultimate formation and birth—to the Pythagorean esoteric doctrine of metempsychosis, so erroneously interpreted by critics.' Thus, she explained the 'Kabbalistic axiom', 'a stone becomes a plant; a plant a beast; a beast a man.' During gestation, after three or four weeks, the ovum would assume a plant-like appearance and the stone would have been changed, 'by metempsychosis', into a plant. The embryo then developed into an 'animal'.[14] Finally, the baby would be born.

> At the birth of the future man, the monad, radiating with all the glory of its immortal parent which watches it from the seventh sphere, becomes *senseless*. It loses all recollection of the past, and returns to consciousness but gradually, when the instinct of childhood gives way to reason and intelligence. After the separation between the life-principle (astral spirit) and the body takes place, the liberated soul-Monad, exultingly rejoins the mother and father spirit, the radiant Augoeides, [Divine Spirit] and the two, merged into one, forever

[14] Ibid., 388–389. See also her definition of metempsychosis, xxxvi–xxxvii, which refers to the same 'kabbalistic axiom'.

ISIS UNVEILED AND METEMPSYCHOSIS
53

form, with a glory proportioned to the spiritual purity of the past earth-life, the Adam who has completed the circle of necessity, and is freed from the last vestige of his physical encasement. Henceforth, growing more and more radiant at each step of his upward progress, he mounts the shining path that ends at the point from which he started around the GRAND CYCLE.[15]

In other words, at birth, the child would forget its previous mineral and animal existences. After death (i.e., the 'separation of the body from the life-principle') the soul, if it were to achieve immortality, would conjoin with the spirit (referred to here by the Greek term *Augoeides*). This would only occur if immortality has been won during Earth-life, which was conditional on the purity of that life. Once this immortality had been achieved, the 'circle of necessity' would be complete. When such a person died, their conjoined soul-spirit entity would travel upwards through the spheres on its 'shining path' towards completion of the 'grand cycle', the return of the monad to its divine parent through the transmigrations of metempsychosis. The 'grand cycle' included the smaller cycle termed the 'circle of necessity', the section of the process leading to the achievement of immortality.

What was a person who had achieved immorality like? Blavatsky imagined them as being like the great religious figures of the Bible.

In the very first remark made by Jesus about John the Baptist, we find him stating that he is 'Elias, which was for to come'. This assertion, if it is not a later interpolation for the sake of having a prophecy fulfilled, means again that Jesus was a kabalist; unless indeed we have to adopt the doctrine of the French spiritists and suspect him of believing in reincarnation.

In fact, in *Old Truths in a New Light*, Lady Caithness had taken the verse as evidence for just that—French Spiritist reincarnation—and Blavatsky may well have been correcting her here.[16] According to Blavatsky, the

[15] Ibid., 303.
[16] Caithness, *Old Truths,* 330 f.

fact Jesus thought John the Baptist was the prophet Elijah proved Jesus was a Kabbalist because he knew of an esoteric teaching allowing for this possibility. That tenet was *not*, however, reincarnation as taught by the Spiritists of the Kardec school or by Lady Caithness. It was another, esoteric, Kabbalistic notion.

> Except the kabalistic sects of the Essenes, the Nazarenes, the disciples of Simeon Ben Iochai, and Hillel, neither the orthodox Jews, nor the Galileans, believed or knew anything about the doctrine of *permutation*. And the Sadducees rejected even that of the resurrection. 'But the author of this *restitutionis* was Mosah, our master, upon whom be peace! Who was the *revolutio* (transmigration) of Seth and Hebel, that he might cover the nudity of his Father Adam—*Primus*,' says the Kabala. Thus, Jesus hinting that John was the *revolutio*, or transmigration of Elias, seems to prove beyond any doubt the school to which he belonged.

According to Blavatsky, the esoteric teaching now revealed as 'revolution' or 'permutation' was not metempsychosis in the sense described above, since there was nothing in that theory that allowed for Moses to have been either Abel or Seth. Confirming this, she explained, 'until the present day uninitiated Kabalists and Masons believe permutation to be synonymous with transmigration and metempsychosis. But they are as much mistaken in regard to the doctrine of the true Kabalists as to that of the Buddhists.' She then quoted an extract from the Kabbalistic work the *Zohar*:

> True, the *Sohar* says in one place, 'All souls are subject to transmigration ... men do not know the ways of the Holy One, blessed be He; they do not know that they are brought before the tribunal, both before they enter this world and after they quit it,' and the Pharisees also held this doctrine, as Josephus shows (*Antiquities*, xviii. 13). [. . .] But this doctrine of permutation, or *revolutio*, must not be understood as a belief in reincarnation. That Moses was considered the transmigration of Abel and Seth, does not imply that the kabalists—those who were *initiated* at least—believed that the identical spirit of either of Adam's sons reappeared under the corporeal form of Moses. It only

shows what was the mode of expression they used when hinting at one of the profoundest mysteries of the Oriental Gnosis, one of the most majestic articles of faith of the Secret Wisdom. It was purposely veiled so as to half conceal and half reveal the truth. It implied that Moses, like certain other god-like men, was believed to have reached the highest of all states on Earth:—the rarest of all psychological phenomena, the perfect union of the immortal spirit with the terrestrial *duad* had occurred. The trinity was complete. A *god* was incarnate. But how rare such incarnations!

Blavatsky stated Moses, like Cain and Abel, was among the few to have conjoined soul and spirit and become immortal. In a previous extract, we saw Blavatsky had referred to those who achieve immortality as 'gods'. She continued:

That expression, 'Ye are gods,' which, to our biblical students, is a mere abstraction, has for the kabalists a vital significance. Each immortal spirit that sheds its radiance upon a human being is a god—the Microcosmos of the Macrocosmos, part and parcel of the Unknown God, the First Cause of which it is a direct emanation. It is possessed of all the attributes of its parent source. Among these attributes are omniscience and omnipotence. Endowed with these, but yet unable to fully manifest them while in the body, during which time they are obscured, veiled, limited by the capabilities of physical nature, the thus divinely-inhabited man may tower far above his kind, evince a god-like wisdom, and display deific powers; for while the rest of mortals around him are but *overshadowed* by their divine SELF, with every chance given to them to become immortal hereafter, but no other security than their personal efforts to win the kingdom of heaven, the so chosen man has already become an immortal while yet on earth. His prize is secured. Henceforth he will live forever in eternal life. Not only he may have 'dominion' over all the works of creation by employing the 'excellence' of the NAME (the ineffable one) but be higher in this life, not, as Paul is made to say, 'a little lower than the angels'. The ancients never entertained the sacrilegious thought that such perfected entities were incarnations of the One Supreme and for ever invisible God. No such profanation of the awful Majesty entered into their conceptions. Moses and his antitypes and types were to them but complete men, gods on earth, for their *gods* (divine spirits) had entered unto their hallowed tabernacles, the purified physical bodies.[17]

Here, Blavatsky found an explanation for the Hindu doctrine of *avatars* (the incarnation of deities on Earth), which was congruent with metempsychosis and didn't portray human beings as gods 'sacrilegiously'. Rather, the divine was said to overshadow such spiritually advanced individuals, and as a consequence, they were divine themselves. Those who achieved immortality by conjoining soul and spirit fulfilled or consolidated that divinity through their personal effort. Such god-like men, who included Moses, Cain, and Abel, shared in each other's divine, conjoined nature. In a sense each was an individual expression of the same divine reality. This was the true meaning of 'revolutio' or 'permutation', and *not* that Moses was the 'reincarnation' of Cain or Abel, in the Spiritist sense, or as Lady Caithness understood it.

Blavatsky's Letters: Immortality and Metempsychosis

Clarifications and confirmations of Blavatsky's early doctrines can be found in her letters, which often expressed her opinions more lucidly than her books and other writings. This is probably because of the difference in means of production. Her major works were apparently produced in a state of trance or through an imaginative, clairvoyant-style process (as well as being heavily edited by others). Her letters seem to have been written in a straightforward manner. Blavatsky's elaborations of metempsychosis in these early letters is unequivocal.

In a letter to C. C. Massey of February 1876, she stated that belief in the (normative) return to life on Earth of the same soul (like that of the Spiritists) was anti-evolutionary, and therefore incorrect. She reinforced the centrality of the evolutionary, progressive, or perfecting character of metempsychosis. Death would be followed by an ascent through the spheres.

[17] Blavatsky, *Isis II*, 152–153.

This philosophy of the evolution of species by flux and reflux from matter to spirit and back again is the only true one; ... the whole trouble of Kardec, and other reincarnationists lies in their misunderstanding the hermetic philosophy upon this point. While it is true that there is a reincarnation in one sense, in the other it is untrue. Nay, more, it is absurd and unphilosophical, doing violence to the law of evolution, which is constantly carrying matter and spirit upward toward perfection. When the elementary dies out of one state of existence he is born into a higher one, and when man dies out of the world of gross matter, he is born into one more ethereal; so on from sphere to sphere, man never losing his trinity, for at each birth a new and more perfect astral body is evolved out of elementaries of a correspondingly higher order, while his previous astral body takes the place of the antecedent, external earthly body. Man's soul (or Divine Spirit, for you must not confound the divine with the astral spirit) constantly entering into new astral bodies, there is an actual reincarnation; but that when it has passed through any sphere into a higher one, it should re-enter the lower sphere and pass through other bodies similar to the one it has just quitted, is as unphilosophical as to fancy that the human foetus could go back into the elementary condition, or the child after birth re-enters its mother's womb.[18]

The flux and reflux from matter to spirit was the 'grand cycle' of metempsychosis, which carried the cosmos toward perfection. Blavatsky's use of the term 'reincarnation' as synonymous with metempsychosis was potentially confusing, although what she meant was that metempsychosis involved a type of 'reincarnation' in which the conjoined soul-spirit entity 'reincarnated' into bodies of increasing ethereality as it travelled upwards. This letter helps explain a passage in *Isis Unveiled* that might otherwise be confusing:

Philosophers held, with the Hindus, that God had infused into matter a portion of his own Divine Spirit, which animates and moves every particle. They taught that men have two souls, of separate and

---

[18] Blavatsky, 'Letter number 65, to C. C. Massey', 248–249.

quite different natures: the one perishable—the Astral Soul, or the inner, fluidic body—the other incorruptible and immortal—the Augoeides, or portion of the Divine Spirit; that the mortal or Astral Soul perishes at each gradual change at the threshold of every new sphere, becoming with every transmigration more purified.[19]

In this passage from *Isis Unveiled*, 'transmigration' indicated the passage from one sphere to the next. At each sphere, a new 'astral soul' would be acquired.

In the spring of 1877, Blavatsky wrote to her aunt, Nadyezhda de Fadeev (1829–1919). She stated that immortality could not be taken for granted since it was conditional and occurred as the result of the shedding of attachment to the earthly elements necessary to incarnation on Earth.

> *Per se* the soul is not immortal. The soul outlives the man's body only for as long as it is necessary for it to get rid of everything earthly and fleshly; then, as it is gradually purified, its essence comes into progressively closer union with the Spirit, which alone is immortal. The tie between them becomes more and more indissoluble. When the last atom of the earthly is evaporated, then this duality becomes a unity, and the Ego of the former man becomes forever immortal. [. . .] And so not all of us human beings are immortal. As Jesus expresses it, we must take the kingdom of Heaven by violence. [. . .] When the soul is imprisoned in a sinning body, it is as if in jail, and in order to get rid of its chains, it has to progressively to aspire upward towards its spirit. The soul is a chameleon. It becomes either a copy of the spirit or of the body. In the first case, it acquires the faculty of separating itself from the body with ease, and of setting forth, travelling all over the wide world, having left in the body a provision of vital forces, or animal, instinctive mental movements. [. . .] In the measure of its union with the spirit it becomes more or less clairvoyant.[20]

---

[19] Blavatsky, *Isis I*, 12.
[20] Letter to N. de Fadeyev, c. May or June 1877, in Blavatsky, *Letters*, 306.

During Earth-life, the soul would experience a choice. It could either aspire downwards, towards matter, or upwards, in the direction of spirit. If it aspired downwards, then, at death, the divine spirit that had 'over-shadowed' it during Earth-life would withdraw and the mortal soul would be annihilated. If the soul aspired upwards, however, it could purify itself and conjoin with the divine spirit. That soul, or 'Ego', would then become immortal. This purification, through which the soul could became 'a copy of the spirit' was achieved through learning to separate the soul from the impure physical body, that is, through as-tral travel, a prominent practice in the early Theosophical Society. The proof the practitioner was succeeding in this work was their developing clairvoyance.[21]

The same year, Blavatsky again wrote to her aunt:

All the most ancient philosophies prove that this 'essence' meant the immortal spirit—the spark of the infinite and beginningless ocean, called God, a spark with which every human being is endowed from birth by the Divine, that it may overshadow him during all his earthly life; and after the death of the body either to blend with the soul (*périsprit*) to make him immortal, or,—if the man was a beast during his life—break the spiritual thread uniting the animal soul, the individual intellectuality, to the immortal spirit, leaving the animal entity at the mercy of the elements constituting its subjective being; after that, following the law of *perpetuum mobile*, the soul or *ego* of the former man has unavoidably to dissolve in time, to be *annihilated*. It is this immortal spirit of ours that is and always was called Chrestos or Christos. [. . .] If we behaved as Christ and the Buddha behaved when embodied as two mortal men, we and any one of us would become like Christ and Buddha, namely united and blended with the Christ-Buddha principle in us, with our immortal spirit; but of course only after the death of our sinful flesh, because how could we, with our beastly snout, climb into paradise in this life?[22]

[21] See Deveney, 'Two Theosophical Societies'.
[22] Letter to N. de Fadeyev, 28–29 October 1877, in Blavatsky, *Letters*, 347–349.

Once again, Blavatsky associated her doctrines with 'all the most ancient philosophers', thereby lending them credibility. Christ and Buddha had both succeeded in conjoining their souls and spirits and become immortal. In a letter to W. H. Burr the same year, she elaborated that very few people achieved immortality:

> I deny that immortality is achieved by every man, woman or child. Immortality must be won. [. . .] But a very small percentage of the human race becomes immortal, i.e. very few individuals become *gods*. [. . .] The rest are sooner or later *annihilated*, and their bodies and souls are disintegrated, and while the atoms of one return to the elements of physical nature, the more sublimated atoms of the other, when no longer cemented by the presence of their individual 'spirits'—which are alone immortal, as everything real becomes subjective—are violently torn loose from each other and return to the more sublimated elements of spiritual nature.[23]

Following the departure of the divine spirit at death, the body and the soul of one who had failed to achieve immortality disintegrated. Its 'atoms' would be recycled back into the elements of physical nature and the 'atoms' of the soul would return to the 'more sublimated elements'. For those who didn't achieve immortality during Earth-life but had a good reason (they died too young or were not of sound mind), the spirit would once again overshadow the soul, incarnating into a new physical body. It would negate the justice of the universe for annihilation to take place in cases such as these. This is why in an article of 1878, Blavatsky stated a dead child was 'a failure of nature' and the child had to be reincarnated. Together with the rebirth on Earth of the congenital idiot, these were the 'only cases of human reincarnation'.[24]

> Nature never leaves her work unfinished; if baffled at the first attempt, she tries again. When she evolves a human embryo, the

---

[23] Letter to W. H. Burr, 19 November 1877, in Blavatsky, *Letters*, 371.
[24] H. P. Blavatsky, 'Fragments from Madame Blavatsky', in *Blavatsky Collected Writings*, ed. Boris de Zirkoff, vol. 1, 368. [Translation from the French, originally published in *La Revue Spirite* (April 1878).]

intention is that a man shall be perfected—physically, intellectually, and spiritually. His body is to grow mature, wear out, and die; his mind unfold, ripen, and be harmoniously balanced; his divine spirit illuminate and blend easily with the *inner* man. No human being completes its grand cycle, or the 'circle of necessity', until all these are accomplished. As the laggards in a race struggle and plod in their first quarter while the victor darts past the goal, so, in the race of immortality, some souls outspeed all the rest and reach the end, while their myriad competitors are toiling under the load of matter, close to the starting point. Some unfortunates fall out entirely, and lose all chance of the prize; some retrace their steps and begin again.[25]

Occasional same-soul reincarnation, the 'supplementary doctrine' of *Isis Unveiled*, was an aspect of the justice of the universe as Blavatsky understood it at the time, before she had assimilated a theory of karma as part of the theodicy of her later period.

Further Exceptional Occurrences

In 1877, Blavatsky explained, 'the evil spirit is not the devil of popular fancy; it is the malicious, wicked soul of any sinner who has died without repentance, and who will go on existing until it dissipates into the dust of the elements.' In other words, the (unconjoined) spirits and souls of those who failed to achieve immortality could linger on Earth for some time before finally disappearing. These 'larvae' could receive a second chance and repent, thereby achieving rebirth in human flesh, and this could be understood as a type of reincarnation, although it was rare. This possibility was presented as a reason for the *apparent* belief in reincarnation of ancient Kabbalists.

It is for these carnal terrestrial larvæ, degraded human spirits, that the ancient kabalists entertained a hope of reïncarnation. But when, or how? At a fitting moment, and if helped by a sincere desire for his amendment and repentance by some strong, sympathising person,

[25] Blavatsky, *Isis I*, 345–346.

or the will of an adept, or even a desire emanating from the erring spirit himself, provided it is powerful enough to make him throw off the burden of sinful matter. Losing all consciousness, the once bright monad is caught once more into the vortex of our terrestrial evolution, and it trespasses the subordinate kingdoms, and again breathes as a living child. To compute the time necessary for the completion of this process would be impossible. Since there is no perception of time in eternity, the attempt would be a mere waste of labor.[26]

In other words, Kabbalists didn't believe in reincarnation in the Spiritist sense (i.e., the return of the same soul repeatedly to Earth-life). Instead, they upheld this other, exceptional type of reincarnation, in which the failed spirit and soul duo would be sent back to complete their journey of metempsychosis for a second time, passing through all the lower kingdoms until reborn in human form. For this, the repenting individual would need an exceptionally strong will and/or the assistance of an adept.

Another uncommon occurrence was what was known as 'the transfer of a spiritual entity'. Blavatsky referred to the novel *Ghost Land* (1876) by Spiritualist Emma Hardinge Britten (1823–1899) to explain another exceptional type of 'reincarnation' in which an adept transferred his or her 'spiritual entity' to a student upon the adept's death.

There were even those among the highest epoptæ of the greater Mysteries who knew nothing of their last and dreaded rite—the voluntary transfer of life from hierophant to candidate. In Ghost-Land this mystical operation of the adept's transfer of his spiritual entity, after the death of his body, into the youth he loves with all the ardent love of a spiritual parent, is superbly described. As in the case of the reincarnation of the lamas of Thibet, an adept of the highest order may live indefinitely. His mortal casket wears out notwithstanding certain alchemical secrets for prolonging the youthful vigor far beyond the usual limits, yet the body can rarely be kept alive beyond ten or twelve score of years. The old garment is then worn out, and

[26] Ibid., 357.

the spiritual Ego forced to leave it, selects for its habitation a new body, fresh and full of healthy vital principle.[27]

Blavatsky didn't elaborate further on this unique form of 'reincarnation', but its presence and difference to other forms of rebirth she proposed at the time underscore the need to distinguish between the different forms of 'reincarnation' in *Isis Unveiled* very carefully indeed.

Conclusions

In *Isis Unveiled* and letters contemporary with it, Blavatsky's ideas were consistent, if not always perspicuous. The primary reason for the confusion was the terminology. Blavatsky used various terms for rebirth: reincarnation, metempsychosis, revolution, permutation, the transfer of an entity, and the reincarnation of terrestrial larvae. To compound the problem, sometimes a term was given multiple meanings. For example, 'reincarnation' could refer to four different things:

1. The 'supplementary doctrine' of *Isis Unveiled*, namely, that in the case of unfinished business, a spirit is reborn on Earth with the same soul.
2. The rebirth of the immortalised soul-spirit entity into a new astral body on each sphere as it ascends through the spheres towards nirvana in metempsychosis.
3. The transfer of an adept's 'spiritual Ego' to his or her young disciple, potentially enabling them to live forever.
4. The 'reincarnation' of repenting terrestrial larvae, possibly with the assistance of an adept.

Metempsychosis was the main rebirth doctrine of *Isis Unveiled* and it was associated with the indestructibility of spirit and matter, progressive evolution, human effort, and cyclicity. Blavatsky gave the stages of metempsychosis as follows:

---

[27] Blavatsky, *Isis II*, 563.

1. The monad is 'exhaled' from the divine source and sent on its journey into matter.

2. It lives on a different planet before it reaches Earth. (The specific details of the monad's journey from other planets to this one were not given at this stage.)

3. Once it reaches Earth, it passes through mineral, animal, and vegetable forms.

4. It 'relives' those forms in utero.

5. It is born as a human on Earth. During this incarnation, it is constituted of spirit, soul, and physical body. The incarnated person has a chance at achieving immortality during Earth-life through the conjoining of their soul with their spirit through occult practices such as astral travel.

6. Most individuals are annihilated at death, having failed to achieve immortality. In such cases, the body and soul return to nature after a period as terrestrial larvae.

7. There is still hope for some of the terrestrial larvae to repent and 'reincarnate'. Adepts can help them do this.

8. A select few succeed in conjoining soul and spirit and achieve immortality. Their reason becomes 'active and discriminative', and they progress to the next sphere after the death of their physical body with the same personality they had during Earth-life.

9. Those few who achieve immortality transmigrate through higher spheres, each time acquiring a new astral body. By this act, the continuously maintain a 'trinity' of principles.

10. Eventually, they achieve nirvana, meaning absorption into the divine, in the seventh sphere.

Blavatsky scattered allusions to, and explanations of, each of these stages throughout her early occult writings and letters. The foregoing detailed reading makes sense of her sometimes apparently contradictory statements and provides a basis on which to better understand Blavatsky's teachings on reincarnation in her second major work, *The Secret Doctrine*. These will be considered in the following chapter.

3

Reincarnation in *The Secret Doctrine*

UNLIKE IN *ISIS UNVEILED* (1877), in *The Secret Doctrine* (1888), Blavatsky taught it was normal for a person to live many lives on Earth (as well as other planets).[1] This was the fundamental difference between metempsychosis and reincarnation. The new teaching was also much more complex than the previous one had been. Blavatsky described the countless deaths and regenerations humans underwent as part of a pilgrimage during which they would evolve physically, psychically, and spiritually. She now stated people were composed of seven principles, rather than three, and that each one played a vital role in the death and rebirth process. (The seven could be grouped into three, to correspond to the previous classification, according to Blavatsky.) Her new theory of reincarnation was intricate, and to begin to understand it, we must start with its cosmology.[2] One of the fundamental tenets of that cosmology was that every aspect of the cosmos mirrors every other. Just as a person lives, dies, and is born again, so do planets and even the cosmos live, die, and 'reincarnate'.

Blavatsky taught that our universe is one of many in a great 'cosmic chain' of universes, each of which arose ('reincarnated') after the demise

---

[1] A version of this chapter appeared in *Correspondences* 5 (2017).
[2] For an account of Blavatsky's thought in terms of 'macrohistory', understood as a 'representation of the human past in terms of a vast panorama', see Gary Trompf, 'Imagining Macrohistory? Madame Blavatsky from *Isis Unveiled* (1877) to *The Secret Doctrine* (1888)', *Literature and Aesthetics* 21, no. 1 (June 2011).

of the previous one.[3] Over the course of its life, each universe was said
to repeatedly manifest and disappear, as though sleeping and waking.[4]
The ultimate goal of the cyclic appearances and disappearances of the
universes was supposed to be the increasing 'self-consciousness' of the
Divine. Blavatsky said the Divine would achieve this self-consciousness
through the periodic exhibition of different aspects of itself to 'finite
minds', in other words, humans.[5] It would attain this through the evolution of humans from lower forms of life.[6] How was this to take place?
According to Blavatsky, universes were living entities constituted of
spirit and matter, in fact, two aspects of the same substance. She considered spirit primary because matter arose from it. Spirit carried the
ideas that gave rise to matter, and consciousness arose from the union of
spirit with matter at a specific point in evolutionary history. Although
they would separate during the course of the universe's lifetime, on a
deeper level, spirit and matter were inseparable, and continuously and
simultaneously repelled and attracted one another. 'So do Spirit and
Matter stand to each other,' Blavatsky wrote, 'The two poles of the same
homogeneous substance, the root-principle of the universe.'[7] Blavatsky
claimed spirit and matter were linked by something called Fohat, which
functioned like a bridge by which divine ideas were impressed on the
material world as 'laws of nature'. It was an animating principle that
brought atoms to life.[8] Describing Fohat in terms of *eros*, or attraction,
she characterised it as a kind of 'affinity', 'intelligence', or even 'guide',
although she was adamant it was not a personal God.[9]

From a state of cosmic rest, spirit was said to 'fall' into matter and
be required to find its way back to its original condition. Blavatsky
called the change from matter to spirit evolution, and from spirit to
matter, involution. During involution, spirit would 'involve' into
matter and 'appear'. Thereafter, it would gradually evolve back into

[3] For example, Blavatsky, *Secret Doctrine I*, 43.
[4] For example, Ibid., 16.
[5] Blavatsky, *Secret Doctrine II*, 487.
[6] Blavatsky, *Secret Doctrine I*, 106–107.
[7] Ibid., 247.
[8] Ibid., 15–16.
[9] Ibid., 119, 139.

spirit again, disappearing. Blavatsky described the periodic appearance and disappearance of the universe as the 'outbreathing' and
'inbreathing' of the great breath.[10] The time it took for the cosmos to
complete one out-breath and one in-breath was known in Sanskrit as
a *manvantara*.[11] During the involutionary phase of the cosmos at the
beginning of a *manvantara*, the divine source (known in Sanskrit as
parabrahman) emitted *mulaprakriti* (matter). Subsequent levels were
thereafter emanated. As stated previously, in the simplest possible
terms, emanation as a concept is evocative of the image of a champagne fountain in which the wine descends from the top glass like a
waterfall, cascading into the glasses that are stacked beneath it, more
or less in the shape of a pyramid. In the various Hermetic, Gnostic,
neo-Platonic and Kabbalistic versions of emanation, the metaphorical bottle was seen as pouring continuously. The Divine was seen
as emanating creation constantly and without diminishing Itself in
any sense.

In Blavatsky's version, after the Divine had emitted *mulaprakriti*, a
second level emerged. This was known as the 'first' or 'un-manifested'
logos. It was followed by the second logos, known as 'the demiurge',
which amounted to an aggregate or 'army' of sentient beings called
dhyan chohans, who functioned as the architects of the universe and
agents of karma.[12] The next emanation was the Universal Soul, the
source of a finite number of monads, or immortal, reincarnating
entities.[13] Blavatsky described the Universal Soul as 'a compound unity
of manifested living Spirits, the parent-source and nursery of all the

[10] Ibid., 43.

[11] It is important to note that Blavatsky used the term *manvantara* to describe different
periods. I refer here to a *manvantara* of the universe.

[12] See Blavatsky, *Secret Doctrine I*, 380. Describing the roles of these different emanations, the first logos has the 'idea' and the second logos, constituted of the *dhyan
chohans*, draws up the 'plan' (Ibid., 279–280). Blavatsky considered these beings
analogous to angels in Christianity, the 'elohim' of Jewish scriptures, and the *Dhyani-
Buddhas* of Buddhism (Ibid., 10, 38, 274). There are inferior beings among them, but
no 'devils' (Blavatsky, *Secret Doctrine II*, 487). On *dhyan chohans* as agents of karma,
see Blavatsky, *Secret Doctrine I*, 122–123.

[13] Blavatsky, *Secret Doctrine I*, 16–17, note. The term 'monad' can have a wider meaning
too, but we will focus here on this meaning. For example, see Ibid., 21.

mundane and terrestrial monads, *plus* their *divine* reflection'.[14] In other words, the Universal Soul was not merely a collective of monads but was also independent of and mirrored them.

All monads were said to enter the cycle of incarnation at the beginning of the universe's *manvantara*. With each incarnation, a monad would acquire a new personality. Through the monad's assimilation of successive temporary personalities, it would spiritualise, overcoming what Blavatsky called 'the delusions of *maya*'.[15] It would thus become increasingly aware of the impermanent and illusory nature of the cosmos and more conscious of its own identity with the Universal Soul. Finally, it would be reabsorbed into the Divine.[16] Blavatsky termed this reabsorption *paranirvana*. *Paranirvana* was followed by a pause, called a *pralaya*, during which the universe rested before repeating the whole process once more.[17]

Blavatsky conceived all of life as participating in this reincarnationary journey. Those incarnated today as humans were previously less evolved life forms such as animals and plants, and those incarnated as *dhyan chohans* were once people.[18] Even the *dhyan chohans* had not finished evolving, and would go on to become still higher beings. Evolution, Blavatsky maintained, was endless, but what compelled it? Blavatsky gave three answers to this question. The first was the universe's inherent tendency to evolve, the second was the assistance of higher beings, and

[14] Ibid., 573.

[15] 'The Universe is called, with everything in it, MAYA, because all is temporary therein, from the ephemeral life of a fire-fly to that of the Sun. Compared to the eternal immutability of the ONE, and the changelessness of that Principle, the Universe, with its evanescent ever-changing forms, must be necessarily, in the mind of a philosopher, no better than a will-o'-the-wisp. Yet, the Universe is real enough to the conscious beings in it, which are as unreal as it is itself.' Ibid., 274.

[16] Ibid., 130–131, 268.

[17] Again, there are different types of *pralaya*, and I refer here to the cosmic variety. On *pralaya*, see Blavatsky, *Secret Doctrine II*, 307. On the re-awakening of monads after *pralaya*, see Blavatsky, *Secret Doctrine I*, 21.

[18] Blavatsky, *Secret Doctrine I*, 277.

the third was the action of karma. Let's look at each of these in more detail.

The Monad's Planetary Journey

Groups of monads were said to evolve more or less together. The group of which present-day humans were a part had progressed through the earlier stages of cosmic evolution together. Karma only became a factor in their evolutionary journey at a specific point. Before then, they had not experienced karma because they had possessed no egos and no intellectual faculties (*manas*). Nevertheless, they still evolved. This was because the evolutionary process of a life wave was rather like a conveyor belt (my simile, not Blavatsky's). Higher beings had assisted the monads in getting onto this conveyor belt in the first place, and, once on it, everyone evolved no matter what. When the monads reached a certain stage of human evolution, it was as though the life wave had reached the end of the conveyor belt and the monads would thereafter have to continue through their own effort. In other words, they had to get off the belt and start walking. This was because by this point, humans had evolved egos as well as intellectual and rational faculties, and were now held responsible for their actions.[19] Karma had a decisive role during this stage of evolution because rational apprehension of its effects could impel a person to think and behave in a more spiritual way.

Blavatsky claimed that there were many solar systems and that within them, each planet was merely the visible globe within a system of seven spheres, the other six of which were invisible and existed on different planes of reality.[20] Thus, six invisible spheres surrounded the

[19] *Manas* (the principle associated with the ego) was 'held responsible for all the sins committed through, and in, every new body or personality—the evanescent masks which hide the true individual through the long series of rebirths.' Blavatsky, *The Key to Theosophy* (London and New York: The Theosophical Publishing Company, 1889), 136.

[20] Blavatsky, *Secret Doctrine I*, 166. Describing the six invisible spheres that surrounded planet Earth, Blavatsky explained they 'blended with our world—interpenetrating it and interpenetrated by it'. Ibid., 605.

other planets of our solar system, as well as the moon. The Earth with its six invisible planets was known as the Earth Chain. In a diagram Blavatsky provided in *The Secret Doctrine*, she represented the Earth as the lowest globe (Globe D), with six more above it (three on each side) in ascending order of spirituality.[21] On the left of the Earth were Globes A, B, and C, and on the right Globes E, F, and G. Moving down from the top of this diagram, Globes A and G were on the highest level of spirituality, B and F the next down, and C and E followed. Within the Earth Chain, evolution began on Globe A before continuing on Globes B, C, D, and so forth. Humans incarnated on Earth today formerly evolved on Globe C, a sphere slightly more spiritual and less material than the Earth.[22] Once they had completed their evolution there, they incarnated on Earth. Once evolution on Earth was complete, life would withdraw and continue its evolution on Globe E, which was as spiritual as Globe C had been. Despite the equivalence in spirituality of Globes C and E, it was not the case that humanity would simply return to the same spiritual condition on Globe E that it experienced on Globe C. Through having lived numerous lives on Earth and assimilating those experiences, the monads would have become more conscious, and moved closer to the divine absorption that was the ultimate goal of their peregrinations.

Blavatsky termed a tour of a life wave around the seven globes a 'round'. Just as the universe experienced a *manvantara* (active period) followed by a *pralaya* (rest period), so too did the planetary chain. There were seven rounds in each active period of the planetary chain, meaning the monads circled through Globes A–G seven times. Every time a life wave completed a round, there was a period of rest called an 'obscuration'. Once the life wave had been around seven times, however, the planetary chain itself would begin to die out. This was known as a 'planetary dissolution' and the life wave would thereafter transfer to a different planetary chain.[23] According to Blavatsky, the Lunar Chain was where the beings now within the Earth Chain previously

---

[21] Ibid., 172.
[22] Ibid., 158–159.
[23] Ibid., 158–159.

evolved.[24] She wrote that occultists termed the transference of life from one planetary chain to another the 'rebirth of planetary chains'. Just as humans left behind shells (i.e., dead physical bodies), so did planets. Said Blavatsky: 'Every such chain of worlds is the progeny and creation of another, *lower*, and *dead* chain—*its reincarnation*, so to say.'[25]

Those incarnated as humans today were thought to have already completed three and a half rounds within the Earth chain, meaning they had travelled from Globe A to Globe G three times before arriving again at Globe D. From its spiritual state at entry, as it progressed through the first three and a half rounds, the monad gradually became more material, only beginning to re-spiritualise after passing the midpoint of the planetary chain on globe D, the Earth. Entering the chain at the ethereal Globe A, the monad was 'shot down by the law of Evolution into the lowest form of matter—the mineral'. The precise order in which it would then inhabit the different forms on each globe was never made entirely clear, although there were some indications. Quoting an 'extract from the teacher's letter on various topics', Blavatsky wrote: 'During the 1st round ... (heavenly) man becomes a human being on globe A (rebecomes) a mineral, a plant, an animal, on globe B and C, etc. The process changes entirely from the second round.'[26] The idea seems to have been that at least during the first round, on each globe, the monad would pass through what we might call mineral, vegetable, animal, and human forms before doing the same on the next globe. Blavatsky clarified that the so-called stones, plants, animals, and humans on other globes were not as we know them, but rather the

---

[24] Ibid., 172.

[25] Ibid., 152.

[26] An undated letter from Mahatma Koot Hoomi states: 'At each round there are less and less animals—the latter themselves evoluting [*sic*] into higher forms. During the first Round it is *they* that were the "kings of *creation*". During the seventh men will have become *Gods* and animals—intelligent beings. Draw your inferences. Beginning with the second round already evolution proceeds on quite a different plan. Everything is evolved and has but to proceed on its cyclic journey and get perfected. It is only the first Round that man becomes from a human being on Globe B. a mineral, a plant, an animal on Planet C. The method changes entirely from the second Round; but—I have learned prudence with you; and will say *nothing* before the time for saying has come.' Letter 23 B in Barker, ed., *The Mahatma Letters*, 177–178.

'germ seeds' of what we would now recognise.[27] This is because on each globe, these forms were appropriate to the overall level of materiality of that particular globe.[28] In other words, a spiritual monad enters Globe A at the lowest level of matter for that globe, something that resembles the stones we are familiar with on this globe.

Blavatsky explained that the most developed of the monads entering the Earth Chain 'reach the human germ-stage in the first Round; become terrestrial, though very ethereal human beings towards the end of the Third Round, remaining on it (the globe) through the "obscuration" period as the seed for future mankind in the Fourth Round, and thus become the pioneers of Humanity at the beginning of this, the Fourth Round'.[29] From the middle turning point of the fourth round no more monads would be allowed to enter the human kingdom; if they hadn't made it to the human stage yet, they would have to wait until the next *manvantara*.[30] Although Blavatsky referred to beings from previous rounds as representing humanity, strictly speaking she claimed that the monad was not a 'man' as such until 'the Light of the Logos' was awakened in him. Until then, he should not 'be referred to as "MAN", but has to be regarded as a Monad imprisoned in ever changing forms'.[31] For 'man' to develop, the monad had to acquire 'a spiritual model, or prototype'. It needed 'an intelligent consciousness to guide its evolution and progress'. This is where the *pitris* came in, higher beings who descended to assist in the evolution of humanity by deliberately blending spirit with matter, and this occurred at a specific point in the evolution that took place on Globe D, the Earth.[32]

---

[27] Blavatsky, *Secret Doctrine II*, 186.
[28] Ibid., 180.
[29] Blavatsky, *Secret Doctrine I*, 182.
[30] Although all the rocks, plants, and animals in the world today would eventually become men, this wouldn't occur in this *manvantara*. Ibid.
[31] Blavatsky, *Secret Doctrine II*, 42.
[32] Blavatsky, *Secret Doctrine I*, 247.

The Monad's Racial Journey

On Earth, the development of human life was divided into seven consecutive stages, known as 'root races', each containing seven sub-races.[33] A monad was required to pass through all seven of these root races during its evolutionary journey.[34] Blavatsky only described in detail the root races of the Earth, stating that 'we are not concerned with the other Globes in this work, except incidentally'.[35] In her account, previous root races lived on continents that no longer existed and their periods of existence were divided from one other by great convolutions of nature, resulting in a lack of physical evidence for their existence.[36] These convolutions weren't punishments but simply the natural course of events. Wrote Blavatsky, 'Such is the fate of every continent, which—like everything else under our Sun—is born, lives, becomes decrepit, and dies.'[37] After the appearance and disappearance of every continent with its root race there was said to be a period of rest before the next race appeared on the next continent. Root races were initially more ethereal, gradually becoming more material, evolving physically and morally and becoming more solid until their physical evolution had reached its fullest extent. This was human incarnation as we know it, the midpoint of the Earth Chain's cycle. After this, the process of spiritualisation could begin again.[38]

Evolution on Earth began when lunar *pitris* (the evolved beings of the Lunar Chain) created the first root race by oozing them out of their own bodies.[39] The first root race was ethereal and Blavatsky called them 'the self-born'.[40] They multiplied by 'budding' and lived on a continent known as 'The Imperishable Sacred Land'.[41] They were sexless

---

[33] Blavatsky, *Secret Doctrine II*, 434–435. Each sub-race has seven branch or family races.
[34] Blavatsky, *Secret Doctrine I*, 160. See also Blavatsky, 'Theosophy and Spiritism', 45.
[35] Blavatsky, *Secret Doctrine I*, 160.
[36] 'Our globe is subject to seven periodical *entire* changes which go *pari passu* with the races. ... It is a law which acts at its appointed time, and not at all blindly, as science may think, but in strict accordance and harmony with *Karmic* law.' Blavatsky, *Secret Doctrine II*, 329.
[37] Ibid., 350.
[38] Blavatsky, *Secret Doctrine I*, 224–225.
[39] Blavatsky, *Secret Doctrine I*, 160, 180 and *II*, 110, 174.
[40] Blavatsky, *Secret Doctrine II*, 164.
[41] Ibid., 6, 17–18, 132.

and could not be injured or die. They gradually turned into their more solid descendants, the second root race, known as 'the sweat born'. This second race was intellectually inactive, and was 'constantly plunged in a kind of blank or abstract contemplation, as required by the conditions of the Yoga state'.[42] Neither of the first two root races was solid enough to have left any physical remains. The 'Hyperborean' continent on which the second race lived stretched southwards and westwards from the North Pole and comprised what is now northern Asia.[43] Like the first root race, they were sexless, but since they were more material, they were affected by the physical conditions of the Earth.

The third root race was the first to develop physical bodies. Blavatsky called it the Lemurian race, because it lived on a continent named Lemuria, which used to occupy the Indian and Pacific Oceans before it sunk because of earthquakes and subterranean fires.[44] The first Lemurians reproduced by exuding drops of sweat that became eggs.[45] These eggs initially produced hermaphroditic beings, but very gradually they produced offspring in which one sex predominated over another. Eventually, male or female Lemurians were born.[46] At the close of the third root race, the Lemurians looked like gigantic apes, but they could already think and speak, and were relatively civilised.[47] Nevertheless, some of them were morally irresponsible and mated with lower animals, creating the remote ancestor of today's ape.[48] This, according to Blavatsky, was how occultists explained how apes evolved from 'men', and not the other way around, as the Darwinists claimed.[49] During the early Lemurian root race, higher beings had produced those who would eventually become human adepts by a process called *Kriyasakti*. These

[42] Blavatsky, *Secret Doctrine I*, 207.
[43] Blavatsky, *Secret Doctrine II*, 7, 116.
[44] Ibid., 266, 332–333. Sri Lanka, Madagascar, Australia, and Easter Island were its remains, Blavatsky claimed (Ibid., 7).
[45] Ibid., 116.
[46] Ibid., 132.
[47] Blavatsky, *Secret Doctrine I*, 191 and *II*, 446.
[48] Blavatsky, *Secret Doctrine I*, 190.
[49] Blavatsky, *Secret Doctrine II*, 180, 263, 635.

proto-adepts, known as the 'Sons of Will and Yoga', remained entirely apart from the rest of mankind.[50]

At around the midpoint of the Lemurian root race, some Lemurians were endowed by higher beings with *manas*, or reason.[51] From then onwards, *manas* would continue to develop, and would eventually become 'entirely divine'.[52] Before they had been endowed with *manas*, the Lemurians had been sinless because they were without egos. They had therefore not created any karma.[53] Their death and rebirth process had consequently been a lot less complicated that that of humans today; they would simply 'resurrect' out of an old body and into a new one.[54] As soon as they were endowed with *manas*, however, they started creating karma and became subject to death and reincarnation in a recognisable form.[55]

The fourth root race was the Atlantean. Their home was the continent of Atlantis, which rose out of the sea in the eastern Atlantic Ocean and was eventually submerged by a deluge.[56] The Atlanteans were more intellectual than the Lemurians and they perfected language.[57] During the highest point of its civilisation, knowledge, and intellectuality the Atlantean Race divided into those who followed the (good) right-hand path of knowledge, and those who followed the (evil) left-hand path.[58] The evolution of the Atlantean race led it down to the very bottom of materiality in its physical development.[59] They diminished in stature and the length of their lives decreased.[60] During the evolution of the Atlantean race, what had been 'the holy mystery of procreation' gradually turned into animal indulgence. As a result, the Atlanteans changed physically and mentally. According to Blavatsky,

[50] Blavatsky, *Secret Doctrine I*, 207.
[51] Blavatsky, *Secret Doctrine II*, 244–245, 248, 275.
[52] Ibid., 161–2.
[53] Ibid., 410.
[54] Ibid., 610.
[55] Ibid., 610.
[56] Ibid., 8, 332–334.
[57] Blavatsky, *Secret Doctrine I*, 189.
[58] Ibid., 192.
[59] Blavatsky, *Secret Doctrine II*, 446.
[60] Blavatsky, *Secret Doctrine I*, 609 and *II*, 331.

from having been 'the healthy King of animal creation of the Third Race, man became in the Fifth, our race, a helpless, scrofulous being and has now become the wealthiest heir on the globe to constitutional and hereditary diseases, the most consciously and intelligently bestial of all animals!'[61] The 'curse of karma' was called down on the Atlanteans, Blavatsky wrote, not for seeking *natural* union, but for 'abusing the creative power' and 'wasting the life-essence for no purpose except bestial personal gratification'.[62]

Present-day humanity, the fifth root race, was known as the Aryan, and it could trace its descent through the Atlanteans from those more spiritual races of the Lemurians.[63] The Aryan race arose in Asia and spread south and west. It had been in existence for about one million years.[64] Blavatsky described the development of the Aryan race from the Atlantean as gradual and complex.[65] As with the emergence of all root races, there was some overlap, so that the remnants of the Atlanteans were still present at the dawn of the Aryan root race. Some of these remnants inhabited lands that eventually became islands, where 'the undeveloped tribes and families of the Atlantean stock fell gradually into a still more abject and savage condition'.[66] After the submersion of the last remnant of the Atlantean race, 'an impenetrable veil of secrecy was thrown over the occult and religious mysteries'. This secrecy led the Aryans to the establishment of the religious mysteries, 'in which ancient truths might be taught to the coming generations under the veil of allegory and symbolism'.[67] Blavatsky considered the Aryan root race to be an evolutionary stage of pivotal importance since it was positioned at the exact midpoint of the involutionary-evolutionary process.[68] Humanity had just 'crossed the meridian point of the perfect adjustment of Spirit and Matter', which represented the 'equilibrium

---

[61] Blavatsky, *Secret Doctrine II*, 411.
[62] Ibid., 410.
[63] Ibid., 318, 433, 444.
[64] Ibid., 435.
[65] Ibid., 433–435.
[66] Ibid., 743.
[67] Ibid., 124.
[68] Blavatsky, *Secret Doctrine I*, 182, 185–86.

between brain intellect and Spiritual perception'.[69] A practical consequence of the turn towards spiritualisation was that phenomena such as thought transference, clairvoyance, and clairaudience would become more common.[70]

The Aryan root race was to be followed by sixth and seventh root races in the future, and Blavatsky claimed the germs of the sixth were already to be found in America.[71] This sixth race, she claimed, would be 'rapidly growing out of its bonds of matter, and even of flesh'.[72] Once evolution had been completed through all the rounds and races of the planetary chain, the monad would 'find itself as free from matter and all its qualities as it was in the beginning; having gained in addition the experience and wisdom, the fruition of all its personal lives, without their evil and temptations'.[73] The monad would then become a *dhyan chohan*.[74] These *dhyan chohans* would be transferred, in the next cycle, to 'higher, superior worlds, making room for a new hierarchy, composed of the elect ones of our mankind'.[75] Highly evolved *dhyan chohans* would move through solar systems in this way until the time arrived for the cosmic *pralaya*, when the entire cosmos would rest. At that point they would achieve 'the highest condition of Nirvana'.[76]

The *Saptaparna*

In Blavatsky's later thought, the human microcosm reflected the septenary macrocosm, and each of the seven elements of the human constitution played an indispensable role in the death and rebirth process.[77]

---

[69] Blavatsky, *Secret Doctrine II*, 300.

[70] Blavatsky, *Secret Doctrine I*, 536–37.

[71] Blavatsky, *Secret Doctrine II*, 444–445.

[72] Ibid., 446.

[73] Ibid., 180–181.

[74] Blavatsky, *Secret Doctrine I*, 159.

[75] Ibid., 221.

[76] Blavatsky, 'Nirvana', *The Theosophist* 5, no. 10 (July 1884), 246.

[77] Blavatsky reconciled the earlier tripartite and the later septenary spiritual anthropologies by explaining that the seven could be condensed into three, or the three expanded into seven, with the two lowest principles forming the physical body, the next two forming the soul, and the top three the spirit. Blavatsky, *Secret Doctrine II*, 602–603. On the saptaparna, see Chajes, Julie (née Hall), 'The Saptaparna: The Meaning

Known as the *saptaparna* (seven-leafed plant), these seven principles represented the balance of material and spiritual elements within the human being, or the spiritual, emotional, mental, and physical levels on which a person was said to operate throughout his or her life.[78] The seven principles were given, in ascending order of spirituality, as the body (Sanskrit: *stula sarira*), vitality (*prana* or *jiva*), astral body (*linga sarira*), animal soul (*kama-rupa*), human soul (*manas*), spiritual soul (*buddhi*), and spirit (*atma*).[79] All seven of these principles were considered necessary for life.[80] In Blavatsky's later esoteric instructions she taught that each of these principles was itself sevenfold: there was an *atma* of the *kama-rupa*, a *buddhi* of the *kama-rupa*, and so forth.[81]

The physical body (*stula sarira*) was composed of the lowest form of matter present in the human constitution. It was animated by *prana*, which Blavatsky described as 'the breath of life', or the active power producing all vital phenomena.[82] She also depicted the physical body as the vehicle (*upadhi*) of the life force. The third principle, the astral body or 'astral double', was an ethereal duplicate of the physical body.[83] The matter of the physical body was formed and moulded over this astral body by the action of *prana*. The fourth principle, the animal soul, was the vehicle of the will and desire. It was associated with feelings

and Origins of the Theosophical Septenary Constitution of Man', *Theosophical History* 13, no. 4 (October 2007).

[78] 'Do not imagine that because man is called septenary ... he is a compound of seven ... entities; or, as well expressed by a Theosophical writer, of skins to be peeled off like the skins of an onion. The "principles", as already said, save the body, the life, and the astral eidolon [*lingha-sharira*], all of which disperse at death, are simply aspects or states of consciousness.' Blavatsky, *Key*, 100.

[79] Blavatsky, *Secret Doctrine I,* 153 and *II,* 593, 596.

[80] Blavatsky, *Secret Doctrine I,* 158 and *II,* 241–242.

[81] Blavatsky, 'Esoteric Instruction Number Three' and 'Esoteric Instruction Number Five', in vol. 12 of *Blavatsky Collected Writings*, ed. Boris de Zirkoff (Wheaton, IL: Theosophical Publishing House, 1980), 648 and 693.

[82] Blavatsky, *The Theosophical Glossary* (Krotona: Theosophical Publishing House, 1918), 242; Blavatsky, *Secret Doctrine II,* 593. This idea is, of course, is reminiscent of her claim that the seven root races each had seven sub-races.

[83] Blavatsky, *Theosophical Glossary*, 35; 'Esoteric Instruction Number Two', in vol. 12 of *Blavatsky Collected Writings*, ed. Boris de Zirkoff (Wheaton, IL: Theosophical Publishing House, 1980), 547; 'Esoteric Instruction Number Five', 704.

and emotional consciousness and Blavatsky described it as 'the subjective form created through mental and physical desires and thoughts
in connection with things of matter, by all sentient beings'.[84] Blavatsky
considered the animal soul 'the grossest of all our principles'. It was the
'medium through which the beast in us acts all its life'. Hinting perhaps
at the temptations of sexuality, she added, 'every intellectual theosophist
will understand my real meaning'.[85] Just as the first principle was the
vehicle of the second, the fourth was the vehicle of the fifth. Bestowed
on humanity when it was incarnated as the Lemurian root race, the
fifth principle, the 'human soul' or *manas,* was associated with memory
and reason. Blavatsky described it as the mind, intelligence, or consciousness assimilating and reflecting the two principles above it. It was
what made a person an intelligent or moral being, distinguishing them
from an animal.[86] Blavatsky also described *manas* as the conception
of self and associated it with 'embodied consciousness' or the 'higher
ego'.[87] Until the third root race, humanity had not possessed an animal
soul sufficiently developed to be able to act as the vehicle of *manas.*[88]
Even among the Aryans, human *manas* was not fully developed, and
only in the future would the full development of *manas* be achieved.[89]

   Manas was crucial to Blavatsky's account of reincarnation because
the spiritual evolution of persons who had reached the Aryan race was
said to depend on the ability of their *manas* to overcome the pull of
the lower principles and attach itself to the higher ones.[90] Blavatsky explained the process as follows: *Manas* was constituted of a higher and
a lower part. The higher aspect was attracted to the principle above it,
buddhi, but the lower aspect to the principles below it, the '*animal* soul
full of selfish and sensual desires'.[91] Although *manas* was drawn down

---

[84] Blavatsky, *Theosophical Glossary*, 159.
[85] Blavatsky, *Secret Doctrine I*, 260.
[86] Blavatsky, *Theosophical Glossary*, 188; *Key*, 92, 135–136.
[87] Blavatsky, *Key*, 100, 174.
[88] Blavatsky, *Secret Doctrine II*, 161–162.
[89] Ibid., 300–301.
[90] Blavatsky, *Key*, 92.
[91] Blavatsky, *Secret Doctrine II*, 495–496. In *The Key to Theosophy*, she explained that
the 'lower, or personal ego' referred to the 'false personality', the combination of the
physical body, etheric double, and the lower self, including all the principles up to the

by these desires, if the 'better man' or higher manas escaped that 'fatal attraction', then buddhi would conquer and carry manas with it 'to the realm of eternal spirit'. This meant the higher manas and buddhi would join together and go on to the next incarnation in a more evolved state.[92] Blavatsky wrote that the higher manas existed on the 'plane of Sutratma, which is the golden thread on which, like beads, the various personalities of this higher Ego are strung'.[93]

The two highest principles (atma and buddhi) formed the monad, the true, immortal essence of a person.[94] Buddhi was the 'divine soul', or the faculty of cognising, the conscience, and the channel through which divine knowledge reached the ego, allowing discernment of good and evil.[95] In other words, through absorbing the higher part of manas in each incarnation, the person evolved and his or her buddhi would become increasingly conscious.[96] Blavatsky stated that buddhi was the vehicle of the seventh principle. Atma was the 'higher self', a 'ray' of the universal spirit inseparable from its divine source.[97] Atma, Blavatsky wrote, 'Is neither your Spirit nor mine, but like sunlight shines on all. It is the universally diffused "divine principle", and is as inseparable from its one and absolute Meta-Spirit, as the sunbeam is inseparable from the sunlight.'[98] Atma was 'the God above, more than within, us. Happy the man who succeeds in saturating his inner Ego with it!'[99]

According to Blavatsky, it was the separation of the higher principles from the physical body that caused death. At death, the three lower principles (the physical body, the vitality, and the astral body)

---

lower part of manas. This false personality therefore indicated the animal instincts, passions and desires (Key, 176).

[92] Blavatsky, Secret Doctrine I, 244–245.

[93] Blavatsky, Secret Doctrine II, 79.

[94] 'Properly speaking, the term "human monad" applies only to the dual soul (Atma–Buddhi), not to its highest spiritual vivifying Principle, Atma, alone. But since the Spiritual Soul, if divorced from the latter (Atma) could have no existence, no being, it has thus been called.' Blavatsky, Secret Doctrine I, 178.

[95] Ibid., xix.

[96] Ibid., 244.

[97] Blavatsky, Key, 175; 'Esoteric Instruction Number Three', 648; 'Esoteric Instruction Number Five', 693; Theosophical Glossary, 40.

[98] Blavatsky, Key, 135.

[99] Ibid., 175.

were cast off. The physical body decomposed, but the astral body could hang around for a while as a ghost and appear during séances. The four higher principles then entered *kama loka*, an astral locality where their experience depended on their level of spiritual achievement. (The more spiritual the person, the shorter their stay in *kama loka*.) At the end of the *kama loka* period, the fifth principle, *manas*, was purified and divided by a struggle between the principles above (*atma* and *buddhi*) and below it (the *kama-rupa* or emotional body). The three highest principles (*atma, buddhi*, and the higher part of *manas*) then entered a 'spiritual ante-natal state', preparing for the bliss of the realm of *devachan*, which would be entered having left behind the emotional body. *Devachan* closely paralleled Earth life, and within it, individuals were said to experience growth, maturity, and decline. There were an infinite variety of levels of well-being within *devachan* to suit different degrees of merit.[100] Blavatsky depicted it as a sort of heaven that provided a rest between lives just as sleep offered rest between days and as *pralayas* occurred between *manvantaras*. Blavatsky remarked on how this teaching reflected the life and death of a human being:

> It thus becomes apparent how perfect is the analogy between the processes of Nature in the Kosmos and the individual man. The latter lives through his life-cycle, and dies. His 'higher principles', corresponding in the development of a planetary chain to the cycling Monads, pass into Devachan, which corresponds to the 'Nirvana' and states of rest intervening between two chains. The Man's lower 'principles' are disintegrated in time and are used by Nature again for the formation of new human principles, and the same process takes place in the disintegration and formation of Worlds. Analogy is thus the surest guide to the comprehension of the Occult teachings.[101]

As with *kama loka*, the length of time spent in *devachan* varied from individual to individual, but it was never less than 1,000 years. It generally

---

[100] Blavatsky, 'The Various States of Devachan', in *Blavatsky Collected Writings*, vol. 5, 90.
[101] Blavatsky, *Secret Doctrine I*, 173.

lasted around 1,500, but could be as long as 3,000 years. Blavatsky wrote that the length of time between rebirths accounted for the fact that we were still working off the karma created in Atlantean bodies.[102]

After a long period in *devachan,* the monad—now composed of *atma, buddhi,* and the higher part of *manas*—would feel the attraction of Earth life. Reincarnation was said to occur because of a thirst for life on the part of the monad. The monad then 'descended', acquiring a new set of lower principles, and the whole process would begin again. Although the principles themselves were considered new, Blavatsky said they were made of the same 'life-atoms' that had formed the lower principles in previous incarnations. These atoms were once again drawn together by the returning individuality under the guidance of karmic law. Adding a scientific angle to this explanation, Blavatsky stated these life-atoms were partially transmitted from father to son by heredity.[103]

Karma

Karma determined the details of the new life.[104] Blavatsky portrayed karma as an impersonal law of the universe, an 'eternal and immutable decree' that brought about harmony in the spirit-matter cosmos.[105]

> Karma creates nothing, nor does it design. It is man who plans and creates causes, and Karmic law adjusts the effects; which adjustment is not an act, but universal harmony, tending ever to resume its original position, like a bough, which, bent down too forcibly, re-bounds with corresponding vigour. If it happen to dislocate the arm that tried to bend it out of its natural position, shall we say that it is the bough which broke our arm, or that our own folly has brought us to grief? ... KARMA is an Absolute and Eternal law in the World of manifestation.[106]

---

[102] Blavatsky, *Key,* 90, 98, *and Secret Doctrine II,* 303.
[103] Ibid., 671–672.
[104] Ibid., 303.
[105] Blavatsky, *Secret Doctrine I,* 643 and *II,* 303.
[106] Blavatsky, *Secret Doctrine II,* 304–305.

Blavatsky saw karma as playing a role in the perfection of humanity.

> Occultists … recognise in every pain and suffering but the neces-
> sary pangs of incessant procreation: a series of stages toward an
> ever-growing perfectibility, which is visible in the silent influence of
> never-erring Karma, or *abstract* nature—the Occultists, we say, view
> the great Mother otherwise. Woe to those who live without suffering.
> Stagnation and death is the future of all that vegetates without a
> change. And how can there be any change for the better without pro-
> portionate suffering during the preceding stage? Is it not those only
> who have learnt the deceptive value of earthly hopes and the illusive
> allurements of external nature who are destined to solve the great
> problems of life, pain, and death?[107]

However, to reiterate, although it played a role in evolution, karma
was not ubiquitous throughout Blavatsky's cosmos. Prior to the late
Lemurian period, 'humanity' had not experienced karma. Karma was,
in fact, only a feature of one of the latest phases in human evolution,
and was associated with intellectuality and the human ego.

As I claimed previously, Blavatsky's discussions of karmic reincarnation typically had the intention of vindicating divine justice by
demonstrating life's apparent inequalities to be the results of individual
or group karma.[108] Had there been no karmic reincarnation, wrote
Blavatsky in *The Secret Doctrine*, the origin and cause of suffering could
not be accounted for.[109]

---

[107] Ibid., 475.
[108] Blavatsky argued that the 'social evils' of the distinction between social classes, or
the sexes, and the unequal distribution of capital and labour were due to karma, but
that the particular conditions of life were not solely the result of individual action but
also the result of group karma. Group karma was the aggregate of individual karma,
so that the sum of the karma of everyone within a particular nation became national
karma and the aggregate of all national karmas was world karma (*Key*, 203–205). The
most important point for Blavatsky here was that the reality of karma didn't mean
that people were entitled to ignore the suffering of others. For example, she argued
it is every individual's responsibility to give what they can of their money, time, and
'ennobling thought' in order to 'balance' or improve the national karma (*Key*, 205).
[109] Blavatsky, *Secret Doctrine I*, 183.

It is only the knowledge of the constant re-births of one and the same individuality throughout the life-cycle; the assurance that the same MONADS ... rewarded or punished by such rebirth for the suffering endured or crimes committed in the former life; ... it is only this doctrine, we say, that can explain to us the mysterious problem of Good and Evil, and reconcile man to the terrible and *apparent* injustice of life. Nothing but such certainty can quiet our revolted sense of justice. For, when one unacquainted with the noble doctrine looks around him, and observes the inequalities of birth and fortune, of intellect and capacities; when one sees honour paid fools and profligates, on whom fortune has heaped her favours by mere privilege of birth, and their nearest neighbour, with all his intellect and noble virtues—far more deserving in every way—perishing of want and for lack of sympathy; when one sees all this and has to turn away, helpless to relieve the undeserved suffering, one's ears ringing and heart aching with the cries of pain around him—that blessed knowledge of Karma alone prevents him from cursing life and men, as well as their supposed Creator.[110]

Having looked at Blavatsky's ideas in some detail, we are now in a position to assess the place of reincarnation vis à vis karma. Karma had a role in Blavatsky's account of evolution, but only from around the middle of the Lemurian period onwards and alongside other evolutionary factors such as the assistance of higher beings and the inherent evolutionary impulse of the cosmos. The compound of *karmic reincarnation* was presented as accounting for inequality and human suffering, and was believed to offer an opportunity for self-perfection and hence accelerated evolution through the endurance of suffering. Furthermore, reincarnation in all its forms was depicted as a microcosmic reflection of the universe's macrocosmic cyclicity.

[110] Blavatsky, *Secret Doctrine II*, 303–304. She made the same point in *Key*, 142.

Conclusions

Presumably, Blavatsky found her later doctrine of reincarnation more appealing than the metempsychosis theory she had discarded around 1882. If one had adhered to the doctrines of *Isis Unveiled*, one wouldn't have expected to meet deceased loved ones at séances, since they would either have achieved immortality and transmigrated to the next sphere, or failed to do so and been annihilated. The latter outcome was considered the lot of the majority and it was not particularly comforting. Not so with reincarnation. In Blavatsky's later theory, one would still not expect to converse with the spirits of the dead (as Spiritualists claimed to), but one might be consoled by the idea of them (in all probability) enjoying their good karma in *devachan* and eventually returning to life on Earth in a more advanced human form. Nevertheless, Blavatsky's reincarnation doctrine still placed a greater distance between the living and the dead than did its main reincarnationist competitor, French Spiritism. Referring to enormous timescales in contrast to the shorter ones of Spiritism, according to Blavatsky, reincarnation never occurred during the lifetimes of family members. As explained by Blavatsky's theory of the seven principles, it also always involved the birth of a completely different person from the one who had died. There was therefore no chance the new baby could be the reincarnation of the deceased grandparent, for example. Thus, Blavatsky deemphasised the personal in favour of an impersonal evolutionary trajectory whose ultimate destination was more important than the details of any particular life. To be sure, despite individual differences, all humans were ultimately alike in that their immortal element, *atma*, derived from—and would return to—the same source. All else was temporary and illusory, including earthly attachments. Blavatsky's reincarnation doctrine was, therefore, arguably quite democratic, and could be seen as supporting the notion of universal brotherhood that was promoted in Theosophy.

It could also be seen as pointing towards the inherent power of mankind and the fundamental importance of the present moment. As such, it reflected that fin-de-siècle apprehension—so common in the literature of the period—that a pivotal moment in history had been reached. For Blavatsky, human incarnation in the fifth (Aryan) root race of the fourth round of the Earth Chain was the critical juncture in the progression of the spirit-matter cosmos, the point of exact equilibration, after which the upward turn would once again begin. Sometimes, Blavatsky made it seem as though everything hinged on humanity's contemporary choices, a position consistent with an occultist emphasis on personal agency, power, and will. On the other hand, reincarnating monads could also be made to seem like twigs in a stream in that no matter what one did, humanity—and the cosmos—would inevitably evolve, karma or no karma. Karmic reincarnation played a supporting role in this evolutionary cosmic drama at the same time as it vindicated divine justice by explaining the meaning of suffering. Nirvana, Blavatsky argued, could be reached only through 'æons of suffering' and by attaining 'the *knowledge* of EVIL as well as of good, as otherwise the latter remains incomprehensible'.[111] The tension between the inherent progressive impulse of the cosmos and human agency was present here too, as it wasn't always clear whether Blavatsky was saying that suffering itself compelled evolution, or whether one's response to that suffering was the key to progress. One suspects both to have been the case.

---

[111] Blavatsky, *Secret Doctrine II*, 81.

4

Spiritualism

BLAVATSKY WAS NOT THE only one to deny reincarnation, at least at first. Similar opinions were expressed in *Ghost Land* and *Art Magic* (both 1876) by the British medium Emma Hardinge Britten (1823–1899), in the writings of the American occultist Paschal Beverly Randolph (1825–1875), and in the teachings of the occultist order, the Hermetic Brotherhood of Luxor (H. B. of L). Joscelyn Godwin described these thinkers as offering an alternative vision within the Spiritualistic milieu of the 1870s. They denied a normative return to Earth after death and postulated progress on higher worlds with a return to Earth-life considered possible in exceptional circumstances.[1] Godwin noted Blavatsky's rejection of the French reincarnationist school of Allan Kardec, despite her close friendships with prominent French Spiritists such as the Leymarie family.[2] He commented on tensions between continental reincarnationists and British and American Spiritualists (who usually denied reincarnation), observing that the debate in the pages of the Spiritualist periodical press was vociferous and that there were counter-schools on both sides.

This chapter builds on Godwin's analysis by exploring in greater detail the similarities and differences between Blavatsky's doctrine of metempsychosis and those of the individuals mentioned above, contextualising them more broadly in reincarnation-denying British and

---

[1] Godwin, *Theosophical Enlightenment*, 303.
[2] Ibid., 281.

American Spiritualism. The Anglo-American currents Blavatsky's ideas had the most in common with all accepted human immortality in some sense but perceived its nature differently. One of the most salient issues was that of personal continuity. Would the same personality live again, or would life continue in the form of a new personality? The contours of such debates within the trans-Atlantic Spiritualist milieu provided the parameters for Blavatsky's discussions of metempsychosis.

The present chapter also evaluates the resemblances and distinctions between Blavatsky's ideas and those of Kardec, which she publicly repudiated. It shows that despite her disavowal, Blavatsky's theories couldn't help having elements in common with French Spiritism because both Theosophy and French Spiritism emerged in related discursive contexts. Overall, therefore, the chapter shows Blavatsky's rebirth theories must be understood in light of her simultaneous reception and rejection of certain specific elements present in Anglo-American Spiritualism and French Spiritism. This shows that there is no straightforward answer to the question of whether Blavatsky was or was not a Spiritualist, an issue that has preoccupied more than one historian since the beginnings of the Society.[3]

Blavatsky and Spiritualism

The beginning of Spiritualism, at least as a public movement, is usually dated to the Hydesville Rappings of 1848.[4] From America, Spiritualism

---

[3] An early historian of Spiritualism, Frank Podmore, described Theosophy as a 'vigorous offshoot of the spiritualist movement'. Frank Podmore, *Studies in Psychical Research* (London: Kegan Paul, Trench, Trübner & Co., 1887), 40. Much more recently, Jeffrey Lavoie has framed Theosophy as 'A Spiritualist Movement'. Jeffrey D. Lavoie, *The Theosophical Society: The History of a Spiritualist Movement* (Boca Raton, FL: Brown Walker Press, 2012).

[4] This date is problematic, however. As Arthur Vesluis notes, studies that repeat the idea that Spiritualism began in Hydesville in 1848 echo 'a long critical tradition of ignoring European and even American esoteric precedents for these phenomena of spirit manifestation. In fact, there is a long history of such phenomena in both Europe and North America.' See Arthur Versluis, *The Esoteric Origins of the American Renaissance* (Oxford: Oxford University Press, 2001), 55.

quickly spread to Britain, Europe, and beyond.[5] Recent studies have portrayed Spiritualism as a central cultural force related to many other aspects of nineteenth-century intellectual and religious life. As Sarah Wilburn and Tatiana Kontou recently concluded, Spiritualism arose in the context of 'a widespread cultural grappling with what it meant to be a modern individual who was curious, scientifically-minded, technologically current, and spiritually advanced'.[6] Spiritualism had no centralised authority or creed and was only loosely organised. The only belief all Spiritualists could be said to have shared was that it was possible to contact the dead. Additionally, Spiritualists tended to believe in spiritual progress in this life as well as after death, and in universal salvation. Spiritualism developed in Protestant and Catholic contexts, and many Spiritualists considered themselves Christian, although Spiritualism could exist in non- and even anti-Christian forms too.[7] American and British Spiritualists had a propensity to deny reincarnation. Spiritism—the French variety of Spiritualism based on the thought of Allan Kardec—had features in common with British and American varieties but it also had some distinct characteristics, notably a strong proclivity towards reincarnationism.

[5] An excellent recent study is Cathy Gutierrez, *Plato's Ghost*. For a short summary, see Gutierrez, 'Spiritualism: Communication with the Dead', *Religion Compass* 4, no. 12 (2010).

[6] Tatiana Kontou and Sarah Wilburn, *Ashgate Research Companion to Nineteenth-Century Spiritualism and the Occult* (Farnham and Burlington: Ashgate, 2012), 4. For some, this grappling led in progressive directions, and Spiritualism has typically been depicted as a democratic, populist, and feminist movement, closely associated with reform agendas such a vegetarianism, abolitionism, dress reform, and women's rights. For example, see Alex Owen, *The Darkened Room: Women, Power, and Spiritualism in Late Victorian England* (London: Virago Press, 1989) and Anne Braude, *Radical Spirits: Spiritualism and Women's Rights in Nineteenth-Century America* (Boston: Beacon Press, 1989). However, Spiritualism was by no means homogenous, and, as Christine Ferguson has emphasised, it incorporated a wide spectrum of political identifications, including the conservative and even the highly reactionary. See Christine Ferguson, 'Recent Studies in Nineteenth-Century Spiritualism', *Literature Compass* 9, no. 6 (2012), 432.

[7] In Britain, anti-Christian Spiritualism was associated with a working-class, secularist context, especially in the north of England. On Christian and non-Christian Spiritualism, see Oppenheim, *The Other World*, 63–110.

Towards the end of the 1870s, when Blavatsky published *Isis Unveiled* in New York, about two decades had passed since the highpoint of American enthusiasm for Spiritualism. Nevertheless, it was still very popular. During the early 1870s, Blavatsky's attitude had been equivocal. Already in 1872 she had expressed serious reservations, claiming the spirits contacted were not real spirits but empty shells from which the immortal component had departed.[8] This position denigrated séance phenomena and denied Spiritualist interpretations of them. However, in a letter to the Russian Spiritualist A. N. Aksakoff in 1874, she referred to Spiritualistic phenomena as resulting from the actions of 'the spirits of the departed', an interpretation that could be interpreted as consistent with Spiritualist perspectives.[9] She also referred to herself as a Spiritualist.[10] Nevertheless, in the same year, she wrote to her relatives, 'The more I see of Spiritualistic *séances* in this cradle and hotbed of Spiritualism and mediums, the more clearly I realise how dangerous they are for humanity.'[11] Despite this, in 1878, she once again described herself as a Spiritualist.[12] This was an ambiguous assortment of statements that may have depended on to whom she was writing. It reflected the fact that Blavatsky was as indebted to Spiritualism as she was critical of it.

Blavatsky and French Spiritism

Blavatsky's bugbear was reincarnation as taught in French Spiritism. Spiritist reincarnationism had roots in previous European theories,

---

[8] 'Their spirits are no spirits but spooks—rags, the cast-off second skins of their personalities that the dead shed in the astral light.' Letter to her relatives, c. March or early April 1872, in Blavatsky, *Letters*, 20.

[9] Letter to A. N. Aksakoff, 28 October 1874, in Blavatsky, *Letters*, 34. Aksakoff was a prominent Russian Spiritualist. See Carlson, *No Religion Higher*, 24.

[10] Letter to H. S. Olcott, Oct/Nov 1874, in Blavatsky, *Letters*, 36.

[11] Letter to her relatives, 1874, in Blavatsky, *Letters*, 52.

[12] 'While the *Spiritualist* and the Banner of Light in days past have classed me as a *non* Spiritualist, the "Indian Daily News" of Calcutta and various secular papers in other countries abuse me and my book for its author being a "Spiritualist"!! This is comical and perplexing. *I am a Spiritualist*, but of another sort, and I flatter myself of a little more philosophical sort.' Letter to P. C. Mitra, 10 April 1878, in Blavatsky, *Letters*, 410–411.

such as that of the Swiss naturalist and philosopher Charles Bonnet (1720–1793), who proposed a theory of *palingenesis*, understood as regeneration on a series of planetary worlds. Bonnet's ideas were adopted by the French philosopher Pierre-Simon Ballanche (1776–1847), and Ballanche, in turn, influenced the early nineteenth-century French socialist Saint-Simonians Pierre Leroux (1797–1871) and Jean Reynaud (1806–1863), who argued that successive lives could occur on Earth or other planets.[13] French Spiritism drew on these currents but went much further in popularising reincarnation belief.

Allan Kardec (1804–1869) was the pen name of Frenchman Hippolyte Léon Denizard Rivail, author of (among others) *Le livre des esprits* (*The Spirits' Book*, 1857) and *Le livre des médiums* (*The Mediums' Book*, 1861).[14] He was also editor of the journal *Revue Spirite*. According to Kardec, the universe was populated with spirits living in the spirit world. These spirits would repeatedly incarnate on Earth or other planets in increasingly better conditions. Incarnation was seen as an aid to the spiritual and moral progress of spirits, who would eventually evolve to perfection and experience a state of pure bliss. According to the 'law of progress', only improvement was possible, never deterioration. Thus, human reincarnation would always take place in another human form, never as an animal, and animals could never evolve into humans. They were a separate kingdom and evolved within that kingdom. The speed of evolutionary progress was said to depend on a spirit's efforts, and reincarnation was supposed to explain the diversity of aptitudes and abilities in humans as well as the conditions into which they incarnated.

As Lynn Sharp has argued, Kardec's reincarnationism was part of a secular version of spirituality popular with those who favoured science (perhaps to the detriment of Catholicism) but who nevertheless retained a religious outlook. Sharp described the development of this secular spirituality as quintessentially modern.[15] She noted that believers

---

[13] See Arthur McCalla, '*Palingenesie philosophique* to *Palingenesie sociale:* From a Scientific Ideology to a Historical Ideology', *Journal of the History of Ideas* 55, no. 3 (July 1994) and Lynn L. Sharp, *Secular Spirituality: Reincarnation and Spiritism in Nineteenth-Century France* (Lanham, MD: Lexington Books, 2006).

[14] Allan Kardec, *Le livre des esprits* (Paris: E. Dentu, 1857) and *Le livre des médiums* (Paris: Didier et cie, 1861).

[15] Sharp, *Secular Spirituality*, xii.

found reincarnation consoling, and Spiritists used it to argue for social and political change.

> Believers in reincarnation imagined an evolutionary, perfectible soul, improving as it moved through a series of lives. [. . .] As humans progressed towards perfection, they would also become less selfish, more able to create a society that recognized the needs, rights, and interests of all, including the working class and especially women.[16]

However, as John Warne Monroe has submitted, although the reincarnationism of Kardec was felt by many to be consoling, it didn't aim for social and political change in any revolutionary sense, but rather a gradual betterment that would result naturally from spiritual progress. Kardec adapted romantic socialist notions of reincarnation such as those of Leroux and Reynaud but gave his ideas a broader appeal by eliminating the revolutionary implications reincarnationism had acquired in the 1840s. Rather than being an incentive for rebellion, reincarnation now became, for Kardec, a way of justifying existing inequalities. The idea was that the rich would eventually become more compassionate and generous and a redistribution of wealth would occur naturally, without recourse to revolution. Additionally, social inequality was said to serve a purpose. Conditions experienced during life depended on past sins, which had to be atoned in the present incarnation for progression to take place.[17] As Kardec summarised, 'spiritism revives faith in the future, raises the courage of those who are depressed, and enables us to bear the vicissitudes of life with resignation.'[18]

[16] Ibid., xv.
[17] John Warne Monroe, *Laboratories of Faith: Mesmerism, Spiritualism, and Occultism in Modern France* (Ithaca, NY, and London: Cornell University Press, 2008), 106–107 and John Warne Monroe, 'Crossing Over: Allan Kardec and the Transnationalism of Modern Spiritualism', in *Handbook of Spiritualism and Channeling*, ed. Cathy Gutierrez (Leiden: Brill, 2015).
[18] Allan Kardec, *The Spirits Book*, trans Anna Blackwell (Boston: Colby and Rich, 1875), 413.

French Spiritism had arrived in Russia by 1854.[19] Since educated Russians commonly spoke French (Blavatsky included), French Spiritism was especially accessible to them. Blavatsky had been familiar with Spiritism at least from the early 1870s, and probably earlier. In 1871, she established a *Société Spirite* in Cairo for the investigation of phenomena according to the philosophy of Allan Kardec.[20] When visiting Paris in 1873, she stayed with the prominent Spiritists the Leymaries.[21] Joscelyn Godwin observed that despite her antagonism towards Spiritism, all her known Parisian contacts were Spiritists.[22] Blavatsky commented on this:

> I find fault with [Spiritists] for one thing [. . .] they are *reincarnationists* and zealous missionaries for the same. They could never do anything with me in that way, so they gave me up in disgust. But we are still friends with Mr and Madame Leymarie who are both of them highly cultured people and—truthful and sincere as gold. [. . .] Prince Wittgenstein is an old friend of my youth, but has become a *reincarnationist*, so we had a fight, or two for it and parted half friends half enemies.[23]

What was it Blavatsky found so objectionable? The major point of disagreement was the identity of the individual who reincarnated. Kardec was adamant that death and rebirth didn't result in any change of identity; the being who died was the same who was reborn. Blavatsky disagreed, arguing that the same spirit would be reborn with a new personality and body. According to Kardec, during incarnation, a human being was constituted of body, soul (or spirit), and the link

[19] It was introduced by General Apollon Boltin. Carlson, *No Religion*, 23.
[20] Godwin, *Theosophical Enlightenment*, 279.
[21] Joscelyn Godwin, *The Beginnings of Theosophy in France* (London: Theosophical History, 1989), 4–6.
[22] Ibid., 7.
[23] Letter to H. Corson, 20 March 1875, in Blavatsky, *Letters*, 113–114.

uniting soul and body, known as the *périsprit*.[24] The *périsprit* played a
role in the continuity of the person's identity through incarnations.[25]
At death, the 'soul' (in Kardec, the highest principle) would disengage
and enter a state of confusion before re-entering the world of spirits,
where it awaited a new incarnation after spending some time as a wandering spirit, before reincarnating. Although Blavatsky's spiritual anthropology reflected Kardec's, Blavatsky used the three principles to
argue the person who was reborn was fundamentally different to the
one who died: only the highest element (in Blavatsky, the 'spirit') was
immortal and continued from life to life. The other principles, namely,
the soul and the body, were usually only attached to the spirit for the
duration of one life on Earth. Furthermore, in Kardec, reincarnation
happened relatively quickly. In Blavatsky, it would happen only after
many centuries.

Wouter Hanegraaff argued Kardec's Spiritism 'combined two things
resented by Blavatsky: popular spiritualism [. . .] and a pronounced
Christian emphasis'. Considering the competition between Spiritism
and Theosophy, it made sense for Blavatsky to denounce the supposedly vulgar Spiritist doctrine of reincarnation in favour of a more
sophisticated Theosophical perspective.[26] This interpretation is consistent with Stephen Prothero's contention that Theosophy began as
an elite attempt to reform what the founders considered a lowbrow
Spiritualism. According to Prothero, Blavatsky (and Olcott) hoped to
'uplift' the Spiritualist 'masses out of their supposed philosophical and
moral vulgarities'.[27] During the earlier period, this had involved a denial of Kardecist reincarnation and affirmation of metempsychosis.[28]

[24] This is normally invisible but it may appear in exceptional circumstances, such as in
the case of apparitions.
[25] 'How does the soul preserve the consciousness of its individuality, since it no longer
has its material body?' the imaginary enquirer asked in Kardec's text. The answer: 'It
still has a fluid peculiar to itself, which it draws from the atmosphere of its planet, and
which represents the appearance of its last incarnation—its perispirit.' Allan Kardec,
The Spirits Book, trans Anna Blackwell (Boston: Colby and Rich, 1875), 63.
[26] Hanegraaff, *New Age Religion*, 481.
[27] Stephen Prothero, 'From Spiritualism to Theosophy: "Uplifting" a Democratic
Tradition', *Religion and American Culture* 3, no. 2, 198.
[28] For a denial of Kardec's ideas consistent with the theory of metempsychosis, see
'Fragments from Madame Blavatsky'. Blavatsky's article was first published in Kardec's

In the later reincarnationist period, Blavatsky still repudiated French Spiritism, even though it may, superficially, have seemed as though she had come around to it because she had started affirming the truth of reincarnation.

British and American Spiritualism

Across the English Channel and even further, across the Atlantic, the situation was somewhat different to that in France. Kardec's ideas were made accessible to an English-speaking audience by such translations as Emma Wood's *The Book on Mediums* (1874)[29] and Anna Blackwell's *The Spirits' Book* (1875). Blackwell also advocated reincarnation belief in such works as *The Philosophy of Existence: The Testimony of the Ages* (1871). Be that as it may, in Britain and America, Spiritualists tended to deny reincarnation on Earth, believing instead in the progress of the soul from one level to another. The soul was believed to work out its faults before moving on in an indefinite series of worlds, each one higher and more perfect than the one before.[30] The first major American theologian of Spiritualism, Andrew Jackson Davis (1826–1910), elaborated a non-reincarnationist notion of evolutionary planetary ascent that was influential and reminiscent of Blavatsky's metempsychosis.[31] Describing

periodical, *La Revue Spirite*, in April 1878. For a refutation of Kardec consistent with her later reincarnation doctrine, see Blavatsky, 'The Teachings of Allan Kardec', *The Theosophist* 4, no. 11 (August 1883), 281.

[29] Allan Kardec, *The Book on Mediums Or; Guide for Mediums and Invocators*, trans. Emma Wood (Boston: Colby and Rich, 1874).

[30] Oppenheim, *The Other World*, 170.

[31] Davis endorsed the 'beautiful laws of progression and development', according to which mankind would progress, after death, through concentric spheres of increasing refinement surrounding the Earth until they reached the seventh sphere. He was influenced by the Swedish visionary Emanuel Swedenborg (1688–1772), who claimed to have discussed the inhabitants of other planets with spirits. Among Blavatsky's source texts, *The Unseen Universe* (1875) by the physicists Balfour Stewart and Peter Guthrie Tait referred to Swedenborg's accounts of different planets and their dwellers. Balfour Stewart and Peter Guthrie Tait, *The Unseen Universe, or, Physical Speculations on a Future State* (New York: Macmillan, 1875), 38–42. Blavatsky was aware of Swedenborg's visions but she didn't take them too seriously. '[Swedenborg] *saw*, in "the *first Earth* of the astral world*", inhabitants *dressed as are the peasants in Europe*; and on the *Fourth*

seven spheres, Davis wrote, the 'first Sphere is that of the natural world, the habitable earths of the planets, the circle of manifested things.' Like Blavatsky, Davis believed in multiple 'earths' or planets on which life could exist. He maintained that after death on the physical planet, a second sphere would be reached. This was the 'Summerland', which contained 'all the beauties of the first [sphere], combined and perfected', gardens, unity, and celestial love.[32] From the second sphere, rebirth would take place on increasingly lovely spheres.[33] The seventh sphere was described as the 'Infinite Vortex of love and wisdom and the Great Spiritual Sun of the Divine Mind'.[34] Davis insisted that no matter how advanced, individuals would not merge into one another or into the Divine. They would retain their own separate identities.[35] During roughly the thirty years before the publication of *Isis Unveiled* in 1877, his works provided theoretical foundations for Anglo-American Spiritualist discussions of after-death states, which generally affirmed post-mortem progress and denied reincarnation.

Despite the broad non- or even anti-reincarnationist consensus in the English-speaking world, Spiritualists debated the issue at length, as evidenced in the Spiritualist periodical press. The following example is taken from the London Spiritualist periodical *The Medium and Daybreak,* which published the following letter on 23 April 1875:

'To the Editor.—Sir,—I was pleased to see in last week's MEDIUM that the doctrines of metempsychosis and re-incarnation have been made the subject of consideration by Dr. Sexton [...] the doctrine of re-incarnation is a distinct contravention of [the great law of progress] and of the fundamental truth of Spiritualism, [...] To introduce doctrines like those of re-incarnation and metempsychosis in *any* connection with Spiritualism, is to obscure its great philosophy,

Earth women clad as are the shepherdesses in a *bal masque.*' Blavatsky, *Secret Doctrine II*, 33.

[32] *The Harmonial Philosophy: A Compendium of the Works of Andrew Jackson Davis, edited by A Doctor of Hermetic Science* (London: William Rider, 1923) , 138–139.
[33] Ibid., 140–143.
[34] Ibid., 144.
[35] Ibid., 120.

and create those sectarian differences which have proved the weakness of dogmatic creeds.—'I remain, Sir, yours faithfully, S. E. G-. *Croydon,* April 11th, 1875.

The editors appended the following:

We publish the foregoing letter as representative of numerous other expressions of opinion on the subject to which it refers. Some there are whose minds receive this peculiar doctrine recently brought forward in Mrs. Tappan's discourses. The great majority of English Spiritualists discard it.[36]

The two individuals mentioned here in connection with the reincarnation debates were Dr. George Sexton (1825–1898), a popular lecturer who, for some years, advocated Spiritualism, and Cora Scott Tappan (1840–1923), one of the best-known mediums of the era.[37]

Dr. Sexton was mentioned again in the July issue of the same periodical, as lecturing on the 'doctrine of metempsychosis, ancient and modern', demonstrating that 'in modern times, it had turned up in a somewhat changed form, as advocated first by Fourier and more recently by Allan Kardec, Miss Blackwell, and other well-known

---

[36] 'Metempsychosis and Reincarnation', in *Medium and Daybreak* 6, no. 264 (23 April 1875), 266. The reference to British druidism is compelling, the notion of Gallic druidic reincarnationism having been popularised by Jean Reynaud in the early nineteenth century in what Lynn Sharp termed a 'fascinating use of history as nationalist propaganda'. Sharp, *Secular Spirituality*, xviii. The idea of druidic reincarnationism entered French Spiritist discourse via Reynaud, but it existed in British versions too, as in the extract above, as well as in several of Blavatsky's sources, which discussed the reincarnationism of English, Irish, and Gallic druids. See, for example, Richard Payne-Knight, *The Symbolical Language of Ancient Art and Mythology* (New York: J. W. Bouton, 1876), 179 and Godfrey Higgins, *Anacalypsis: An Attempt to Draw Aside the Veil of The Saitic Isis* (London: Longman, Rees, Brown, Green and Longman, 1836), vol. 2, xvi. Blavatsky herself argued for druidic reincarnation in *The Secret Doctrine* and in the context of her later doctrines of reincarnation. Blavatsky, *Secret Doctrine II*, 760.
[37] Cora married four times, each time taking the name of her husband: Hatch, Daniels, Tappan, and Richmond, and we meet her here during her third marriage. Thanks to Marc Demarest for helping me identify these figures. For more on George Sexton, see Timothy Larsen, *Crisis of Doubt: Honest Faith in Nineteenth-Century England* (Oxford: Oxford University Press, 2006), 197–227.

Spiritualists.' He concluded with the 'reasons for rejecting the theory in all its forms'.[38] Cora Scott Tappan reached different conclusions. She had also lectured at Cavendish Rooms some months previously, on 21 February 1875. The theme had been 'metempsychosis, various forms of transmigration and re-incarnation'. She responded to arguments posed against reincarnation, saying, in contradistinction to Dr. Sexton, that since the ancients had all believed in reincarnation, there must be some truth in it. As Blavatsky would later maintain, Mrs. Tappan argued for the need to 'unlock' these ancient teachings, particularly because of the dangers of materialism and mistranslation.

Mrs. Tappan went on to outline a theory in which individuals were dual, possessing a personality, which distinguished them from one another, and an identity, meaning 'the actual individual consciousness of the soul itself'. She described the soul's progression:

> [the soul] passes through the regular succession of cherubim, seraphim, archangelic and angelic hosts, down through the spiritual spheres of soul existence until it reaches a planet, this earth being, of course, only one of many planets and not being especially selected for its age or spiritual advancement, but being in progress of development under the administration of souls, angels, and divinities.[39]

A particularly striking parallel between Mrs. Tappan's and Blavatsky's early thought appeared in the following section of the article:

> All souls must have equal opportunities in eternity. [. . .] Since all souls do not have equal opportunities in a single expression of life, since some die in infancy and other have maimed, deformed, and useless bodies, [. . .] Every soul in the great cycles of eternity must have equal opportunities of advancement to perfection.[40]

---

[38] 'Dr Sexton at Cavendish Rooms', *Medium and Daybreak* 6, no. 275 (9 July 1875), 439.
[39] 'Metempsychosis: Mrs. Tappan's Oration at Cavendish Rooms', *Medium and Daybreak* (26 February 1875), 138.
[40] Tappan, *Metempsychosis*, 138.

Mrs. Tappan here displayed the same concern as Blavatsky did in both her rebirth doctrines that cases of child death or deficiency were simply not *fair* and that something would be adjusted to compensate for them.

Emma Hardinge Britten

Closely associated with the early Theosophical Society and present at the founding meeting, the British medium Emma Hardinge Britten presented tenets very similar to the metempsychosis of Blavatsky's early period.[41] John Patrick Deveney highlighted the striking similarities between Britten's views on rebirth and Blavatsky's early teachings, showing, for example, that they both discussed human gestation and even resembled each other on a verbal level, both mentioning the 'pilgrim'.[42] The notion of 'discarded shells', a prominent theme in Blavatsky's writings, was also present in Britten, who described an apparition as an 'astral shell', not a true 'departed spirit'.[43]

Britten's views on reincarnation are stated most explicitly in an article she published in the Boston Spiritualist periodical over which Blavatsky and Olcott had much influence, *The Spiritual Scientist*, edited by E. Gerry Brown (1849–1928). In her article, Britten referred to reincarnation as an 'obnoxious and repulsive side issue' that had been 'ruthlessly engrafted upon the pure and fruitful soil of Spiritualism'. She elaborated that although Cora Scott Tappan now affirmed reincarnation, she had previously taught 'endless spiritual progression' and that her past utterances contained not 'the least allusion to the doctrine of

---

[41] In her two major works, *Ghost Land* and *Art Magic* (both 1876), Britten claimed that the real author was a living person she had known for a long time who went under the alias of Chevalier Louis de B——. Robert Mathiesen identified the Chevalier as Ernst Christian Ludwig von Bunsen (1819–1903), a member of an occult society known as the 'Orphic Circle', for which Emma had been a mesmeric subject as a child. Robert Mathiesen, *The Unseen Worlds of Emma Hardinge Britten: Some Chapters in the History of Western Occultism* (Fullerton: Theosophical History, 2001), 26–32. See Emma Hardinge Britten, *Ghost Land; Or Researches into the Mysteries of Occultism* (Boston: Published for the editor, 1876) and *Art Magic* (New York: Published by the author, 1876).

[42] See Deveney, *Randolph*, 35f.

[43] Britten, *Ghost Land*, 60.

Re-incarnation'.[44] Britten objected to Mrs. Tappan's turnaround in the strongest terms, objecting that 'countless millions' of spirits communicating through other channels had no knowledge of Re-incarnation and even emphatically denied it.[45] She concluded, 'the theory of Re-incarnation, to my apprehension, [is] a doctrine more loathsome, horrible and repulsive than even annihilation itself.'[46]

Britten summarised her position on what actually did take place after death in one of her major and most influential works, *Art Magic* (1876):

> Man lives on many earths before he reaches this. Myriads of worlds swarm in space where the soul in rudimental states performs its pilgrimages ere he reaches the large and shining planet named the Earth, the glorious function of which is to confer *self-consciousness*. At this point only is he man; at every other stage of his vast, wild journey he is but an embryonic being—a fleeting, temporary shape of matter—a creature in which *a part*, but only a part, of the high, imprisoned soul shines forth; a rudimental shape, with rudimental functions, ever living, dying, sustaining a fleeting, spiritual existence, as rudimental as the material shape from whence it emerged; a butterfly, springing up from the chrysolitic shell, but ever as it onward rushes, in new births, new deaths, new incarnations, anon to die and live again, but still stretch upward, still strive onward, still rush on the giddy, dreadful, toilsome, rugged path, until it awakens once more—once more to live and be a material shape, a thing of dust, a creature of flesh and blood, but now—*a man*.[47]

Blavatsky quoted this passage in *Isis Unveiled*, confirming the similarity between her early views and those of Britten.[48] However, although

---

[44] Emma Hardinge Britten, 'The Doctrine of Re-Incarnation', *The Spiritual Scientist* 2, no. 11 (20 May 1875), 128.

[45] Ibid., 129.

[46] Ibid., 140.

[47] Britten. *Art Magic*, 28. The account supposedly came from the Sanskrit automatic writing of a twelve-year-old Hindu girl. Deveney quoted the extract as it appears in *Isis Unveiled* in *Randolph*, 269. There are some small typographical errors in the Blavatsky version, such as 'flitting' for 'fleeting'.

[48] Blavatsky, *Isis I*, 368.

Britten's and Blavatsky's early views were very similar, they were not identical. In contradistinction to Blavatsky (who claimed immortality had to be won on Earth otherwise annihilation would result), Britten's writings claimed annihilation was impossible because the human being was intrinsically self-conscious and immortal.[49]

Paschal Beverly Randolph

Britten's and Blavatsky's views on post-mortem progression had further parallels in those of Paschal Beverly Randolph, a black American Spiritualist and magician significantly influenced by Andrew Jackson Davies who was notorious for his magic mirrors and sexual practices.[50] Randolph and Blavatsky hardly mentioned one another, but Randolph's biographer, John Patrick Deveney, concluded there was an 'elusive and indirect relationship' between them.[51] In *Dealings with the Dead; The Human Soul, Its Migrations, and Transmigrations* (1862) and its sequel, *After Death; Or; Disembodied Man* (1868), Randolph described his visions and cosmology. He referred to souls as monads or 'human seeds'. (Britten had written of 'germ-seeds'.) According to Randolph, there was a perpetual flow of these 'world-souls' and 'monads' from the 'Fountain', incarnating on every 'perfected earth in the universe' as intelligent, deathless beings.[52] Randolph explained matter was 'alive with imprisoned Spirit' because it contained these monads, which sought to escape their bonds in matter by travelling through the various stages of mineral, plant, and animal life until they reached the human level.[53] He

[49] Britten, *Ghost Land*, 318–320.
[50] Randolph didn't mention Britten by name, and Britten only mentioned him once, and slightingly, in her history, *Modern American Spiritualism* (New York: Published by the author, 1870), 242. See Deveney, *Randolph*, 35. Randolph didn't mention Blavatsky either. Olcott was certainly familiar with Randolph's works before he developed a friendship with Blavatsky and gave them to her as gifts. Apparently, she read and valued them, although she hardly mentioned Randolph. Ibid., 260.
[51] Ibid., 253, 257–258.
[52] Paschal Beverly Randolph, *After Death; or; Disembodied Man* (Boston: Printed for the Author, 1868), 89.
[53] In a visionary account, Randolph described the transmigrations of his own monad as it travelled together with others from its home in a fiery comet that cooled into a world that was shaken by an earthquake freeing the monads from the granite in

referred to the process as 'the great law of Transmigration' and claimed it explained the similarities between humans and animals.[54] When the monad reached the human level, it would be born intrinsically immortal. (In this, Randolph agreed with Britten but disagreed with Blavatsky, who argued immortality had to be won.) Nevertheless, he echoed Blavatsky's idea that the embryo developed in utero according to stages corresponding to its previous transmigrations through plant and animal forms.[55] After death, the individual would find a new home 'in the starry heavens', where they would learn 'lessons far more important than any ever studied here'.[56] He elaborated on these starry heavens, describing them as 'spiritual belts' around planets, the sun, the solar system, and even the galaxy.[57] After death, progress would continue in the zones surrounding the Earth (or any other planet on which monads

which they were housed, allowing them to change their outer form into that of moss. From moss, the monads became plants of increasingly 'higher character', followed by lower and higher forms of fish, reptiles, birds, mammals, apes, and finally different types of human, including Negros, Indians, and Chinese and leading up to the final three: 'Gaul, Briton, and American!' (The exclamation point is original, and seems apt.) Randolph, *Dealings with the Dead; The Human Soul, Its Migrations and Transmigrations* (Utica, NY: M. J. Randolph, 1861–1862), 45–48.

[54] It was not the case that humans had previously been animals, but rather that their monads had transmigrated by *associating* themselves with animals. 'Dogs and owls were originally made in order that the human monad, in passing a sort of gestation period in them, might be ripened slowly, and prepared for what he is now.' Ibid., *Dealings*, 205.

[55] 'The foetus [. . .] rapidly passes through a series of strange mutations, successively resembling bird, beast, and simia (apes), until finally the strictly human plane is reached [. . .] if the foetus dies before it has reached the strictly human body, it dies forever, and its monad escapes, because it requires the chemical and other properties of the human body to properly elaborate the human spirit and fashion it for eternity. But if that human shape be reached before it dies in the womb, then that it is a true child, and is, of course, immortal, for it, though weak, survived the physical death.' Randolph, *After Death*, 55–56. This was an interpretation of recapitulationism, the contemporary scientific theory that the human embryo passes through stages of development that correlate to the stages of that organism's evolutionary development.

[56] Randolph, *After Death*, 29. The notion of 'starry heavens' is reminiscent of Thomas Lake Harris's work, *An Epic of the Starry Heaven* (New York: Partridge and Brittan, 1855). In *Dealings with the Dead*, Randolph acknowledged his admiration for Harris. Randolph, *Dealings*, 254.

[57] Randolph, *After Death*, 29.

incarnated), situated beyond the outer limits of the Earth's atmospheric envelope. From there, the monad would progress to the third stage, on 'the solar belt', and the fourth, in the 'zone which engirdles the entire solar system'. The fifth stage would take place in the zone encircling the star cluster to which the solar system belonged, and the sixth would be on 'an immense belt or zone that surrounds another dark sun'. Finally, the seventh stage would take place in a belt surrounding entire galaxies and crossing the Milky Way at right angles.[58] The similarities to Blavatsky's seven spheres are clear, but there were differences too, as Blavatsky never described the spheres in this way.

Significantly, like Britten, Blavatsky, and Mrs. Tappan, Randolph discussed the issue of 'special cases' such as the deaths of foetuses and idiots.[59] In *After Death*, Randolph didn't postulate that in such special cases reincarnation would take place as Blavatsky had, but rather that in some instances, the individual would be immortal and in others not. He gave various details and included consideration of groups Blavatsky had not discussed, such as murderers and prostitutes. His style and some of his conclusions were different to Blavatsky's, but the echoes with Blavatsky and Mrs. Tappan were undeniable.[60] Finally, a noteworthy difference of perspective was that Randolph considered the idea of the ultimate absorption of the spirit to be problematic and undesirable.[61] Clearly, this was an issue that divided the Spiritualist community, and one on which Blavatsky and Randolph did not agree.

---

[58] There were also six more grand zones just like the seventh zone. The transcendent glories of the first grand zone were said to 'exceed the power of a seraph to describe' and in the other six, 'there is absolutely nothing whatever resembling anything pertaining to the first'. Ibid., 90–92.

[59] Deveney, *Randolph*, 278.

[60] Randolph's full discussion can be found in *After Death*, 54f.

[61] 'Immortality can be the prerogative of man only so long as God and man are not blended into one single Personality. So long as each soul shall think, feel, suffer, enjoy, cogitate and have a continuity of self-knowing, just so long will it be possessed of an invincible conviction of personal identity, under which circumstance alone, and only, can its immortality be truly predicated and affirmed. But, should any soul ever be reabsorbed into Deity—again become a portion of Divinity—an utter, total, and complete annihilation of the individual must ensue; and that destruction of the human self-hood would be [. . .] effective, utter and complete.' Randolph, *Dealings*, 166.

The Hermetic Brotherhood of Luxor

Godwin, Chanel, and Deveney identified the Hermetic Brotherhood of Luxor (H. B. of L.) as a possible connection between Blavatsky and Randolph. The H. B. of L. was an organisation teaching practical occultism through a correspondence course that began its public work in 1884 but may have been in existence, in one form or another, for much longer.[62] The H. B. of L. started functioning within a 'small Randolphian coterie already existing in England'.[63] It had many influential members and its ideas impacted on subsequent esoteric movements.[64] A document on reincarnation circulated as part of the H. B. of L. correspondence course, but this has not survived. Deveney reconstructed it using extracts from *The Light of Egypt* (1889) by Thomas Henry Burgoyne, born Thomas Dalton (1855–1895). Burgoyne had acted as a medium for the entities considered the founders of the H. B. of L.[65] *The Light of Egypt* was based on the teachings of the H. B. of L. and broke its secrecy.[66] Just as in early Blavatsky, the document denied reincarnation, saying it was a poisonous doctrine and 'the true Hindu and Buddhist religions' didn't teach it.[67] Instead, the H. B. of L. proposed a theory much like Blavatsky and Randolph's:

> Thus we see the atom of life commencing at the mineral in the external world. The grand spiral of its evolutionary life is carried forward slowly, imperceptibly, but always progressively. [. . .] The soul in rudimental states performs its pilgrimages until its cyclic progress

---

[62] The H. B. of L. became public with the appearance of a discreet advertisement requesting potential members to make contact. Godwin, Chanel, and Deveney, *The Hermetic Brotherhood of Luxor*, 3.

[63] Ibid., 44.

[64] Ibid., ix. Amongst its leaders were Peter Davidson (1842–1916), who may have been initiated by Randolph (and responsible for incorporating his teachings into the curriculum), and the Reverend William Ayton (1816–1909). Godwin, *Theosophical Enlightenment*, 258, 351.

[65] Godwin, Chanel, and Deveney, *The Hermetic Brotherhood of Luxor*, 4–5.

[66] Joscelyn Godwin, *The Beginnings of Theosophy in France* (London: Theosophical History Centre, 1989), 19; Godwin, Chanel, and Deveney, *The Hermetic Brotherhood of Luxor*, 38.

[67] Godwin, *Theosophical Enlightenment*, 358, 360.

enables it to reach the magnificently organised planet whose glorious function it is to confer upon the soul self-consciousness. At this point alone does it become man. At every other step of the wild, cosmic journey it is but an embryonic being. [. . .] The grand, self-conscious stage, humanity, is attained, and the climax of earthly incarnation is reached. Never again will it enter the material matrix or suffer the pains of material incarnation. Henceforth its rebirths are in the realm of spirit. Those who hold the strangely illogical doctrine of a multiplicity of human births have certainly never evolved the lucid state of soul consciousness within themselves.[68]

The H. B. of L. document on reincarnation contained another pertinent extract:

Each race of human beings is immortal in itself; so likewise is each round. The first round never becomes the second, but those belonging to the first round become the parents or originators of the second so that each round constitutes a great planetary family which contains within itself races, sub-races and still minor groups of human souls; each state being formed by the laws of its karma, and the laws of its form and the laws of its affinity—a trinity of laws.[69]

This bears a marked similarity to Blavatsky's theory of the root races, which was present in Blavatsky's later (reincarnationist) works, but not in the earlier (non-reincarnationist) ones. This suggests Blavatsky's *later* perspective was also consistent with this current of thought in some aspects, even though she changed her mind about reincarnation. As we have already seen several times, despite Blavatsky's change of doctrinal direction, there were important continuities between her earlier and her later views.

[68] Godwin, Chanel, and Deveney, *The Hermetic Brotherhood of Luxor*, 189–191.
[69] Ibid., 192.

Conclusions

It is undeniable there were strong similarities between Blavatsky's early doctrine of metempsychosis and the teachings of Britten, Randolph, and the H. B. of L. Small but significant differences were present too, such as the question of whether the being who incarnates on Earth is intrinsically immortal or has to win immortality during life. Blavatsky's views were not identical to those of Britten et al., although this remains the current with which her early ideas had the most in common. The exact relationship between the different proponents remains elusive but, as Deveney has shown, it is clear there was some sort of (possibly mutual) influence. This was the 'immediate family' of Blavatsky's metempsychosis. The 'extended family' included Andrew Jackson Davis, Mrs. Tappan, Dr. Sexton, and other British and American Spiritualists. They tended to believe in the participation of higher beings in human progress, and differentiated between metempsychosis and reincarnation, approving or disapproving of one or the other. Some highlighted ancient reincarnationist currents and some even affirmed belief in 'exceptional circumstances' in which normal processes were supervened.

When Blavatsky embraced the idea of a normative return to Earth-life around 1882, she had not turned to Kardec's Spiritism. The tension between Blavatsky's teachings (first metempsychosis, later, reincarnation) and Kardec's reincarnationist Spiritism was constant despite changes in perspective. In both her metempsychosis and her reincarnation-affirming periods, Blavatsky referred to and incorporated Spiritist ideas and terminology (such as the *périsprit*), but she also denied central Spiritualist tenets (e.g., immediate reincarnation, the return of the same personality). Theosophy and Spiritism came from related discursive worlds, but there was a constant strain between them; Spiritism was the extended family member with whom Blavatsky did not get on and never had.

Stephen Prothero's observation that the Theosophists aimed to 'uplift' Spiritualism was astute. If the proposition of metempsychosis had already been part of Blavatsky's attempt to 'uplift' the dogmas of Spiritualism into something more sophisticated, then her later theory of reincarnation endeavoured to 'raise' them even higher, by offering a resplendent vision of a fractal cosmos of reincarnating planets, solar systems, and universes. One of the ways Blavatsky probably felt she was raising the tone of the conversation was through reference to highbrow topics, such as the ancient Greeks, new scientific theories, and Oriental religions. In the following chapters, I show how Blavatsky's discussions of reincarnation drew on contemporaneous debates related to each of these areas, revealing fundamental aspects of how Blavatsky transmuted Spiritualist conceptions into Theosophical ones.

5

Platonism

ALFRED NORTH WHITEHEAD'S STATEMENT that the 'safest general char-
acterisation of the European philosophical tradition is that it consists
of a series of footnotes to Plato' has often been quoted.[1] M. H. Abrams
spoke instead of a long series of footnotes to Plotinus.[2]

Indebted to Spiritualism but taking her engagement with the Greeks
much further than the Spiritualists generally did, Blavatsky's discussions of metempsychosis and reincarnation are important—and hitherto unacknowledged—sites for the intersection of occultist thought
with nineteenth-century (neo-)Platonism. As I will demonstrate, her
constructions of the Greeks shifted to reflect her changing rebirth doctrines. Her doctrines therefore provide a window into wider historical
issues related to how Classical civilisation was construed during the
period.

In Blavatsky's rebirth doctrines, both Plato and Plotinus had their
place, especially because, together with Pythagoras, these figures were
often noted as exponents of reincarnation or metempsychosis. Blavatsky
discussed them in this context, and so did many of her sources. She referred to Pythagoras, Plato, and the various neo-Platonists much more
frequently in *Isis Unveiled* than in *The Secret Doctrine*. In her first major

---

[1] Alfred North Whitehead, *Process and Reality: An Essay in Cosmology* (New York: Free
Press, 1979), 39.
[2] M. H. Abrams, *Natural Supernaturalism: Tradition and Revolution in Romantic
Literature* (New York and London: W. W. Norton 1973), 146–147.

work, such references were always interpreted as corroborations of met-empsychosis and conditional immortality. This makes sense inasmuch as the term 'metempsychosis' is of Greek origin. In Blavatsky's later publications, she still occasionally referred to Platonism, but much less frequently (the main focus having shifted to India) and always in veri-fication of reincarnation and related ideas such as *devachan*. Again, this seems logical: no emphasis on 'metempsychosis', a lot less mention of the Greeks. They hadn't disappeared completely, however.

Blavatsky's interest in Hellenism was part of a wider nineteenth-century fascination evident in the large number of her source texts dealing explicitly with ancient Greece. In her works, she discussed books specifically devoted to the subject, such as *Plato und die Alte Akademie* (1876) by the German theologian and philosopher Eduard Zeller, *Mythologie de la Grèce antique* (1886) by the French scholar Paul Decharme, and many others.[3] References to Classical philosophy, his-tory, and civilisation could also be found throughout source texts of Blavatsky's that had a broader, usually comparative, scope.[4] The rather long list of books to which Blavatsky referred that made some reference to the Greeks spanned professional, amateur, scholarly, and heterodox works that dealt with many different topics. This points towards the widespread nineteenth-century interest in the Classics and its inter-section with various other subjects, especially the comparative study of religion and mythology.

Certain themes tended to recur in these sources' discussions of Greek religious doctrines. The Greeks were said to have taught a theory of

---

[3] Other sources include B. F. Cocker, *Christianity and Greek Philosophy* (New York: Harper and Brothers, 1870) and J. Lempriere [sic], *Classical Dictionary* (London: J. Cadell and W. Davies, 1812).

[4] Discussions of Greek philosophy and reincarnation theories can be found in plenty of these works, including, for example, Samuel Fales Dunlap, *Sōd: The Son of Man; Sōd: The Mysteries of Adoni* (London: Williams and Norgate, 1861); and *Vestiges of the Spirit-History of Man* (New York: D. Appleton and Company 1858). Also important are: Joseph Ennemoser, *The History of Magic*, trans. William Howitt (London: George Bell and Sons, 1893); Alexander Winchell, *World Life* (Chicago: S. C. Griggs and Company, 1883); Isaac Myer, *Qabbalah* (Philadelphia: Published by the author, 1888); and William Howitt, *The History of the Supernatural* (London: Longman, Green, Longman, Roberts and Green, 1863). Some of these works are listed in Gómes, *Bibliography*, 150–177.

rebirth (referred to as metempsychosis, reincarnation, or transmigration) in which the body was considered the 'tomb of the soul' and in which repeated return to Earth-life was said to result in the soul's purification. Another theme was a link between the Greeks, Egypt, and India. Although rooted in ancient sources, the influence of the East on ancient Greece was a speculation that had become especially popular since the end of the previous century. The notion was found throughout Blavatsky's source texts, and versions of it appeared in the works of the German-born Oxford Orientalist Max Müller (1823–1900), the French barrister and author Louis Jacolliot (1837–1890), and the Tyrolean Mesmerist Joseph Ennemoser (1757–1854). Other notable sources to link the Greeks with India include Edward Upham's *The History and Doctrine of Buddhism* (1829) and Edward Pococke's *India in Greece* (1852), but there were many others.

Blavatsky affirmed the influence of India on ancient Greece with enthusiasm. 'Pococke,' she wrote in *Isis Unveiled*, 'in his most ingenious work, [. . .] endeavours to establish still more firmly the identity of the Egyptian, Greek, and Indian mythology.'[5] She elaborated, the 'primitive history of Greece is the primitive history of India' and concluded, 'the primitive history of Judea is a distortion of Indian fable engrafted on that of Egypt.'[6] In other words, the two 'great civilisations', as they were perceived in the nineteenth century—Hellenism and Hebraism—came from the same (Indian) source.

Nineteenth-Century Constructions of the Greeks

The fact that Blavatsky considered it essential to demonstrate that the ancient Greeks corroborated her teachings points towards the contemporary cultural importance of the Classics. Blavatsky's rebirth theories must, therefore, be situated within wider nineteenth-century constructions of the Greeks. Interest in ancient Greece had intensified following the Enlightenment, first in Germany, and eventually spreading to the

[5] Blavatsky, *Isis II*, 438.
[6] Ibid., 471.

rest of Europe and America.[7] This nineteenth-century interest in (or even obsession with) the Greco-Roman Classics has been documented in some excellent studies, which have focused on various aspects of scholarship, literature, politics, art, and music.[8] They have demonstrated that a fascination with the Classics was shared by many of the greatest intellectual, literary, and artistic figures of the century, as well as by many lesser figures, and indeed by the wider public. Many of the authors of works on the history of ancient Greece (including Blavatsky's source texts) were amateur scholars, and both amateur and professional scholarship was commonly influenced by the authors' theological agendas and ideologies. Nineteenth-century scholars of Greece believed their work could have a real impact on contemporary politics, aesthetics, religion, morals, and other areas of life. Many of them felt a close kinship with the figures they studied, whom they considered distant contemporaries.[9]

Despite the wealth of academic literature on the Greeks in the nineteenth-century imagination, no study as yet has been dedicated to the intersection between the Classics and occultism. Cathy Gutierrez's excellent *Plato's Ghost* (2009) comes closest by exploring the 'elective affinity' between Platonic ideas about the nature of the soul, the cosmos, and education in Spiritualist thought. As Gutierrez argued, although Spiritualists were not necessarily deeply concerned with Platonism, they were influenced by Platonic 'structures of thought' thanks to new translations of Plato such as those of Bohn's Library (begun in 1848), which made the dialogues and other writings available to middle-class people in inexpensive editions.[10]

Classicism has most commonly been associated with the elite, political conservatism, imperialism, and colonialism, and with the preparation of men for the church or other offices of power. Instruction in

---

[7] Franck M. Turner, *The Greek Heritage in Victorian Britain* (New Haven and London: Yale University Press, 1981), 2.

[8] Ibid.; Richard Jenkins, *The Victorians and Ancient Greece* (Oxford: John Wiley and Sons, 1981); Simon Goldhill, *Victorian Culture and Classical Antiquity: Art, Opera, Fiction, and the Proclamation of Modernity* (Princeton: Princeton University Press, 2011).

[9] Turner, *The Greek Heritage*, 8 and xii.

[10] Guttierez, *Plato's Ghost*, 7–8.

the Classics usually involved reading the great works of the established canon in Greek and Latin, and the study of ancient history. As Franck Turner noted, 'General familiarity with the classics was once one of the distinguishing and self-defining marks of the social and intellectual elite of Europe.'[11] On the other hand, Classicism could also be associated with revolutionary and radical ideas. Simon Goldhill highlighted the challenge posed to traditional Christian faith by the study of critical history, implicating Classicism (alongside science) in the challenge faced by conventional forms of Christianity during the nineteenth century. In Romantic thought, radical tendencies had stood alongside interest in the Classics from the beginning of the century, for example in the propensity of some Romantic poets to see a plausible alternative to Christianity in Greek mythology.[12] A little later, this unconventional attitude was evident in the literary and philosophical movement of American Transcendentalism, which tended to reject received religion and embrace 'natural laws', the divine spirit in nature, and an intuitive grasp of truth over and above the purely 'rational'. From the 1860s, writers associated with the late-Romantic aesthetic movement also took their Hellenism in transgressive directions.[13]

Blavatsky's vision of ancient Greece was inclined towards culturally radical readings. The 'establishment' constantly came under fire in her works and this, for her, meant the Protestant and Catholic churches, materialist science, and 'erroneous' academic scholarship. Like many

---

[11] Turner, *The Greek Heritage*, 4.

[12] Ibid., 77–78.

[13] Stefano Evangelista's study of literary aestheticism highlighted Hellenism's transgressive potential, examining the reception of ancient Greece by writers linked to the aesthetic movement from the 1860s to the end of the century. The aesthetic movement included figures such as the English poet Algernon Charles Swinburne (1837–1909); the English historian, critic, and poet John Addington Symonds (1840–1893); the English critic Walter Pater (1839–1894); and Oscar Wilde (1854–1900). These men were all trained in Classics at Oxford, the main centre of classical learning in nineteenth-century Britain. Evangelista concluded, 'the experience of ancient Greece stands at the very heart of literary aestheticism in its polemical and counter-cultural identities: it is to the Greeks that the aesthetes turn to formulate their late-Romantic theorisation of the aesthetic as a discourse of dissent from the dominant culture of the mid-Victorian decades.' Stefano Evangelista, *British Aestheticism and Ancient Greece: Hellenism, Reception, Gods in Exile* (Basingstoke: Palgrave Macmillan, 2009), 2.

of her contemporaries, Blavatsky identified with the Greeks, but this was because she considered herself an advocate of the same subversive secret doctrine they had taught. George Mills Harper observed the neo-Platonist scholar Thomas Taylor (1758–1835) had a similar perspective, believing Plato not to have been the originator of Platonic philosophy but rather the greatest philosopher in a chain in which Taylor himself was the latest link.[14] The similarity between Blavatsky's and Taylor's perspectives is not surprising, since the influence of Taylor on Blavatsky was both direct and indirect. In addition to reading Taylor's works, his ideas were also mediated through a prominent early friend of Blavatsky's, the American physician and Platonist Alexander Wilder, himself a representative of an American Platonic tradition that we will consider presently.

Another important figure in Theosophical Classicism was George Robert Stowe Mead (1863–1933). Mead studied Classics at Cambridge, taking his BA in 1884, and reading Sinnett's recently published introduction to Theosophical doctrines, *Esoteric Buddhism* (1883) while still at university. He joined the Theosophical Society the same year, becoming Blavatsky's private secretary in 1889. By the time Mead took on this role, Blavatsky had already published *The Secret Doctrine* (1888), but she continued writing. Mead assisted her, holding this secretarial post until Blavatsky's death in 1891. At her cremation, he referred to the life that had just ended as merely one brief incarnation.[15] Mead prepared Blavatsky's *Theosophical Glossary* for publication in 1892. That year, he was mentioned in the Theosophical periodical *Lucifer*, which he now edited together with Blavatsky's successor, Annie Besant (1847–1933).[16] The article went on to detail the many lectures Mead had subsequently given in different cities, including some on the topic of reincarnation.

---

[14] George Mills Harper, *The Neoplatonism of William Blake* (Chapel Hill: University of North Carolina Press, 1961), 15.

[15] http://www.katinkahesselink.net/his/mead.html.

[16] 'Our General Secretary read a paper [at the Convention of the American Section of the Theosophical Society] on Reïncarnation, and is described as having "made a strong argument for the rationalism of the belief that men live many times on earth". Brother Mead seems to be winning golden opinions among the Americans, and it is pleasant to read kind words of one whom we so highly value here.' Besant, Annie. 'On the Watch-Tower', *Lucifer* 10, no. 57 (May 1892), 182–183.

In 1895, he published *Select Works of Plotinus*, a title originally published by Thomas Taylor. He wrote on many topics, and among his work on the Greeks were writings on Orpheus and Orphic religion, Ammonius Saccas, Porphyry, and Iamblichus.[17] He also published a series of articles on reincarnation in the thought of the Church Fathers.[18] As important as G. R. S. Mead was in the history of Theosophical Classicism and reincarnationism, however, it was really only after Blavatsky's death that he started publishing and speaking extensively on these topics. For this reason, it is here that we will leave our discussion of him.

Alexander Wilder

It is within an American current influenced by Transcendentalism and Thomas Taylor, among other things, that we must situate Blavatsky's interpretations of the Greeks.

Alexander Wilder (1823–1908) was a noteworthy early Theosophist who played a significant role in the writing and editing of *Isis Unveiled*.[19] He met Blavatsky when he was in his fifties, becoming a close friend and regular visitor at Blavatsky's 'Lamasery' in 1870s New York.[20] Wilder was a doctor and an advocate of what was at the time termed 'irregular' medicine (usually by its detractors)—the ancestor of today's holistic medicine. Among other things, he was also an amateur Platonist.[21] Although not a professional scholar of the Classics,

---

[17] Clare Goodrick-Clarke and Nicholas Goodrick-Clarke, *G. R. S. Mead and the Gnostic Quest* (Berkeley, CA: North Atlantic Books, 2005), 2–12.

[18] 'A Proposed Enquiry Concerning "Reincarnation in the Church Fathers"', *The Theosophical Review* 37 (December 1905), 329–330; 'Origen on Reincarnation', *The Theosophical Review* 37 (February 1906), 513–527; 'Irenaeus on Reincarnation', *The Theosophical Review* 38 (March 1906), 38–48; 'Justin Martyr on Reincarnation', *The Theosophical Review* 38 (April 1906), 129–136; 'Reincarnation in the Christian Tradition', *The Theosophical Review* 38 (April 1906), 253–259.

[19] Olcott spoke of 'Dr. Alexander Wilder's numerous notes and text paragraphs in the Introduction and throughout both volumes, and others which add so much to the value and interest of the work'. Olcott, *Old Diary Leaves First Series*, 206.

[20] Ibid., 412–413.

[21] Wilder was a one-time member of the religious community founded in 1848 by John Humphrey Noyes (1811–1886) that was based in Oneida, New York, and which practiced complex marriage and male sexual continence. Wilder fought against slavery and mandatory vaccinations and wrote a 900-page introduction to the history of

Wilder had a vast knowledge of the topic. He was a translator, editor, lecturer, and prodigious writer who wrote or edited some of the works on Classical thought to which Blavatsky referred. These included articles such as 'Paul and Plato' (1881), just one of many Wilder published in the New York journal *The Evolution*.[22]

Blavatsky called Wilder 'one of the best Platonists of the day'. In a letter of around December 1876, she wrote him:

> 'Pon my word, without any compliment, there's Taylor alone and yourself, who seem to grasp truth *intuitionally*. I have read with the greatest pleasure your edition of the *Eleusinian and Bacchic Mysteries*. You are right. Others know Greek better, but Taylor knew Plato a thousand times better; and I have found in your short fragments much matter which for the life of me I do not know where you could have learned it. Your *guesses* are so many *hits* right on the true spot. Well, you ought to go East and get initiated.[23]

Here Blavatsky echoed a statement Wilder had previously made about Thomas Taylor.[24] It was Taylor's first complete English translations of Plato and Aristotle, as well as sections of Plotinus and some of the minor neo-Platonists, which first brought these works to the attention

---

medicine. For an excellent survey of Wilder's life, see Ronnie Pontiac, 'The Eclectic Life of Alexander Wilder: Alchemical Generals, Isis Unveiled, and Early American Holistic Medicine', *Newtopia Magazine*, 15 Feb 2013. https://newtopiamagazine. wordpress.com/2013/02/15/the-eclectic-life-of-alexander-wilder-alchemical-generals-isis-unveiled-and-early-american-holistic-medicine/.

[22] Mentioned in Blavatsky, *Isis II*, 90. Other titles include 'Bacchus the Prophet-God' (June 1877), mentioned in Blavatsky, *Isis II*, 523 and 'Paul, the Founder of Christianity' (September 1877), mentioned in Blavatsky, *Isis II*, 536. Wilder also contributed essays to *The Metaphysical Magazine of New York* around 1894–1895, as well as to *The Word*, from 1904 onwards, but his earlier articles are more important in this context as influences on the formation of Blavatsky's Theosophy. See Boris de Zirkoff, 'Dr. Alexander Wilder', in *The Later Platonists and Other Miscellaneous Writings of Alexander Wilder* (Henry County, Ohio: Kitchen Press, 2009), 631.

[23] Letter to Alexander Wilder, c. 6 Dec 1876, in Blavatsky, *Letters*, 283–284.

[24] Harper, *William Blake*, v. See also 12, 17, and 29. Regarding Taylor's popularity and reputation, see Cees Leijenhorst, 'Neoplatonism III: Since the Renaissance', in *Dictionary of Gnosis and Western Esotericism*, ed. Wouter Hanegraaff, 845.

of Romantics and Transcendentalists. A prodigious translator, Taylor had produced more than 100 titles. Notable works of his to which Blavatsky referred included the above-mentioned *Dissertation on the Eleusinian and Bacchic Mysteries* (1790), edited by Wilder in 1875,[25] as well as *Works of Plato* (1804),[26] *Select Works of Plotinus* (1817),[27] and a translation of Iamblichus' *Life of Pythagoras* (1818).[28]

Blavatsky's acknowledgement of his deficient Greek alludes to the fact that Taylor's work had been criticised within the academy. Together with Floyer Sydenham (1710–1787), Taylor had published the first complete English translation of Plato's dialogues, but Taylor's neo-Platonic tendencies and inadequate Greek meant it came to be ignored soon after its publication, having been attacked in the Edinburgh review in 1809.[29] In *Isis Unveiled*, Blavatsky responded to the criticisms of Taylor's 'mistranslations' that had been levelled by contemporary Classicists. Echoing her letter to Wilder, she wrote Taylor's memory was dear to the 'true Platonist', in contradistinction to Taylor's 'dogmatic' detractors within the academic establishment. In an echo of the Transcendentalist themes of interiority and intuition, she opined that the true Platonist learnt the 'inner thought' of Plato rather than the mechanical elements of his work. Blavatsky allowed for the existence of more accurate phraseology than Taylor's but maintained Taylor revealed Plato's true meaning. She chided the prominent scholars Eduard Zeller (1814–1908) and Benjamin Jowett (1817–1893) for not revealing this message, and she concluded by quoting Wilder's statement that Taylor had a superior intuitive perception of Plato.[30]

With his debt to Taylor's neo-Platonic interpretations, Alexander Wilder was a representative of a middle-class American Midwestern Platonic movement that has been described by Paul Anderson in *Platonism in the Mid-West* (1963). According to Anderson, this Platonic

[25] Blavatsky, *Isis I*, xxiii, 213, 253; Blavatsky, *Isis II*, 81, 88, 91, 98.

[26] Blavatsky, *Isis I*, 218.

[27] Ibid., xlix, 221.

[28] Taylor also wrote *The Mystical Hymns of Orpheus* (1787) and *Aristotle* (1806–1812). See Blavatsky, *Isis I*, 222, 253, 283.

[29] Turner, *The Greek Heritage*, 371.

[30] Blavatsky, *Isis II*, 98.

movement was closely related to Transcendentalism, influencing American culture particularly between the 1860s and 1890s. By the 1860s, the peak of Transcendentalism had already passed, having reached its greatest popularity between the 1830s and 1850s. Nevertheless, its influence could still be felt. The influence of the prominent Transcendentalist Ralph Waldo Emerson (1893–1882) on Americans around the midcentury was enormous, and the Platonic movement that flourished in the Midwest in the later part of the century was directly indebted to it.

The Plato Club was founded in 1860 in Jacksonville, Illinois. It was a society where amateur middle-class enthusiasts could read Plato together in Greek. The club had an egalitarian ethos that valued education for people of all backgrounds. Its teachings included the idea the 'creator' could best be understood as a form of 'absolute energy' that produced a hierarchy of being, in which man was at the centre and above him were sub-deities. Below him were spheres 'antagonistic to the good'. The soul was resident in the body and needed to be purified, leading to union with the creator.[31] These late-nineteenth (neo-Platonic) readings of Plato were very similar to Blavatsky's views.

Around twenty years later, the Plato Club inspired the establishment of the American Akademe, a society that held monthly meetings during the winter. Alexander Wilder was secretary of the Akademe and later its vice president.[32] He also edited the *Journal of the American Akademe* for its first four volumes and wrote many papers.[33] At each meeting of the society, a paper was read and discussed. There was a general emphasis on 'high thought', and although membership was based in the American Midwest, there were members from all over the world. Among them were many physicians, like Wilder.[34] The Akademe was associated with various international publications, such as *The Platonist*, the *Bibliotheca Platonica*, and the *Journal of the American Akademe*.[35] The nucleus of membership was the Plato Club, which still operated and continued

[31] Paul Anderson, *Platonism in the Midwest* (New York: Columbia University Press), 48.
[32] Ibid., 52–53.
[33] Ibid., 59.
[34] Ibid., 57.
[35] Ibid., 6.

to do so even until after the Akademe ceased.[36] The last meeting of the American Akademe took place in 1892.

The Plato Club and the Akademe overlapped with another society, the Transcendentalist Concord School of Philosophy. This was a summer school founded in 1879 in Concord, Massachusetts, by the reformer and writer Amos Bronson Alcott (1799–1888), a friend of Emerson and the father of the American novelist and poet Louisa May Alcott (1832–1888). Bronson Alcott was an even more enthusiastic Platonist than Emerson. His Concord School lasted until 1888, and Wilder lectured there many times.

Anderson has convincingly argued the Platonic movement represented by the Plato Club, American Akademe, and Concord School was an expression of 'the temper of the age'. The Plato Club was established just before the outbreak of the Civil War in 1861, a time of great tension between different sections of American society. These tensions led to a desire for an inclusive, universalistic philosophy and a universal law of morality. The members 'were not exponents of social programs; they were interpreters of social events on a cosmic scale', finding solutions to moral problems 'based on religious and metaphysical principles. It was to these principles that they gave attention, rather than to active participation in ameliorative measures.'[37] In Anderson's analysis, serious American interest in Plato was 'partly the result of a desire for philosophic knowledge which would provide a gospel of social unity'.[38] In this context, Platonism provided them with a sense of the harmony of reality.[39]

These aims are congruent with those of Blavatsky, who, although she wrote after the Civil War, was heavily indebted to the American Platonism of Wilder, which, in turn, was based on the neo-Platonism of the earlier English Platonist, Thomas Taylor. Wilder had other influences too, though. Among his many other publications, he was the author of a pamphlet entitled *New Platonism and Alchemy: A Sketch of*

[36] Paul Anderson estimated there were around 200 active members of the Akademe at any given time. Ibid., 56.
[37] Ibid., 20–21.
[38] Ibid., 21.
[39] Ibid., 22.

the Doctrines and Principal Teachers of the Eclectic or Alexandrian School (1869).[40] Jean-Louis Siémons has demonstrated that Wilder drew many of his statements from the work of the German Lutheran theologian Johann Lorenz von Mosheim (1694–1755), author of *Ecclesiastical History* (1726).[41] Siémons established that Wilder ignored Mosheim's criticisms of Ammonius Saccas, portraying the neo-Platonic philosopher in a purely positive light.[42] This selective reading of Wilder's was probably influenced by Thomas Taylor's favourable evaluations of Ammonius Saccas.[43] Wilder's point of view was especially influential on Blavatsky. She initially perceived the Theosophical Society as a re-creation of this Alexandrian Eclectic School as it was depicted in Wilder's work.[44] In an echo of one of Wilder's statements, and in the spirit of American Platonism in general, Blavatsky wrote that the Alexandrian School's purpose had been to 'reconcile all religions, sects and nations under a common system of ethics, based on eternal verities'.[45] This sounded remarkably close to the goals of the Theosophical Society.

Blavatsky and Greek Rebirth

Blavatsky's doctrines of metempsychosis and reincarnation had affinities with Greek ideas. Nevertheless, the similarities between Blavatsky's teachings and Greek thought were superficial enough that we cannot

[40] Blavatsky, *Isis I*, 437.
[41] Johann Lorenz von Mosheim, *Institutionum historiae ecclesiasticae antiquioris et recentioris libri IV* (Helmstedt: 1726–1755). The first English translations were those of Archibald Maclaine (1764) and James Murdoch (1832). See the second edition of James Murdock, *Mosheim's Institutes of Ecclesiastical History, Ancient and Modern* (London: William Tegg, 1867), xxii and xxv.
[42] Jean-Louis Siémons, *Ammonius Saccas and His 'Ecclectic Philosophy' as presented by Alexander Wilder* (Fullerton: Theosophical History, 1994), 3, 6–7, 13–17.
[43] On Taylor's favourable evaluation of Saccas and his love of Greek religion, see Harper, *William Blake*, 12.
[44] She gave the Alexandrian School pride of place in her first published article on Theosophy. H. P. Blavatsky, 'What Is Theosophy?', in *Blavatsky Collected Writings*, ed. Boris de Zirkoff [Originally published in *La Revue Spirite* (November 1880)]. See also Blavatsky, *Key*, 1. In *Old Diary Leaves*, Olcott said that the spirit 'John King' had brought a Master to his attention, a representative of the neo-Platonist Alexandrian school and 'a very high one' at that. Olcott, *Old Diary Leaves First Series*, 19.
[45] Blavatsky, *Key*, 1–2.

speak of Blavatsky proposing 'Pythagorean' or 'Platonic' teachings. In any case, the issue here will not be to question 'how Greek' Blavatsky's ideas 'really were'. Rather, the objective will be to show that Blavatsky's construction of the Greeks paralleled her changing perspectives. In Blavatsky's writings, first the Greeks taught metempsychosis, then re-incarnation. This is an example of how, for nineteenth-century thinkers (Blavatsky included), the Greeks could be who you wanted them to be and say what you wanted them to say.

Pythagoras

Greek belief in rebirth is primarily associated with Pythagoras. Accounts of his life are unanimous in stating that from an early age, he travelled widely in search of wisdom, including in Egypt and Chaldea (Babylonia).[46] Pythagoras' doctrines (variously described as 'reincar-nation', 'metempsychosis', or 'transmigration' in nineteenth-century sources) have been noted since the first century BCE, but very little is known of the details of his teaching.[47] This made speculation easy. References to Pythagoras' ideas abound in Blavatsky's sources. For ex-ample, Samuel Fales Dunlap stated Pythagoras taught 'transmigra-tion',[48] Eliphas Lévi's *The History of Magic* discussed Pythagoras' belief in the immortality of the soul and memory of past lives,[49] and Joseph Ennemoser wrote that Pythagoras appeared to have been the first person in Greece to maintain 'belief in transmigration'.[50]

---

[46] David Fideler, 'Introduction', in *The Pythagorean Sourcebook and Library: An Anthology of Ancient Writings Which Relate to Pythagoras and Pythagorean Philosophy*, ed. Kenneth Sylvan Guthrie and David Fideler (Grand Rapids, MI: Phanes Press, 1988), 19–20.

[47] Aristotle, *De Anima*, trans. R. D. Hicks (Amherst, MA: Prometheus Books, 1991), 24; Jan Bremmer, *The Rise and Fall of the Afterlife* (London: Routledge, 2002), 2, 11–12; Herbert Strainge Long, *A Study of the Doctrine of Metempsychosis in Greece from Pythagoras to Plato* (Princeton, NJ: Privately printed, 1948), 15; Walter Burkert, *Lore and Science in Ancient Pythagoreanism*, trans. Edwin L. Minar Jr. (Cambridge, MA: Harvard University Press, 1972), 120, 138.

[48] Dunlap, *Vestiges*, 368–369.

[49] Eliphas Lévi, *The History of Magic*, trans. A. E. Waite (London: Rider and Co., 1974), 96.

[50] Ennemoser, *History of Magic I*, 145.

In *Isis Unveiled,* Blavatsky made numerous references to Pythagoras' doctrine of metempsychosis. As we saw in chapter 2, which focused on Blavatsky's early metempsychosis doctrine, she wrote of Pythagoras' 'allegorical mysticism and metempsychosis'[51] and considered 'Pythagorean metempsychosis' to have an advantage over modern science.[52] She even referred to 'Pythagoreans' from much later periods, especially the Dutch Jewish philosopher Baruch Spinoza (1632–1677) and the Italian Dominican friar and esoteric thinker Giordano Bruno (1548–1600).[53] Socrates and the Gnostics were said to have been exponents of Pythagorean metempsychosis,[54] and Blavatsky associated the theory of metempsychosis with Hindu and Buddhist terms.[55]

Blavatsky discussed Pythagoras much less frequently in *The Secret Doctrine,* in which there were no longer any references to Pythagorean

[51] Blavatsky, *Isis I,* 307.

[52] Ibid., 9.

[53] 'The modern commentators affirm that Bruno, "*unsustained by the hope of another and better worlds* still surrendered his life rather than his convictions;" thereby allowing it to be inferred that Giordano Bruno had no belief in the continued existence of man after death. [. . .] Giordano Bruno, if he adhered to the doctrines of Pythagoras he must have believed in another life, hence, he could not have been an atheist whose philosophy offered him no such "consolation." [. . .] the above words plainly indicate the belief of Bruno in the Pythagorean metempsychosis, which, misunderstood as it is, still shows a belief in the *survival* of man in one shape or another.' Ibid., 93–95.

[54] Ibid., 12.

[55] Blavatsky, *Isis II,* 286. Elaborating on the connection between Pythagoras and India, Blavatsky complained that Lemprière's *Classical Dictionary* (1792–1797) had stated, 'there is great reason to suspect the truth of the whole narrative of Pythagoras's journey into India'. 'If this be so,' she interjected, 'How account for the doctrine of the metempsychosis of Pythagoras, which is far more that of the Hindu in its details than the Egyptian?' Blavatsky, *Isis I,* 347. In fact, Lemprière had affirmed Pythagoras' journey to India: 'The Samian philosopher was the first who supported the doctrine of *metempsychosis* or transmigration of the soul into different bodies, and those notions he seemed to have imbibed among the priests of Egypt, or in the solitary retreats of the Brachmans.' J. Lempriere [*sic*], *Classical Dictionary* (London: T. Cadell and W. Davies, 1820). There are no page numbers. Pythagoras is listed under 'PY'. Blavatsky's attribution was mistaken; the quotation actually came from the *Classical Dictionary* of the American Classicist Charles Anthon (1797–1867): Charles Anthon, *A Classical Dictionary* (New York: Harper and Brothers, 1841), 1153. Be that as it may, the most important points were that Blavatsky affirmed Pythagoras taught metempsychosis and that he had learned it in India.

'metempsychosis' at all. However, she mentioned him in relation to 'reincarnation' in another of her later publications, *The Theosophical Glossary* (1892):

> [Pythagoras] seems to have travelled all over the world, and to have culled his philosophy from the various systems to which he had access. Thus, he studied the esoteric sciences with the Brachmans of India, and astronomy and astrology in Chaldea and Egypt. [. . .] As the greatest mathematician, geometer and astronomer of historical antiquity, and also the highest of the metaphysicians and scholars, Pythagoras has won imperishable fame. He taught reincarnation as it is professed in India and much else of the Secret Wisdom.[56]

In this passage, Blavatsky summed up much of what she had said in *Isis Unveiled* about Pythagoras' connection to India, but she now referred to him as a teacher of reincarnation rather than metempsychosis. This may seem like a small difference—only one word—but taken together with parallel changes throughout her writings, it shows her constructions of the Greeks shifted to reflect her changing rebirth doctrines.

Plato

Plato (427–347 BCE) discussed reincarnation in six dialogues: *Meno, Cratylus, Republic, Phaedo, Phaedrus,* and *Timaeus.* Plato didn't have one fixed theory and apparently never tried to harmonise his accounts. Nevertheless, there were some general features. The idea that humans had one soul, which could be divided, and which survived death, was consistent throughout the dialogues. Souls originally lived in a blissful, ideal world of Forms but 'fell' and were condemned to suffer corporeal life and multiple human and animal incarnations. The *Phaedo* described animal incarnations as punishments for acts committed in the present life. In that dialogue, Socrates proposed a hierarchy of possible future incarnations saying that those who 'carelessly practiced gluttony,

---

[56] H. P. Blavatsky, *Theosophical Glossary* (Krotona: Theosophical Publishing House, 1918), 248.

violence and drunkenness are likely to join a company of donkeys or of similar animals. [. . .] those who have practiced popular and social virtue [. . .] will again join a social and gentle group, either of bees or wasps or ants.'[57] The incurable were annihilated.[58] In the *Timaeus*, two-legged creatures were at the top of the hierarchy, followed by four-legged and many-legged creatures.[59] The *Phaedrus* also described the types of person that less-enlightened souls might be reborn as in a hierarchy that was similar, but different, to that presented in the *Phaedo*, with kings, commanders, and statesmen at the top, and a tyrant at the bottom. Only those who had glimpsed at least some truth could be born in human form.[60] In some dialogues, souls were allowed to choose their rebirth.[61] Once incarnated, the intellect strove to return to its previous blissful state but was impeded by the lower parts of the soul. One therefore had to practice philosophy and fight to transform negative desires into positive ones. The soul could only perceive the Forms in its disembodied state, as contact with the body caused forgetfulness. In the *Phaedrus*, beauty, wisdom, and all good qualities and virtues nourished the soul's wings, while any sort of ugliness or foulness shrunk them.[62] The numbers 1,000 and 10,000 appeared repeatedly. For example, in the *Phaedrus*, souls who practised philosophy returned to where they came from after 10,000 years.[63]

---

[57] *Phaedo* 81 d–82 c, in Plato, *Complete Works*, ed. John M. Cooper (Indianapolis: Hacket, 1997), 71.

[58] *Phaedo* 113 d–114 c, in Plato, *Complete Works*, 96–97.

[59] The most foolish were the 'footless', such as fish and snakes. Men who lived lives of cowardice and injustice were reborn as women. Birds came from innocent but simple-minded men. Land animals came from men who didn't study philosophy. All water-inhabiting animals came from the most stupid and ignorant men of all. *Timaeus* 90 ef–92 a, in Plato, *Complete Works*, 1289–1290.

[60] *Phaedrus* 248 d–e and 249 b, in Plato, *Complete Works*, 1526 and 1527.

[61] For example, *Phaedrus* 249 a–b, in Plato, *Complete Works*, 1526–1527.

[62] *Phaedrus* 246 d, in Plato, *Complete Works*, 1525. See also *Timaeus* 42 a–d, 90 e, and 91 d–92 b, in Plato, *Complete Works*, 1245 and 1290.

[63] *Phaedrus* 249 a, in Plato, *Complete Works*, 1526. For an interpretation of the 10,000-year cycle that squares the *Phaedrus* with the *Timaeus* and with Empedocles and Pindar, see R. S. Bluck, 'The Phaedrus and Reincarnation', *American Journal of Philology* 79, no. 2 (1958), 164.

Like most educated people, Blavatsky would have been acquainted
with the Platonic dialogues, and unsurprisingly, they were discussed
throughout her source texts. To give just one example, Samuel Fales
Dunlap quoted Plato's *Phaedo* that souls returned from the dead. 'What
then is produced from death?' 'Life is!' 'From the dead living things
and living men are produced.'[64] Despite the many discussions of Plato's
doctrines, neither of Blavatsky's rebirth theories reproduced any known
Platonic account. In Blavatsky, reincarnation was progressive whereas
in Plato souls could both rise and fall. Animal reincarnation following
human incarnation was thus a prominent feature of the Platonic
accounts but was considered impossible by Blavatsky. Nevertheless,
Blavatsky's theories of rebirth agreed with the Platonic accounts that
the soul was of divine origin and could be divided into at least two different parts, with the higher struggling against the lower. The soul in
some sense 'fell' and would return to its divine source, but might also
be annihilated, at least in her doctrine of metempsychosis. Blavatsky's
account shared with Plato's dialogues the hierarchical arrangement of
humans above animals, but, according to Blavatsky, the monads now
inhabiting human bodies had only inhabited animal bodies during a
previous round.

Blavatsky referred to Plato in corroboration of her theories in much
the same way as she had Pythagoras. This was consistent with her view
in *Isis Unveiled* that Plato was 'the ardent disciple of Pythagoras' and that
'Pythagoras obtained his knowledge in India [. . .] and Plato faithfully
echoed his teachings'.[65] We recall that in the *Timaeus*, Plato presented
a hierarchy, with two-legged creatures at the top and water-inhabiting
animals at the bottom. In *Isis Unveiled*, Blavatsky referred to Plato's
Timaeus when discussing her theory of the metempsychosis of the
human monad through plant, reptile, bird, and animal phases, until it
reached the human embryo stage.[66] Again, referring to the *Timaeus*, she

---

[64] Dunlap, *Mysteries of Adoni*, 22. See also Myer, *Qabbalah*, 196 and Eduard Zeller,
Plato and the Older Academy, trans. Sarah Frances Alleyne and Alfred Goodwin
(London: Longmans, Green and Co., 1876), 391–394.
[65] Blavatsky, *Isis I*, 9–10.
[66] Ibid., 303.

interpreted the dialogue in terms of her doctrine of metempsychosis, one of the central themes of which was the indestructibility of matter:

> Matter is as indestructible and eternal as the immortal spirit itself, but only in its particles, and not as organized forms. The body of so grossly materialistic a person as above described, having been deserted by its spirit before physical death, when that event occurs, the plastic material, astral soul, following the laws of blind matter, shapes itself thoroughly into the mould which vice has been gradually preparing for it through the earth-life of the individual. Then, as Plato says, it assumes the form of that 'animal to which it resembled in its evil ways' during life.[67]

Here, Blavatsky didn't teach that a person is reborn as an animal in any straightforward sense. Rather, in the context of her early denial that reincarnation on Earth was a normative occurrence, she stated that a materialistic individual would not only fail to achieve immortality but would also be deserted by the overshadowing spirit during life. After death, the astral soul (which, had it achieved immortality, would have proceeded to higher spheres) assumed the form of the animal appropriate to the materialistic individual's behaviour during life. In this way, Blavatsky gave a Theosophical interpretation of the *Timaeus* consistent with her teachings on metempsychosis, as given in *Isis Unveiled*.

In a preceding passage, Blavatsky had discussed Plato's *Gorgias* alongside the *Timaeus* in corroboration of metempsychosis:

> That which survives as an *individuality* after the death of the body is the *astral soul*, which Plato, in the *Timæus* and *Gorgias*, calls the *mortal* soul, for, according to the Hermetic doctrine, it throws off its more material particles at every progressive change into a higher sphere. Socrates narrates to Callicles that this *mortal* soul retains all the characteristics of the body after the death of the latter.[68]

[67] Ibid., 328.
[68] Ibid., 327.

Here, Blavatsky referred to the ascent through the higher spheres characteristic of her theory of metempsychosis, in which, after the death of the body, the soul would conjoin with the spirit and rise. This astral soul was mortal because it had the *potential* to achieve immortality by combining with the spirit. If this had not been achieved, then after death, this astral soul—which looked like the physical body of the individual who just died—would hang around for a while, eventually disintegrating. These astral souls, detached from their spirits, Blavatsky considered to be the cause of Spiritualistic phenomena. Therefore, in this extract, she cited Plato in support of her attack on the misunderstandings of contemporary Spiritualism, a perspective consistent with her early doctrine of metempsychosis.

During her later period, corroboration of the new doctrine of reincarnation—with reference to Plato—could be found in Blavatsky's commentary on the *Pistis Sophia*. This appeared in the Theosophical periodical *Lucifer* in May 1891, shortly before her death. Blavatsky's exegesis followed extracts from a translation of the Gnostic text made by G. R. S. Mead. She explained that the term *metangizein* meant 'to pour from one vessel into another'. *Metangismos*, Blavatsky argued, was the technical term for 'metempsychosis or reincarnation among the Pythagoreans', and *metangizein* and *metangismos* were technical terms, used only in connection with the idea of reincarnation. C. W. King, author of *The Gnostics and Their Remains*, had missed this fact, Blavatsky maintained. She went on to lament that the numerous passages from the Gnostics referring to reincarnation had yet to be collected. She referred to a statement of the Church Father Clement of Alexandria (c. 150–c. 215), which she claimed should be interpreted in light of the Theosophical teaching regarding the higher and the lower parts of the human principle of *manas*. She also referred to a book by E. D. Walker on reincarnation, which she believed demonstrated reincarnation to have been 'the prevailing creed in the first centuries of Christianity'.[69] Blavatsky referred to the need for an authoritative volume, 'supported by the citation of the innumerable passages that are to be found in

---

[69] E. D. Walker, *Reincarnation: A Study in Forgotten Truth* (New York: John W. Lovell, 1888).

the writings of the Gnostics, neo-Platonists and early Church Fathers', and it is likely she was influenced here by G. R. S. Mead, who published a series of articles on the Church Fathers and reincarnation in the early 1890s. Finally, she referred to Thomas Taylor's translation of Plato's *Phaedrus*, in which she claimed to have discerned references to *kama loka* and *devachan*. She argued that the passage from Plato was comprehensible only with the help of Theosophical teachings, and referred to cycles, rounds, races, individual births, monadic evolution, and *manasic* and *kamic* souls. These were all ideas that were inextricably linked with the reincarnation doctrine of her later period.[70]

The Neo-Platonists

The influential neo-Platonist and student of Ammonius Saccas, Plotinus (c. 205–270), referred to reincarnation several times in his most famous work, the *Enneads*.[71] His position on reincarnation was to a degree congruent with that represented in Plato's dialogues, and similar observations about its similarity or dissimilarity to the Blavatskyan accounts can be made. Blavatsky didn't discuss Plotinian rebirth doctrines as such, but Plotinus' ideas nevertheless influenced her rebirth doctrines substantially. Plotinus developed Plato's Form 'the Good' into the ultimate, undifferentiated source of all being, known as 'The One'. Transcendent and unknowable, the One was situated at the top of a cosmic hierarchy, overflowing (emanating) without diminution into existence. In this scheme, immediately below the One was the Divine Mind (*nous*), followed by the Universal Soul. Finally, Matter was said to be furthest from the One, yet still originated in it. The Universal Soul constituted an upper part that transcended the material, and a lower part that was involved in generating the material universe. The similarity to Blavatsky's Theosophy is unmistakable. The idea of the 'Universal Soul' had been popularised as the 'Over-Soul' in

---

[70] 'The Pistis Sophia'. Translated and annotated by G. R. S. M[ead] with additional notes by H. P. B. *Lucifer* 8, no. 45 (15 May 1891), 203–204.

[71] *Ennead* I, 1.12, and *Ennead* III, 4.2, in Plotinus, *The Enneads*, trans. Stephen MacKenna (London: Penguin, 1991), 12, 167–168. See H. J. Blumenthal, *Plotinus' Psychology: His Doctrines of the Embodied Soul* (The Hague: Martinus Nijhoff, 1971), 95.

Transcendentalist Ralph Waldo Emerson's 1841 essay of the same name. In *Isis Unveiled*, Blavatsky mentioned this essay at least twice, once in the introduction, strongly suggesting it was Alexander Wilder's contribution, since Wilder is known to have written and edited much of the introduction.

In *Isis Unveiled*, Blavatsky referred to Plotinus and another neo-Platonic philosopher, Porphyry (c. 234–c. 305), in the context of her doctrine of conditional immortality, which was part of her teaching on metempsychosis.

> We have shown elsewhere that the 'secret doctrine' does not concede immortality to all men alike. 'The eye would never see the sun, if it were not of the nature of the sun,' said Plotinus. Only 'through the highest purity and chastity we shall approach nearer to God, and receive in the contemplation of Him, the true knowledge and insight,' writes Porphyry. If the human soul has neglected during its life-time to receive its illumination from its Divine Spirit, our *personal* God, then it becomes difficult for the gross and sensual man to survive for a great length of time his physical death.[72]

This was another way of saying that Plotinus and Porphyry taught a theory of conditional immortality. The 'human soul' (i.e., the astral soul) either received illumination from its Divine Spirit, thereby becoming immortal, or disintegrated after physical death. Later, alluding to the notion of the emanation of individual human souls and the need for these to be united with the divine spirit during Earth-life, Blavatsky referred to 'the collective aggregation of the numberless spirit entities, which are the direct emanations of the infinite, invisible, incomprehensible FIRST CAUSE—the individual spirits of men'. She stated that Pythagoras, Apollonius, Plotinus, Plato, and Iamblichus were examples of those who had been 'intermittently united' with their spirits during life, becoming 'demi-gods' and leaders of mankind. 'When unburdened of their terrestrial tabernacles, their freed souls, henceforth united forever with their spirits.'[73] In other words, the neo-Platonists had been

---

[72] Blavatsky, *Isis I*, 431–432.
[73] Ibid., 159.

initiates and had achieved conditional immortality of the type outlined in Blavatsky's doctrine of metempsychosis.

There were fewer references to neo-Platonists in Blavatsky's later works. Nevertheless, allusions to them did appear in corroboration of her new doctrine of reincarnation and related concepts. In *The Key to Theosophy* (1889), Blavatsky wrote:

> Ideas on *re-incarnation* and the trinity of man were held by many of the early Christian Fathers. It is the jumble made by the translators of the New Testament and ancient philosophical treatises between soul and spirit, that has occasioned the many misunderstandings. It is also one of the many reasons why Buddha, Plotinus, and so many other Initiates are now accused of having longed for the total extinction of their souls—'absorption unto the Deity', or 'reunion with the universal soul', meaning, according to modern ideas, annihilation. *The personal soul* must, of course, be disintegrated into its particles, before it is able to link its purer essence for ever with the immortal spirit.[74]

This was the same passage that had been cited in *Isis Unveiled* with the terms 'reincarnation' (instead of transmigration) and 'personal soul' (instead of animal soul) substituted.[75] This substitution is one of the most explicit indications we have that Blavatsky changed her terminology to suit her changing doctrines of rebirth. She also changed it to correspond with her changing constructions of the Greeks, first as believers in metempsychosis, and later as believers in reincarnation.

[74] Blavatsky, *Key*, 77.
[75] Here is the passage as it had appeared in *Isis*: 'Ideas on the transmigrations and the trinity of man, were held by many of the early Christian Fathers. It is the jumble made by the translators of the *New Testament* and ancient philosophical treatises between soul and spirit, that has occasioned the many misunderstandings. It is also one of the many reasons why Buddha, Plotinus, and so many other initiates are now accused of having longed for the total extinction of their souls—"absorption unto the Deity", or "reunion with the universal soul", meaning, according to modern ideas, annihilation. The animal soul must, of course, be disintegrated of its particles, before it is able to link its purer essence forever with the immortal spirit.' Blavatsky, *Isis II*, 281.

Conclusions

Like many nineteenth-century authors with an interest in the Classics, Blavatsky was a knowledgeable amateur researcher. She drew her information from a variety of books, including scholarly and amateur ones. As many of her sources did, Blavatsky portrayed Greek thought as teaching the human body to be 'the tomb of the soul' and the spirit to be in need of purification. The origins of Greek thought, she said, lay in the East, specifically in Egypt and/or India. We cannot, therefore, consider Blavatsky's depiction of the Greeks in isolation from her other points of reference, which included currents such as Hinduism, Buddhism, and Gnosticism. As a consequence, Blavatsky's Hellenism was inseparable from her Orientalism. It was also inextricable from her reception of the Anglo-American Spiritualist doctrines explored in chapter 4, which influenced how she interpreted the metempsychosis doctrines of the ancient Greeks. In spite of this debt, and the affinity Cathy Gutierrez has demonstrated Spiritualism had with Platonism, Blavatsky's interpretations of the Greeks were often used to attack Spiritualism, the very current from which Theosophy had emerged.

Blavatsky's writings are an indispensable source for understanding how nineteenth-century occultists appropriated elements from wider nineteenth-century Hellenism. Blavatsky portrayed Greek philosophers as initiates and as guardians of a secret doctrine that had to be understood 'intuitively'. Like many contemporaneous enthusiasts for the Classics, she personally identified with the Greeks, but unlike many of the authors that influenced her, she based her identification on the idea that Theosophy had a place in the chain of tradition that also included the teachings of figures like Pythagoras, Plato, and Plotinus.

This idea was not unprecedented. It echoed the thought of Thomas Taylor, the English Platonist. The academy had already rejected Taylor's translations as faulty, but they were redeemed (at least according to Alexander Wilder and Blavatsky) thanks to Taylor's superior intuitive grasp of Plato, which overrode any technical deficiencies his translations may have had. Taylor influenced Transcendentalism and the American Platonic movement that came from it, which emphasised liberalism, universalism, harmony, and morality, and sought to interpret life's challenges in cosmic terms.

These were perspectives in common with Theosophy, despite the obvious differences. Influenced by Taylor, Wilder, and the American Platonic tradition, Blavatsky's Platonism was of a broadly Romantic type that emphasised intuition, an emphasis that lent itself well to esotericist, universalising interpretations. As such, Blavatsky's Platonism was of a self-consciously 'anti-establishment' variety. She articulated her interpretations of the Greeks (rebirth theories included) in opposition to the religious and scholarly establishments as she perceived them. Taylor's rejection by the academy therefore no doubt only endeared him all the more to Blavatsky and Wilder, both of whom had a tendency towards dissent from what they saw as the mainstream.

When Blavatsky wanted them to, the Greeks taught the Theosophical doctrines of conditional immortality and metempsychosis. When she wanted them to teach the normative repeated return to Earth-life—reincarnation—they did that too. This confirms what is already well established in the scholarly literature, that the Greeks were malleable in the hands of nineteenth-century thinkers. Blavatsky's occultist depictions were part of an ongoing process in which scholars, artists, and the public at large constructed Classical antiquity. Often, these writers were, like Blavatsky herself, amateur scholars with obvious theological or political agendas. Her perspectives on metempsychosis and reincarnation exemplify an occultist woman's voice among the better-known cultural and intellectual movements.

6

Science

IN ADDITION TO THE Platonic and Spiritualistic influences already explored, Blavatsky's theories of rebirth owe a debt to the scientific ideas under discussion at her time of writing.[1,2] This chapter provides a detailed discussion of Blavatsky's engagement with the thought of contemporaneous scientists in the context of issues relevant to her rebirth theories. As such, it focuses more on the background to, and presuppositions of, Blavatsky's rebirth theories, while also making some reference to particulars that were influenced by current scientific theories, such as the idea that the monad 'relives' previous plant and animal incarnations in utero prior to human incarnation.

Blavatsky's belief that Theosophy represented the perfect balance between science and religion was just one position among many. Opinions on the extensive scientific developments of the nineteenth century and how they impinged on wider issues varied. There were commentators who believed science opposed religion and others who thought it complemented it. Secularists embraced science to the exclusion of religion while some theologians accommodated science within natural theologies in which God was seen as governing the universe through natural

---

[1] A version of this chapter was published in *Aries* 18 (2018).
[2] For an introduction to Blavatsky and Science, see Olav Hammer, *Claiming Knowledge*, 218–222 and Egil Asprem, 'Theosophical Attitudes towards Science: Past and Present', in *Handbook of the Theosophical Current*. For background on science and occultism, see Egil Asprem, 'Science and the Occult', in *Handbook of the Theosophical Current*.

laws.[3] Popularising works on science introduced new developments to the reading public, some of whom embraced them, some of whom rejected them, and some of whom simply failed to understand them.

Increasing professionalisation and specialisation meant the sciences had become more and more inaccessible to those not trained within the scientific establishment. Authors of popular works became intermediaries between the universities and an increasingly literate population. As Bernard Lightman demonstrated, popularisers of science (often educated middle-class writers, journalists, clergymen—and sometimes women) offered interpretations of scientific advancements to their readers during the second half of the century.[4] Historians initially viewed the popularisation of science as involving the simplification of elite knowledge in its dissemination to less-educated readers, but Roger Cooter and Stephen Pumfrey disagreed, arguing that the public were not the passive recipients of watered-down science but rather active agents with their own interests and agendas.[5] Blavatsky can be considered such an active agent, albeit one with esoteric interests and an occultist agenda.

Blavatsky, Science, and Materialism

In Blavatsky's construction of science, she divided scientists into two camps, the good and the bad.

> We, Theosophists, would willingly bow before such men of learning as the late Prof. Balfour Stewart, Messrs. Crookes, Quatrefages, Wallace, Agassiz, Butlerof, and several others, though we may not

[3] James R. Moore, 'The Crisis of Faith: Reformation vs Revolution', in *Religion in Victorian Britain*, ed. Gerald Parsons and James R. Moore (Manchester: Manchester University Press, 1988), vol. 2: *Controversies*, 229. Robert M. Young, 'The Impact of Darwin on Conventional Thought', in *The Victorian Crisis of Faith*, ed. Anthony Symondson (London: SPCK, 1970), 22–25.

[4] Bernard Lightman, *Victorian Popularizers of Science: Designing Nature for New Audiences* (Chicago and London: University of Chicago Press, 2007), vii–xi.

[5] Roger Cooter and Stephen Pumfrey, 'Separate Spheres and Public Places: Reflections on the History of Science Popularization and Science in Popular Culture', *History of Science* 32 (1994).

agree, from the stand-point of esoteric philosophy, with all they say. But nothing could make us consent to even a show of respect for the opinions of other men of science, such as Hæckel, Carl Vogt, or Ludwig Büchner, in Germany; or even of Mr. Huxley and his co-thinkers in materialism in England—the colossal erudition of the first named, notwithstanding. Such men are simply the intellectual and moral murderers of future generations; especially Hæckel, whose crass materialism often rises to the height of idiotic *naivetés* in his reasonings.[6]

One of Blavatsky's main criticisms of scientific perspectives she disapproved of was that they were 'materialist', and she often wrote about this in the context of her discussions of biological evolution and Darwinism.[7] In *The Origin of Species* (1859), Charles Darwin (1809–1882) argued that natural selection was a central mechanism in evolution. Organisms were subject to randomly occurring variations within their populations, some of which provided advantages in the context of their struggle to survive, compete for limited resources, and reproduce. Successful variations would be passed on to descendants and unsuccessful ones would not. According to Darwin, species changed gradually over time through the selection of characteristics favourable to survival within particular environments. The English philosopher and social Darwinist Herbert Spencer (1820–1903) dubbed the process 'the survival of the fittest', and the phrase caught on.

Darwinist ideas were associated (but not necessarily identical) with radical materialism, the view that matter is all that exists or that life is reducible to material causes. In Britain, materialism was ascribed to scientific publicists such as the biologist and supporter of Darwinism Thomas Henry Huxley (1825–1895), the physicist John Tyndall (1825–1895), the mathematician and philosopher William Kingdon Clifford (1845–1879), and Herbert Spencer. It was also associated with the

[6] Blavatsky, *Secret Doctrine II*, 651–652.
[7] The term 'evolution' was popularised by Herbert Spencer, although it has a history going back to the seventeenth century. For a history of the use of the term, see Robert J. Richards, *The Meaning of Evolution: The Morphological and Ideological Reconstruction of Darwin's Theory* (Chicago and London: University of Chicago Press, 1992).

positivism of the French philosopher and founding father of sociology Auguste Comte (1798–1857), and in Germany with the thought of scientists such as Karl Vogt (1817–1895), Ludwig Büchner (1824–1899), and Ernst Haeckel (1834–1919).[8] Straightforwardly labelling all these men 'materialists', however, is problematic. As Frank Turner observed, matter could be dealt with in relation to either scientific theory or metaphysics, and in the latter sense, Clifford, Tyndall, and Huxley all backed away from embracing full materialism.[9] Comte and Spencer also explicitly denied the materialist label. Despite this, they have been unproblematically categorised as materialists both by contemporary commentators and by more recent ones. A reason for this, Turner suggested, was that materialism and positivism were often erroneously conflated because both proposed science as the most reliable source of knowledge. Later opponents of the view that empirical science is the only true source of knowledge identified materialism with positivism in their crusades against them. As Turner pointed out, the misunderstanding was understandable, especially since nineteenth-century thinkers defined materialism differently, creating considerable confusion.[10] The individuals in question also encouraged this confusion either by sometimes referring to themselves as materialists (as in the case of Tyndall) or by seeming to (as in the case of Huxley).[11] But perhaps most significantly, Turner noted, the opponents of materialism *wanted* Tyndall and others to be materialists. They wanted a target.[12]

Materialism, portrayed largely monolithically, was one of Blavatsky's primary polemical targets. She decried it as a reprehensible and totally

[8] Especially on Vogt, Büchner, and Haeckel, see Bergunder, '"Religion" and "Science" within a Global Religious History', *Aries* 16, no. 1 (2016), 86–141.
[9] 'Clifford's mind-stuff was essentially an idealistic monism. Huxley always said that if forced to answer the unanswerable question, he would choose idealism over materialism. Tyndall, who called himself a "materialist" and who lectured for several years on a materialistic theory of psychology, still contended that matter had been "defined and maligned by philosophers and theologians, who are equally unaware that it is, at bottom, essentially mystical and transcendental."' Frank Turner, *Contesting Cultural Authority* (Cambridge: Cambridge University Press, 1993), 147.
[10] Ibid., 264.
[11] Ibid., 264–5.
[12] Ibid., 264–5.

erroneous 'denial of Deity, spirit or soul' that admitted 'no intelligence outside the mind of man'.[13] She didn't even hesitate in associating it with the devil himself:

> The Satan of Materialism now laughs at all alike, and denies the visible as well as the invisible. Seeing in light, heat, electricity, and even in the *phenomenon of life*, only properties inherent in matter, it laughs whenever life is called VITAL PRINCIPLE, and derides the idea of its being independent of and distinct from the organism.[14]

If Blavatsky considered materialism poison, then the 'vital principle' was its antidote. Vitalism was the belief that a vital principle distinguished life.[15] With roots in earlier ideas, in the nineteenth century, it was offered in various forms as both a philosophical and scientific alternative to materialism and mechanistic reductionism.[16] As Bruce Clark put it, vitalism involved a 'phantasmagoric remythologization of nature', and its 'master trope' was 'the *life force* that drives living things up the escalator of evolution'.[17] Blavatsky embraced vitalism, endorsing a teleological (end-driven) theory of progressive evolution impelled by a spiritual element internal to the cosmos and its inhabitants. Matter was alive, claimed Blavatsky, and apprehension of this solved the mysteries of evolution.[18] She perceived her view as diametrically opposed to that of materialist science, which, she said, denied the existence of a vital principle. This was a 'grand mistake'.[19] Despite the errors of many scientists, there were, nevertheless, 'men of science' who took

---

[13] Blavatsky, *Secret Doctrine I*, 479.

[14] Blavatsky, *Secret Doctrine I*, 602–603

[15] On earlier forms of vitalism, see Carolyn Merchant, 'The Vitalism of Anne Conway: Its Impact on Leibniz's Concept of the Monad', *Journal of the History of Philosophy* 17, no. 3 (July 1979) and 'The Vitalism of Francis Mercury van Helmont: Its Influence on Leibniz', *Ambix* 26, no. 3 (1979).

[16] Bruce Clarke, *Energy Forms: Allegory and Science in the Era of Classical Thermodynamics* (Ann Arbor: University of Michigan Press, 2001), 72.

[17] Ibid., 72. On Blavatsky's vitalism see Mark S. Morrisson, *Modern Alchemy: Occultism and the Emergence of Atomic Theory* (Oxford: Oxford University Press, 2007), 83.

[18] Blavatsky, *Secret Doctrine II*, 299.

[19] Blavatsky, *Secret Doctrine I*, 538.

'the same view about "things occult" as theosophists and occultists'.[20] As an example, she adduced a statement from *L'Espèce Humaine* (The Human Species, 1877) by the French biologist and anthropologist Jean Louis Armand de Quatrefages de Bréau (1810–1892).[21] Quatrefages acknowledged the contemporary criticism that vitalism had introduced 'into science a vague and mysterious expression' but disagreed that the proposition of a life principle was vague or mysterious, arguing it was perfectly scientific and didn't go beyond 'experiment and scientific observation'.[22]

Nineteenth-century vitalism was associated with German Romantic *Naturphilosophie* or 'philosophy of nature'.[23] Connected to the thought of Johann Gottlieb Fichte (1762–1814), Georg Wilhelm Friedrich Hegel (1770–1831), and Friedrich Wilhelm Joseph Schelling (1775–1854), *Naturphilosophie* saw nature as producing the perfection of the human form through what Michael Ruse called the 'dynamic, forward-moving, purposive thrust to reality'.[24] Blavatsky didn't always agree with Fichte, Hegel, and Schelling entirely, but she was clearly influenced by them.[25] *Naturphilosophische* themes included unity and polarity, metamorphosis, and ideal types, all ideas that resonated strongly with Blavatsky's thought.[26] *Naturphilosophie* was influential in biology throughout the nineteenth century, especially among those who opposed Darwinism.

[20] Ibid., 603.

[21] She quoted him as writing: 'It is very true we do not know *what* life *is*; but no more do we know *what* the force *is* that set the stars in motion.' Blavatsky, *Secret Doctrine I*, 540.

[22] A. De Quatrefages, *The Human Species* (New York: D. Appleton, 1890), 10–12.

[23] Bruce Clarke, *Dora Marsden and Early Modernism: Gender, Individualism, Science* (Ann Arbor: University of Michigan, 1996), 30.

[24] Michael Ruse, *Monad to Man: The Concept of Progress in Evolutionary Biology* (Cambridge, MA: Harvard University Press, 1996), 26–27.

[25] 'This leads the reader naturally to the "Supreme Spirit" of Hegel and the German Transcendentalists as a contrast that it may be useful to point out. The schools of Schelling and Fichte have diverged widely from the primitive archaic conception of an ABSOLUTE principle, and have mirrored only an aspect of the basic idea of the Vedanta.' Blavatsky, *Secret Doctrine I*, 50. Blavatsky knew Sibree's 1856 translation of Georg Wilhelm Friedrich Hegel's *The Philosophy of History* (New York: Dover, 1956). See Blavatsky, *Secret Doctrine I*, 52.

[26] Timothy Lenoir, *The Strategy of Life: Teleology and Mechanics in Nineteenth-Century German Biology* (Dordrecht, Holland, and London: D. Reidel, 1982), 27.

Among them were some of the scientists Blavatsky cited approvingly, such as Karl Ernst von Baer and Richard Owen, although those with whom Blavatsky disagreed—such as Ernst Haeckel—were influenced by *Naturphilosophie* too.

The notion of progress so prominent in *Naturphilosophie*, but also found more widely, had a central place in (re)defining humanity's place in the cosmos for many late nineteenth-century thinkers, especially in response to the perceived threats of Darwinism. Blavatsky proposed a cyclic but continuously forward-moving universe comprising a *scala naturae* of fixed types indebted to Aristotelian and Platonic thought. The immortal monad travelled through it, reincarnating within successive predetermined levels as it ascended the 'great chain of being'. This great chain, as Arthur Lovejoy explained in his classic study, was a conception of the plan and structure of the world that had been accepted by almost everyone from the Middle Ages to the eighteenth century, an immense hierarchy composed of the lowest to the highest existents with God at the top.[27] For Blavatsky, different species each had their place in the hierarchy. The possibility of small mutations notwithstanding, species could not change into one another, as proposed in natural selection. Blavatsky was not alone in rejecting transmutationism and upholding the fixity of species. Many prominent scientists thought along similar lines, including Richard Owen and Karl Ernst von Baer, both of whom Blavatsky admired.

Blavatsky referred to the names and theories of numerous such scientists in her descriptions of the evolving reincarnationary cosmos to justify her views. Choosing to treat science, heuristically, as a cultural construct the boundaries of which were 'fluid and contested',[28] Olav Hammer argued that esotericists like Blavatsky defined science as a body of doctrines rather than a method of enquiry, selectively appropriating elements of scientific discourse. Occultists used contemporary science in two apparently contradictory ways, both as a source

---

[27] Arthur O. Lovejoy, *The Great Chain of Being* (Cambridge, MA, and London: Harvard University Press, 2001), 59.
[28] Hammer, *Claiming Knowledge*, 206–207.

of legitimacy and as an 'Other' against which to define themselves.[29] Hammer described this as 'scientism'. It involved

> The active positioning of one's own claims in relation to the manifestations of any academic scientific discipline, including, but not limited to, the use of technical devices, scientific terminology, mathematical calculations, theories, references and stylistic features—without, however, the use of methods generally approved within the scientific community, and without subsequent social acceptance of these manifestations by the mainstream of the scientific community through e.g. peer reviewed publication in academic journals.[30]

Such scientism was a fundamental process in the construction of modern religion. Kocku von Stuckrad called it the 'scientification of religion', and as a part of it, 'the discursive organization of knowledge around religion in secular environments' became entangled with scientific discourses. Theosophy was 'instrumental in establishing new meanings of religion and science in the twentieth century',[31] and Blavatsky's work can be seen as a 'discursive hub' in which various discursive strands were brought together.[32]

Theosophy between 'Science' and 'Religion'

Although late nineteenth-century commentators depicted science and religion as warring camps in popular works such as *The History of the Conflict between Science and Religion* (1874) by John William Draper (1811–1882), historians today tend see the situation much differently.[33] As James Moore put it, we 'aim to situate religion and science on cultural common ground and so recover the religiosity of science, the

[29] Ibid., 203–4.
[30] Ibid., 206.
[31] Kocku von Stuckrad, *The Scientification of Religion: A Historical Study of Discursive Change 1800–2000* (Boston and Berlin: De Gruyter, 2014), 112 and 180.
[32] Ibid., 94.
[33] See Richard Noakes, 'Spiritualism, Science, and the Supernatural in Mid-Victorian Britain', in *The Victorian Supernatural,* ed. Carolyn Burdett Nicola Bown and Pamela Thurschwell (Cambridge: Cambridge University Press, 2004), 24 and 39.

scientificity of religion, and the integrity of metaphysics occupying that large terra incognita "between science and religion." '[34] Spiritualism had a significant place in discussions surrounding science and religion, and many prominent scientists took an interest in it. While some believed séance phenomena were 'supernatural', others believed natural forces lay behind them. Science had not yet identified these, but they thought it eventually would. William Crookes (1832–1919), one of the scientists named approvingly by Blavatsky above, is a good example. Crookes believed in the existence of spiritual beings. He was attracted to Theosophy and joined the London Lodge in 1883.[35] One of the most celebrated Victorian investigators of Spiritualism, Crookes was also a leading analytical chemist and discoverer of the element thallium. He conducted controversial research throughout the 1870s that led him to believe he had discovered a psychic force, although he failed to convince his colleagues at the Royal Society of its existence.[36]

Another prominent Spiritualist-scientist Blavatsky mentioned approvingly was the co-discoverer (with Darwin) of evolution by natural selection, Alfred Russel Wallace (1823–1913). Blavatsky had sent letters to Wallace, as well as a copy of *Isis Unveiled*.[37] She described him as one of the 'luminaries of the modern Evolutionist School' and praised him for highlighting the inadequacy of natural selection (as understood by Darwin and his followers). Wallace believed human evolution had been guided by the entities revealed in séances.[38] This wasn't precisely what Blavatsky taught (which was that evolution was guided by beings called *dhyan chohans* and *pitris*, as distinct from the entities contacted in séances) but the basic idea was the same: evolution was guided by

[34] James Moore, 'Religion and Science', in *The Cambridge History of Science: Volume 6, the Modern Biological and Earth Sciences*, ed. Peter J. Bowler and John V. Pickstone (Cambridge: Cambridge University Press, 2009), 561.
[35] William Hodson Brock, *William Crookes (1832–1919) and the Commercialization of Science* (Aldershot: Ashgate, 2008), 207.
[36] William Crookes, *Researches in the Phenomena of Spiritualism* (Manchester: Two Worlds, 1926), 17. Blavatsky was familiar with Crookes's work. See Noakes, 'Spiritualism, Science, and the Supernatural', 33–34.
[37] Letter to A. R. Wallace, 7 November 1877, in Blavatsky, *Letters*, 362.
[38] Richard Noakes, 'The Historiography of Psychical Research: Lessons from Histories of the Sciences', *Journal of the Society for Psychical Research* 72, no. 2 (April 2008).

spiritual beings. Blavatsky therefore agreed with Wallace in principle and quoted him in corroboration of her position.[39] She may have been convinced, but like Crookes, Wallace's attempts to persuade his colleagues to take his ideas seriously in the 1860s proved unsuccessful.[40]

Crookes and Wallace's critics believed Spiritualism to be anathema to science and threaten its progress.[41] Some of Blavatsky's source texts put forward similar opinions. For example, in *The Concepts of Modern Physics* (1882), the philosopher Johann Bernhard Stallo (1823–1900) expressed a hope that all metaphysical elements would be eliminated from science, and he even went so far as to attack all metaphysical endeavours as flawed.[42] In *The Doctrine of Descent and Darwinism* (1873), Oscar Schmidt (1823–1886) argued that religious and scientific ideas were incommensurable.[43] He went on to criticise Spiritualism explicitly. 'We have only to look round at the spiritualists and summoners of souls, who now form special sects and societies [. . .] and we can but marvel at the extensive sway of [. . .] superstition [indicating] the very widespread lack of judgment which prevails wherever the supposed enigma of human existence is concerned.'[44] Similarly, in *Science vs. Spiritualism,* Count Agénor de Gasparin (1810–1871) vehemently denounced 'false miracles, spurious sorcery, wonders of every kind, a return to the most foolish and odious credulities of the past, a restoration of the Middle Ages and their least respectable practices'.[45] He

---

[39] 'One of the luminaries of the modern Evolutionist School, Mr. A. R. Wallace, when discussing the inadequacy of "natural selection" as the sole factor in the development of physical man, practically concedes the whole point here discussed. He holds that the evolution of man was directed and furthered by superior Intelligences, whose agency is a necessary factor in the scheme of Nature. But once the operation of these Intelligences is admitted in one place, it is only a logical deduction to extend it still further.' Blavatsky, *Secret Doctrine I,* 107.

[40] Brock, *Crookes,* 126.

[41] Noakes, 'Spiritualism, Science, and the supernatural', 24.

[42] J. B. Stallo, *Concepts and Theories of Modern Physics* (London: Kegan and Paul, Trench and Co., 1882), 8.

[43] Oscar Schmidt, *The Doctrine of Descent and Darwinism* (London: Henry S. King and Co., 1875), 12 and 14–15.

[44] Ibid., 2.

[45] Agénor de Gasparin, *Science vs. Spiritualism: A Treatise on Turning Tables, the Supernatural in General and Spirits,* trans. E. W. Robert, 2 vols. (New York: Kiggins and Kellogg, 1857), vol I, 197–198.

denounced magnetism[46] (i.e., Mesmerism) and stated, 'either science must consent to take one step, or superstition will take ten'.[47] These opinions were not monolithic, but they illustrated a general anti-religious and/or anti-Spiritualist trend with which Blavatsky was familiar, and which she repudiated.

On the other side of the debate were those who denounced materialism. Among Blavatsky's sources who took this stance was *The History of the Supernatural* (1863), by the British Spiritualist William Howitt (1792–1879). Howitt argued, 'it must be admitted that in no age have the deadening effects of a materialistic education been so prominent as in the present.'[48] He claimed to have amassed evidence 'from every age and every people' to prove the existence of spiritual agencies as an antidote to the growth of 'religious infidelity'.[49] Some professional scientists pointed to the supposed limits of materialism too and, like Crookes and Wallace, found in this reason to believe in invisible realms. In another literary source of Blavatsky's, *The Soul of Things* (1863), William Denton, a professor of geology, wrote, 'notwithstanding the disbelief of materialists and material scientists, there lie realms beyond the domain of physical science.'[50]

Other commentators expressed exasperation over the polarisation of materialist and Spiritual positions. John Lucas Tupper (1824?–1879) had expressed it particularly poignantly when he wrote to fellow artist William Holman Hunt (1827–1910) in 1870 about the current struggle between intellectuals positing a 'machine world' devoid of any real humanity and the 'credulous fanatics, the victims of spiritualist imposters'.[51] Some of Blavatsky's most influential literary sources sought similar reconciliations and it is no coincidence that, like Blavatsky, they were often of a heterodox or occult inclination. As Michael Bergunder observed, esoteric movements, Theosophy included, played a decisive

[46] Ibid., vol. 1, 254–255.
[47] Ibid., vol. 2, 424.
[48] Howitt, *The History of the Supernatural*, vol. 2, 461.
[49] Noakes, 'The Historiography of Psychical Research', 67.
[50] William Denton and Elizabeth Denton, *The Soul of Things* (Wellesley, MA: Denton Publishing Company, 1888), 1–3, 11.
[51] Herbert Schlossberg, *Conflict and Crisis in the Religious Life of Late Victorian England* (New Brunswick, NJ: Transaction Publishers, 2009), 275.

role in the conceptual establishment of discourses aimed at fusing the categories 'science' and 'religion' at a time when they were separating.[52] Lady Caithness's *Old Truths in a New Light* (1876), for example, aimed to test the 'old truths' of Spiritualism in the new light of science. She argued although science was essential, it could not stand alone. 'It must go hand in hand with Spiritism, or it will inevitably stumble every third step.'[53] Likewise, the French occultist Eliphas Lévi (1810–1875) maintained that occult science reconciled science and religion. In *La Clef des Grandes Mystères* (1861), he wrote that the three objectives of his work were 'to bring into accord, within religion, science with revelation, reason with faith, to demonstrate, in philosophy, the absolute principles that reconcile all the antinomies, and, finally, to reveal the universal equilibrium of natural forces'.[54] From Lévi's perspective, religion and science were vulgarisations of the true, ancient occult science revealed in his works. The resonances here with Blavatsky were significant, and Lévi was a key influence whose works Blavatsky knew well.[55]

She may have believed that scientific theories were 'faulty, materialistic and biased', but they were still 'a thousand times nearer the truth than the vagaries of theology'.[56] Blavatsky argued that 'belief' and 'unbelief' embraced only a small part of the 'infinite horizons of spiritual and physical manifestations' and that they could not 'circumscribe the whole within their own special and narrow barriers'.[57] She maintained that the 'best and most spiritual men of our present day' could no longer be satisfied with 'either science or theology' since neither had anything better to offer than '*blind* faith in their respective infallibility'.[58] Like

---

[52] Bergunder, 'Religion and Science'.

[53] Caithness, *Old Truths in a New Light*, 1.

[54] 'Accorder, dans l'ordre religieux la science avec la révélation, et la raison avec la foi, démontrer en philosophie les principes absolus qui concilient toutes les antinomies, révéler enfin l'équilibre universel des forces naturelles, tel est le triple but de cet ouvrage, qui sera, par conséquent, divisé en trois parties.' Eliphas Lévi, *La clef des grandes mystères* (Paris: Germer Baillière, 1861), ii–iii.

[55] Blavatsky was very familiar with Lévi's works. She had translated them from French to English in the 1870s and she quoted them throughout her own writings.

[56] Blavatsky, *Secret Doctrine II*, 323.

[57] Blavatsky, *Secret Doctrine I*, 287–288.

[58] Blavatsky, *Secret Doctrine II*, 349.

many of her Spiritualist contemporaries, Blavatsky maintained there were things natural science had not yet discovered, and she called for scientists to be more modest about the reach of their research and not to unfairly condemn the occultists, arguing, 'science has no right to deny to the Occultists their claim to a more profound knowledge of the so-called Forces.'[59]

The Unseen Universe and *Isis Unveiled*

The Unseen Universe (1875) was a dominant source for Blavatsky with regard to this attempted reconciliation, influencing her perception of what science should be as well as her theories of rebirth.[60] Its authors were two Scotsmen: Balfour Stewart (1828–1887), professor of natural philosophy and president of the Society for Psychical Research, and Peter Guthrie Tait (1831–1901), professor of mathematics and later natural philosophy. Responding to ideas like William Draper's about the supposed conflict between science and religion, Stewart and Tait endeavoured to show that 'the presumed incompatibility of Science and Religion' did not exist.[61] They were part of a group of scientists who, between the 1850s and the 1870s, proposed a science of energy, promoting a natural philosophy they believed was in harmony with Christian belief. They offered this in counterpoint to scientific materialism, which they saw as 'pernicious nonsense', in contrast to the 'harmless folly' of Spiritualism.[62] Stewart and Tait saw this destructive materialism exemplified in John Tyndall's 'Belfast Address', a series of lectures given between 1868 and 1874.[63] Analysing the Belfast Address,

[59] Ibid., 520.

[60] For background on Blavatsky's indebtedness to Stewart and Tait see Clark, *Energy Forms*, 173–175.

[61] Stewart and Tait, *The Unseen Universe*, xi. The work was initially published anonymously but most of the scientific community knew who the authors were and they eventually added their names to a later edition. Daniel J. Cohen, *Equations from God: Pure Mathematics and Victorian Faith* (Baltimore: Johns Hopkins University Press, 2007), 166.

[62] Noakes, 'The Historiography of Psychical Research', 75.

[63] P. M. Heimann, 'The "Unseen Universe": Physics and the Philosophy of Nature in Victorian Britain', *The British Journal for the History of Science* 6, no. 1 (June 1972), 73.

however, Ruth Barton has shown that Tyndall's concept of matter was in fact a metaphysical construct with pantheistic implications influenced by the American Transcendentalist Ralph Waldo Emerson and the 'natural supernaturalism' of the influential Scottish philosopher Thomas Carlyle (1795–1881).[64] Be that as it may, Stewart and Tait perceived Tyndall as a materialist and proposed their theory in response to him. Blavatsky did the same.

Attempting to bridge science and religion as they understood them, Stewart and Tait argued for the principle of the continuity of energy, which stated energy could not be destroyed but only change form.

> We thus see that the extreme scientific, as well as the old theological school, have erred in their conclusions, because they have neither of them loyally followed the principle of Continuity. The theologians, regarding matter and its laws with contempt, have without scruple assumed that frequent invasions of these laws could constitute a tenable hypothesis. On the other hand, the extreme school of science, when they were brought by the principle of Continuity into such a position that the next logical step should have been the realisation of the unseen, failed to take it, and have suffered grievously in consequence.[65]

Unsurprisingly, this claim was met with hostility from some quarters. The English philosopher and mathematician William Kingdon Clifford (1845–1879) wrote a critique of *The Unseen Universe* in the influential English periodical *The Fortnightly Review* that was widely celebrated as a triumphant refutation of pseudo-science.[66] As Daniel Cohen observed, for Clifford, 'true scientists and mathematicians shunned inappropriate extrapolations such as this, and thus had no patience for the scientific support of theology.'[67]

---

[64] Ruth Barton, 'John Tyndall, Pantheist: A Rereading of the Belfast Address', *Osiris* 2, no. 3 (1987), 111–134. Carlyle's natural supernaturalism was the idea that people and, more broadly, nature have the power and authority once ascribed to an independent deity.

[65] Stewart and Tait, *The Unseen Universe*, 66.

[66] Cohen, *Equations*, 166 and 219.

[67] Ibid., 167.

A. P. Heimann characterised *The Unseen Universe* as an original contribution to the philosophy of nature. He affirmed that Stewart and
Tait 'rejected any attempt to separate the natural from the miraculous.
Arguing that the natural order included an invisible realm which was in
communication with the visible universe, they explained the manifestations of divine providence in terms of the transfer of energy from the
invisible to the visible realm.'[68] For Stewart and Tait, the totality comprising the invisible and visible realms was a self-contained system.[69]
They referred to the speculation of the English scientist Thomas Young
(1773–1829) that nature constituted a hierarchy of material and imma-
terial levels, and maintained that the visible and invisible realms were
connected through the transfer of energy from one level to another.[70]
The ether (the ethereal medium widely believed to fill space at that
time) was 'not merely a bridge between one portion of the visible universe and another' but was also 'a bridge between one order of things
and another'.[71] These were ideas with clear resonances with Blavatsky.

Stewart and Tait suggested that despite the death of the human body,
a part of the person might live on as a form of energy in an invisible
realm.[72] 'Immortality,' Stewart and Tait wrote, 'may be regarded as a
transference from one grade of being to another' or 'a transference from
the visible universe to some other order of things intimately connected
with it.'[73] All of this was rather close to Blavatsky's doctrine of metempsychosis. It was not a coincidence, since the first volume of *Isis
Unveiled* was full of explicit references to *The Unseen Universe*.[74]

> Of late, some of our learned men have given a particular attention
> to a subject hitherto branded with the mark of 'superstition'. They
> begin speculating on hypothetical and invisible worlds. The au-
> thors of the *Unseen Universe* were the first to boldly take the lead.

[68] Heimann, *Unseen Universe*, 75–76.
[69] Ibid., 76.
[70] Ibid., 77.
[71] Ibid., 77.
[72] Cohen, *Equations*, 166.
[73] Stewart and Tait, *Unseen Universe*, 66–67.
[74] Blavatsky, *Secret Doctrine I*, 114.

[. . .] If scientists, proceeding from a strictly scientific point of view, such as the possibility of energy being transferred into the invisible universe—and on the principle of continuity, indulge in such speculations, why should occultists and spiritualists be refused the same privilege?[75]

Indeed, Blavatsky presented Stewart and Tait's book as *proving* the doctrines she presented in *Isis Unveiled*:

Of all the modern speculators upon the seeming incongruities of the *New Testament*, alone the authors of the *Unseen Universe* seem to have caught a glimpse of its kabalistic truths, respecting the gehenna of the universe. This gehenna, termed by the occultists the *eighth* sphere (numbering inversely), is merely a planet like our own.

Blavatsky cited *The Unseen Universe* in support of the idea that that matter discarded during metempsychosis was recycled on an eighth sphere. Immediately afterward, she outlined her theory of conditional immortality and metempsychosis:

The secret doctrine teaches that man, if he wins immortality, will remain forever the trinity that he is in life, and will continue so throughout all the spheres. The astral body, which in this life is covered by a gross physical envelope, becomes—when relieved of that covering by the process of corporeal death—in its turn the shell of another and more ethereal body. This begins developing from the moment of death, and becomes perfected where the astral body of the earthly form finally separates from it. This process, they say, is repeated at every new transition from sphere to sphere. But the immortal soul, 'the silvery spark', [. . .] remains indestructible.[76]

This was one of the clearest statements of the doctrines of her early period Blavatsky ever gave. She taught humans were required to

---

[75] Ibid., 185.
[76] Blavatsky, *Isis I*, 328–329.

achieve immortality during life on Earth by conjoining their immortal spirits with their mortal souls. Having achieved this, they would ascend through the next six spheres (which, with the Earth gave a total of seven), discarding and acquiring an astral body with each transition, thereby maintaining a trinity of principles. Blavatsky had drawn significant elements of these doctrines from the Anglo-American Spiritualist currents discussed in chapter 4, but she found her interpretations confirmed by Stewart and Tait's account of a hierarchical cosmos in which transferences from one fixed 'grade' to another occurred.

Ernst Haeckel's Monism and *The Secret Doctrine*

Not all attempts to bridge science and religion were equal in Blavatsky's eyes. Monism—the idea that everything is united in a single substance—originated in antiquity and had been present in German Idealism and Romanticism, where F. W. J. Schelling (1775–1854), J. W. von Goethe (1749–1832), and G. W. F. Hegel (1770–1831) had drawn on the philosophies of Baruch Spinoza (1632–1677) and Giordano Bruno (1548–1600), giving them a characteristically nineteenth-century flavour through reference to notions of 'becoming', progress, or development. Nineteenth-century monism could be of different orientations, with materialist versions asserting the primacy of matter and spiritualist ones emphasising spirit.[77] Up until around 1840, variously materialist or spiritualist versions of monism had been in tension with one another, but from the end of the 1840s, materialist monism was the most prominent.[78]

In *General Morphology* (1866), Haeckel proposed a materialist monism that would become particularly influential. Although he didn't invent the term 'monism', he did much to popularise it.[79] He cited Goethe, synthesising Darwinism with *Naturphilosophie* and Lamarckism—an

---

[77] Frederick Gregory, *Scientific Materialism in Nineteenth-Century Germany* (Dordrecht and Boston: D. Reidel Publishing Company, 1977), 46–47.
[78] Gregory, *Scientific Materialism*, 50.
[79] Todd H. Weir, 'The Riddles of Monism: An Introductory Essay', in *Monism: Science, Philosophy, Religion, and the History of a Worldview*, ed. Todd H. Weir (New York: Palgrave Macmillan, 2012), 5.

aspect of the theory of Jean-Baptiste Lamarck (1744–1829), namely, that characteristics acquired by an organism during its life are passed on to the offspring. Haeckel's monism asserted the 'unity of nature', meaning that the universe was composed of one substance and was governed by one set of laws. Although it had spiritual meaning, reality comprised the material world and nothing more.[80] It was a naturalistic, materialistic, and secularising vision that proposed the unity of science and religion under Darwinism and left no room for anything beyond the material realm.

Haeckel's ideas exemplified the interaction of natural science with philosophy and religion in the context of contemporary social tensions.[81] Notions of an immanent divine tended to be associated with anti-confessional rationalism, and monism appealed to many with mystical, heretical, or anti-authoritarian dispositions.[82] One might therefore have expected it to have appealed to Blavatsky. After all, she had an immanent view of the divine, was vehemently anti-clerical, and definitely thought of herself as an anti-establishment thinker. Indeed, there was much about Haeckel's monism that resonated, and Blavatsky even identified Theosophy as a type of monism.[83] However, as Gauri Viswanathan explained, Blavatsky 'sought to disentangle' Theosophy from Haeckel's monism, claiming, 'Theosophy's notion of the unity

---

[80] Gregory, *Scientific Materialism*, 49.

[81] Weir, *Monism*, 3 and 27.

[82] Ibid., 17 and 27. Many of those who attended the International Congress of Freethinkers in Brussels, for example, were drawn to Haeckel's monism. Gathering in 1880 to oppose clerical influence in public life, among them were Freemasons, secularists, and abolitionist radical republicans. Ibid., 5.

[83] She also wrote a couple of articles specifically addressing monism in answer to the secularist Charles Bradlaugh, who wrote an article critical of Theosophy after Annie Besant's conversion to Theosophy. Bradlaugh wrote: 'An Atheist certainly cannot be a Theosophist. A Deist might be a Theosophist. *A Monist could not be a Theosophist. Theosophy must at least involve Dualism.*' Blavatsky answered: 'The Monism of Theosophy is truly philosophical. We conceive of the universe as one in essence and origin. And though we speak of Spirit and Matter as its two poles, yet we state emphatically that they can only be considered as distinct from the standpoint of human, *mayavic* (*i.e.*, illusionary) consciousness. We therefore conceive of spirit and matter *as one in essence* and not as separate and distinct antitheses.' [All emphases original] H. P. Blavatsky, 'Force of Prejudice', *Lucifer* 4, no. 23 (July 1889), 355 and 357.

of matter and spirit constituted a purer expression of monism than found in science or secularism'.[84] Ultimately, Blavatsky was a spiritualist monist and Haeckel a materialist one, and Blavatsky could not forgive him for this fundamental error.

> Such men are simply the intellectual and moral murderers of future generations; especially Hæckel, whose crass materialism often rises to the height of idiotic *naivetés* in his reasonings. One has but to read his 'Pedigree of Man, and Other Essays' (*Aveling's transl.*) to feel a desire, in the words of Job, that his remembrance should perish from the earth, and that he 'shall have no name in the streets'.[85]

Blavatsky had several grievances. She objected to Haeckel's theory that life arose from purely material processes, challenging his account of the origins of life in *monera*, organisms that reproduce through asexual budding. Nevertheless, she incorporated the notion of asexual budding into her account of the evolution of the earlier root races, while complaining that Haeckel's account was incomplete and demanding the input of spiritual elements.

> Occult Sciences admit with Hæckel that (objective) life on our globe 'is a logical postulate of Scientific natural history', but add that the rejection of a like *Spiritual* involution, from *within without*, of invisible subjective Spirit-life—eternal and a Principle in Nature—is more illogical, if possible, than to say that the Universe and all in it has been gradually built by blind forces inherent in matter, without any *external* help.[86]

Then there was Haeckel's advocacy of the detested Darwinian theory of man's descent from the apes, which he tried to prove through reference to recapitulation, the idea that the human embryo passes through stages of development that correlate to the stages of that organism's

---

[84] Gauri Viswanathan, 'Monism and Suffering: A Theosophical Perspective', in *Monism*, ed. Todd H. Weir, 92.
[85] Blavatsky, *Secret Doctrine II*, 651–652.
[86] Ibid., 348.

evolutionary development.[87] Blavatsky incorporated versions of recapitulationism into her doctrines of metempsychosis and reincarnation, in which she argued (differently in each case) that the monad passed through mineral, plant, and animal forms on its way to human incarnation.[88] Haeckel's version of recapitulationism referred only to animal forms and was, therefore, incomplete from Blavatsky's point of view. In *The Secret Doctrine*, she argued the forms the embryo went through were the '*store of types* hoarded up in man, the microcosm'. In other words, they were the fixed forms the monad had already incarnated into during previous rounds on its evolutionary journey. Blavatsky noted that Haeckel and Darwin 'triumphantly' referred to the presence of a tail in the embryonic stages as proof of man's ancestry from the apes. She objected, '*It may also be pointed out that the presence of a vegetable with leaflets* in the embryonic stages is *not explained* on ordinary evolutionist principles. Darwinists have not traced man through the vegetable, but Occultists have. *Why then this feature in the embryo*, and how do the former explain it? [her emphases].'[89] Once again, Blavatsky subsumed an aspect of a scientific theory while maintaining the Theosophical version was *scientifically* superior.

Haeckel's theories had been opposed by the Berlin physiologist Emil Du Bois Reymond (1818–1896), who pinpointed questions—like the origin of consciousness and the origin of motion—he believed were not open to empirical explanation.[90] As Todd H. Weir observed, Du Bois Reymond's map of science allowed for the existence of a transcendent realm, although he insisted the transcendental should not encroach

---

[87] Weir, *Monism*, 5.

[88] In metempsychosis, the monad passes through mineral, plant, and animal forms before achieving immortality on Earth and ascending to the spheres. In reincarnation, the monad passes through these earlier stages in previous rounds. 'The human fœtus follows now in its transformations all the forms that the physical frame of man had assumed throughout the three Kalpas (Rounds) during the tentative efforts at plastic formation around the monad by senseless, because imperfect, matter, in her blind wanderings. In the present age, the physical embryo is a plant, a reptile, an animal, before it finally becomes man, evolving within himself his own ethereal counterpart, in his turn. In the beginning it was that counterpart (astral man) which, being senseless, got entangled in the meshes of matter.' Blavatsky, *Secret Doctrine I*, 184.

[89] Blavatsky, *Secret Doctrine II*, 187.

[90] Weir, *Monism*, 9 and Gregory, *Scientific Materialism*, 49.

on the scientific. Haeckel saw no such limits.[91] His theory was an all-encompassing materialism that subsumed religion by replacing it with empirical science.[92] Blavatsky was well aware of the argument between Haeckel and Du Bois Reymond.[93]

> We are assured that real science is not materialistic; and our own conviction tells us that it cannot be so, when its learning is real. There is a good reason for it, well defined by some physicists and chemists themselves. Natural sciences *cannot* go hand in hand with materialism. To be at the height of their calling, men of science have to reject the very possibility of materialistic doctrines having aught to do with the *atomic* theory; and we find that [. . .] Du Bois Reymond,—the latter probably unconsciously—and several others, have proved it. [94]

Blavatsky knew her citation of Du Bois Reymond might be seen as problematic because he was known as a materialist. Nevertheless, his value as an ally against Haeckel outweighed such minor issues (which also included his rejection of vitalism).[95] This was especially the case if Blavatsky could turn things to her advantage by stating that even 'his own brother materialists' had criticised Haeckel, including 'as great, if not greater, authorities than himself' such as Du Bois Reymond. However, she also explained that Du Bois Reymond was not *really* a materialist, but rather an agnostic, who had 'protested most vehemently against the materialistic doctrine'.[96] One suspects it was a case of trying to have one's cake and eat it, but it may have been fuelled by the generalised lack of clarity over definitions of materialism that Frank Turner highlighted.

[91] Weir, *Monism*, 10.
[92] Ibid., 10–11.
[93] Blavatsky, *Secret Doctrine II*, 650. See also 663–664, 651, and 656.
[94] Blavatsky, *Secret Doctrine I*, 518.
[95] On Du Bois Reymond's opposition to vitalism, see Lenoir, *Strategy of Life*, 217.
[96] Blavatsky, *Secret Doctrine II*, 650. Gabriel Finkelstein, *Emil Du Bois Reymond: Neuroscience, Self, and Society in Nineteenth-Century Germany* (Cambridge, MA, and London: MIT Press, 2013), 255.

Darwinism

In natural selection, evolution was seen as driven by a combination of chance and environmental factors. Robert J. Richards has argued that despite historians' and scientists' portrayals of Darwin as making a complete break with previous Romantic and teleological evolutionary theories, in fact, his theory had its roots in earlier ones, such as recapitulationism, which had 'more than a whiff' of 'guidance in evolution by teleological factors'.[97] Be that as it may, Blavatsky perceived natural selection as non-teleological and materialist, and both these things guaranteed her to hate it.[98] She claimed that natural selection was incomplete and didn't conform to ancient science, the benchmark against which modern ideas had to be judged.[99] She also objected that it excluded spiritual elements and as a result didn't adequately explain the origin of variations in biological organisms. This could only be explained through reference to the divine.[100] In *Isis Unveiled*, she had criticised transformationism, the idea that species gradually change into one another that was associated with Darwinism and Lamarckism. This intervention was so urgent to her that she opened *The Secret Doctrine* by quoting herself:

'While it is positively absurd to believe the "transformation of species" to have taken place according to some of the more materialistic views of the evolutionists, it is but natural to think that each genus, beginning with the molluscs and ending with man,

---

[97] See Richards, *Meaning of Evolution*, esp. 76–77.

[98] She had criticised Darwin already in *Isis Unveiled* but was much more detailed in her rebuttals in *The Secret Doctrine*.

[99] 'Space fails us to present the speculative views of certain ancient and mediaeval occultists upon this subject. Suffice it that they antedated Darwin, embraced more or less all his theories on natural selection and the evolution of species, and largely extended the chain at both ends. Moreover, these philosophers were explorers as daring in psychology as in physiology and anthropology. They never turned aside from the double parallel-path traced for them by their great master Hermes. "As above, so below", was ever their axiom; and their physical evolution was traced out simultaneously with the spiritual one.' Blavatsky, *Isis I*, 427. See also Blavatsky, *Secret Doctrine II*, 426.

[100] Blavatsky, *Isis I*, 154 and 429. Blavatsky, *Secret Doctrine II*, 299.

had modified its own primordial and distinctive forms.' —*Isis Unveiled*, Vol. I., p. 153.[101]

She maintained that despite the possibility of some adaptations leading to variations, each species possessed a primordial or essential form and that modifications due to the environment only took place within those parameters.

If Blavatsky rejected Darwin, then how did she believe evolution occurred? Blavatsky believed evolution was guided, spiritually, both internally and externally. We have already encountered the idea of the evolutionary guidance of spiritual entities in the thought of Alfred Russel Wallace. This was just one of the various alternatives to natural selection propagated during what Peter Bowler referred to as the 'eclipse of Darwinism' from the 1880s through the first decades of the twentieth century. At that time, biologists generally accepted the idea of evolution but doubted that natural selection was its central mechanism. As Blavatsky observed, 'There are many *anti*-Darwinists in the British Association, and "Natural Selection" begins to lose ground. [. . .] Even Mr. Huxley is showing signs of truancy to "Selection", and thinks "natural selection *not the sole* factor".'[102] The four main alternatives to natural selection in the late nineteenth century were saltationism, also known as the 'mutation theory' (evolution through sudden mutations), neo-Lamarckism (transmission of acquired characteristics), theistic evolution, and orthogenesis (evolution driven by something internal). These were proposed in various combinations by different thinkers and the distinctions between them were sometimes blurred.[103] A central issue for evolutionary theorists was whether evolution necessarily involved progress or whether degradation could occur. There was no clear-cut relationship between particular evolutionary theories and a specific view of progress. As Bowler noted, 'Darwinism,

---

[101] Preface to *The Secret Doctrine*. No page number.
[102] Blavatsky, *Secret Doctrine II*, 696. On Huxley's questioning of natural selection as a fully adequate explanation for evolution, see Turner, *Contesting Cultural Authority*, 20.
[103] Peter J. Bowler, *The Eclipse of Darwinism* (Baltimore and London: Johns Hopkins University Press, 1992), 7–8.

Lamarckism and orthogenesis were *all* exploited by *both* progressionists and degenerationists.'[104]

Blavatsky was firm in her progressionism. In addition to the idea of guidance by higher intelligences, her ideas had the most affinity with progressivist versions of orthogenesis. Orthogenetic theories proposed that an internal factor directed evolution along a certain path independently of the environment.[105] In this vein, Blavatsky wrote about matter's 'impulse to take on a higher form'[106] and pitted this perspective against a Darwinism she perceived as materialist and non-teleological. She quoted an extract from *On the Origin of Species*:

> The Occultists believe in an *inherent law* of progressive *development*. Mr. Darwin never did, and says so himself. On page 145 of the 'Origin of Species' we find him stating that, since *there can be no advantage* 'to the infusorian animalcule or an intestinal worm ... to become highly organized', therefore, 'natural selection', *not including necessarily progressive development*—leaves the animalcule and the worm (the 'persistent types') quiet [Blavatsky's emphases].[107]

Blavatsky was inspired by several prominent critics of Darwin, who proposed teleological theories she described as 'veiled manifestations of the universal guiding FOHAT'. [108] In this context she referred to the '*principle of perfectibility*'[109] of the Swiss botanist Carl Wilhelm von Nägeli (1817–1891), who, in *The Origin and Concept of Natural Historical Species* (1865), had argued that natural selection was a not sufficient explanation and had to be supplemented with a 'theory of perfectibility' (*Vervollkommnung*), an inner progressive principle or tendency towards

---

[104] Peter J. Bowler, 'Holding Your Head Up High: Degeneration and Orthogenesis in Theories of Human Evolution', *History, Humanity, and Evolution: Essays for John C. Greene*, ed. James R. Moore (Cambridge: Cambridge University Press, 1989), 330.

[105] Orthogenesis was not necessarily teleological, since trends developing without reference to the environment could lead to extinction, although it often was teleological in orientation. Bowler, *The Eclipse of Darwinism*, 7.

[106] Blavatsky, *Isis I*, xxxii.

[107] Blavatsky, *Secret Doctrine II*, 260.

[108] Ibid., 649.

[109] Ibid., 649.

complexity.[110] Almost twenty years later, in *A mechanico-Physiological Theory of Organic Evolution* (1884), Nägeli reasoned there had to be a fraction of the human egg that was important in inheritance. He called this the 'ideoplasm'.[111] This was suggestively reminiscent of Blavatsky's claim that a 'spiritual potency in the physical cell [. . .] guides the development of the embryo. [. . .] This inner soul of the physical cell—this "spiritual plasm" that dominates the germinal plasm—is the key that must open one day the gates of the terra incognita of the Biologist, now called the dark mystery of Embryology.'[112]

Blavatsky also mentioned Karl Ernst von Baer (1792–1876) in support of her progressivist orthogenetic perspective, referring to his notion of 'striving towards the purpose'.[113] Von Baer was an anti-Darwinist and distinguished member of the St. Petersburg Academy of Sciences with an interest in *Naturphilosophie*.[114] According to Alexander Vucnich, von Baer 'represented the culmination of a strong tradition in pre-Darwinian embryology in Russia built by scientists of German origin'.[115] Like Blavatsky, he allowed for some transformation within types, but none from one to another. Superficially reminiscent of Du Bois Reymond, von Baer also believed there were mysteries of nature inaccessible to science. For him, however, these were better approached through religion, and he objected to materialism because it led to atheism.[116] His objections to Darwinism centred on his dislike of the mechanistic aspects of the theory as well as his teleological views, and his writings were drawn on by many anti-Darwinists, especially in Russia.[117]

[110] *Evolution: Selected Letters of Charles Darwin 1860–1870*, ed. Frederick Burkhardt, Samantha Evans, and Alison M. Pearn (Cambridge: Cambridge University Press, 2008), 210.
[111] Stephen Webster, *Thinking about Biology* (Cambridge: Cambridge University Press, 2003), 16.
[112] Blavatsky, *Secret Doctrine I*, 219.
[113] Blavatsky, *Secret Doctrine II*, 649.
[114] Ruse, *Monad to Man*, 112.
[115] Alexander Vucinich, *Darwin in Russian Thought* (Berkeley and Los Angeles: University of California Press, 1988), 13 and 31–2.
[116] Ibid., 93
[117] Ibid., 94 and 97.

A third teleological evolutionary theorist Blavatsky mentioned was the English biologist and palaeontologist Richard Owen (1804–1892), an anti-Darwinian who had a reputation as Darwin's most vociferous opponent.[118] Blavatsky referred to his notion of a 'tendency towards perfectibility'.[119] Owen had been influenced by *Naturphilosophie* to the extent that Michael Ruse classed him as the 'British *Naturphilosoph*'.[120] Like Blavatsky, he objected to the Darwinian ascription of variation to chance and the notion of man's descent from apes, maintaining evolution involved progression towards a specific predetermined goal. Influenced by German progressivism and by von Baer, he espoused a view that was teleological but not straightforwardly so.[121] As Nicolaas Rupke explained, Owen argued that evolution was determined by an organism's 'innate capacity or power of change'. He combined orthogenesis with mutationism, at the same time adopting elements of Lamarckism too.[122] He proposed a theory of 'archetypes', as a kind of 'blueprint of design for the formation of animal life' in which mutations were 'a logical embroidering on the archetype'.[123] Rupke observed that it has often been stated that Owen's archetype was a Platonic idea. The matter was more complex, however. According to Rupke, Owen's ideas were initially consistent with 'a form of pantheistic *Naturphilosophie* and in contradistinction to a Platonic idea. Yet in due course he came to accept and to promulgate a Platonist connotation, even though his archetype differed significantly from a Platonic idea *sensu stricto*.'[124]

[118] 'It was not cogency of argument, nor even his imposing reputation as a vertebrate anatomist and paleontologist, that made Richard Owen, superintendent of the natural history department of the British Museum, Darwin's most formidable opponent. It was above all his arrogant and underhand manner.' James Moore, *The Post-Darwinian Controversies* (Cambridge: Cambridge University Press, 1979), 87.
[119] Blavatsky, *Secret Doctrine II*, 649.
[120] Ruse, *Monad to Man*, 117.
[121] Ibid., 118 and 125.
[122] Nicolaas Rupke, *Richard Owen: Biology without Darwin* (Chicago and London: University of Chicago Press, 1994), 172–173.
[123] Rupke, *Owen*, 128 and 171.
[124] Ibid., 126.

Conclusions

Blavatsky's engagement with scientific theories serves as an excellent window into the debates of the times and was much more extensive than has been possible to illustrate in this chapter. Nevertheless, the foregoing overview has provided a broad outline of Blavatsky's response to several individual scientists. Of those she approved of, Stewart and Tait, Du Bois Reymond, and Quatrefages were mentioned frequently by Blavatsky in her writings. Others, such as Crookes and Wallace, were important in the history of the Theosophical Society, not just as authors of sources on which Blavatsky drew but as influential early members and correspondents. Blavatsky helped diffuse the ideas of all these men in the context of her occultist agenda.

The second group of scientists was the one against which Blavatsky defined herself. These were the supposed 'materialists', and Darwin, Huxley, and Haeckel were among the most maligned. As we've seen, Blavatsky didn't pull her punches. From her portrayals alone, one might presume all these men to have shared the same foolish stance, but their positions on science and metaphysics were complex and varied. Furthermore, Du Bois Reymond, in whose ideas Blavatsky found ammunition against the materialist Haeckel, took a materialist and anti-vitalist position himself, and although Haeckel was a central target for Blavatsky's hostility, his monism had much in common with her views. In other words, Blavatsky disagreed with those she praised and agreed with those she criticised. She was the first to admit her endorsements were only ever partial.

Blavatsky's progressive theory of reincarnation within a vitalistic cosmos of hierarchically arranged fixed types subsumed, scientistically (according to Olav Hammer's definition), theories such as Stewart and Tait's principle of the continuity of energy, recapitulationism, the idea of reproduction through asexual budding, and more. Sometimes, confirmations coming from scientific quarters weren't particularly substantial, but often all Blavatsky needed was a hint. Aspects of her views were born of the scientistic interaction of nineteenth-century evolutionary biology with Platonic, Romantic, Spiritualist, and occultist thought. This was probably why Janet Oppenheim's apprehended Blavatsky as 'harking back to a neo-Platonic comprehension of scientific enquiry' and depicting a universe 'thoroughly permeated by spirit as a creative, causative agent'.[125] It was a law-governed cosmos, in which spiritual, physical, and psychic evolution went hand in hand in the development of everything from solar systems, continents, and biological organisms, to human beings. Everything progressed in spiral and cyclic fashion, living, dying and being 'reborn' on a higher level. Blavatsky explicitly stated her notion of the monad's reincarnationary journey through seven rounds and seven root races solved every problem in contemporary evolutionary theory.[126] It explained how humanity progressed in minute detail, guided by orthogenetic spiritual potencies reminiscent of Nägeli's ideoplasm, as well as by the spiritual beings Crookes and Wallace had failed to fully comprehend, in Blavatsky's opinion. All this took place within a great chain of being whose existence extending beyond the material realm had been confirmed by Stewart and Tait. Blavatsky's vision was offered against a background of tensions between various materialist and vitalist viewpoints, as well as varied definitions of the scope of science and the relationship between science and religion. I have taken care not to speak about science and religion as if they existed 'out there', but rather of different nineteenth-century constructions of science, religion, and their relationship. These ranged from the well-known conflict model of William Draper and others, to the idea that there's no real contradiction between science and religion when properly understood. The latter was more or less Blavatsky's view. It represented an attempt to define humanity's place in the cosmos in response to the perceived challenges of Darwinism and materialism, the 'others' against whom Blavatsky defined herself.

[125] Oppenheim, *Other World*, 193.
[126] Blavatsky, *Secret Doctrine II*, 696–698.

7

Hindu and Buddhist Thought

BLAVATSKY AND OLCOTT ARRIVED in Bombay in February 1879. In 1880, they travelled to Ceylon and took *pansil*, reciting the five Buddhist precepts before the venerable Akmeemana Dharmàrama at Galle.[1] In Ceylon, they developed relationships with numerous local Buddhists, some of whom wrote articles for *The Theosophist* on topics relating to reincarnation and karma.[2] In June, Blavatsky and Olcott inaugurated the Colombo branch of the Society, and the headquarters became a place where leading monks came to preach.[3] Two particularly note-worthy figures were Megittuwatte Gunananda (1823–1890), chief priest of the Dipaduttama Temple in Colombo, and Hikkaduwe Sumangala (1827–1911), high priest of the temple of Sri Pada (Adam's Peak).[4] Both of them wrote articles for *The Theosophist* on Buddhist topics.[5]

---

[1] Olcott, *Old Diary Leaves Second Series*, 168–169. See also H. N. S. Karuanatilake, 'The Local and Foreign Impact of the Pânadurâ Vadaya', *Journal of the Royal Asiatic Society of Sri Lanka*, New Series, vol. 49 (2004), 72.

[2] Examples include Bulatgama Sumanatissa, chief priest of the principal temple of Galle (Olcott, *Old Diary Leaves Second Series*, 160, 295), and Piyaratana Tiss, high priest at Dodanduwa (Olcott, *Old Diary Leaves Second Series*, 170).

[3] Karuanatilake, 'Local and Foreign Impact', 72.

[4] For more on Sumanagala, see K. N. O. Dharmadasa, *Language, Religion, and Ethnic Assertiveness: The Growth of Sinhalese Nationalism in Sri Lanka* (Ann Arbor: University of Michigan Press, 1992), 99, 334.

[5] H. Sumangala, 'The Buddhist Idea about Soul', *The Theosophist* 1, no. 6 (March 1880), 144; H. Sumangala, 'The Nature and Office of Buddha's Religion I', *The Theosophist* 1, no. 2 (November 1879), 43; H. Sumangala, 'The Nature and Office of Buddha's Religion

Blavatsky and Olcott also had many Hindu friends and colleagues, including several scholars and pandits (teachers).[6] On the boat to Bombay in January 1879, they had met Shyamji Krishna Varma (1857–1930), who would later go on to found the Indian Home Rule Society and was advisor to the leading Orientalist Sir Monier Monier-Williams (1819–1899).[7] Krishna Varma assisted as a translator in the Theosophists' correspondence with Swami Dayananda Saraswati (1824–1883), the Gujarati Vedic scholar who headed the *Arya Samaj* (Aryan Society) with which the Theosophical Society was associated until 1882. In his *Old Diary Leaves*, Olcott described how, in 1879, he and Blavatsky (presumably through the translator) had long conversations with Dayananda, the topics of which included nirvana and *moksha*, themes closely related to reincarnation.[8]

There were many other leading early Theosophists of Indian origin. The Bengali Hindu social reformer and writer Peary Chand Mitra (1814–1883) joined the Society in 1877. Mitra had an interest in Spiritualism and eventually became president of the Bengal Theosophical Society.[9] Another respected Indian Theosophist was Damodar K. Mavalankar (1857–?), who joined in 1879 and took *pansil* with the Theosophists in Ceylon the following year. His biographer, Sven Eek, described Damodar as one of the chief architects of the early Society. He was the

II', *The Theosophist* 1, no. 5 (February 1880), 122; and Mohottivatte Gunanande, 'The Law of the Lord Sakhya Muni', *The Theosophist* 1, no. 2 (November 1879), 43.

[6] On some of the types of individuals who joined the Society in India, see Edward C. Moulton, 'The Beginnings of the Theosophical Movement in India, 1879–1885', in *Religious Conversion Movements in South Asia*, ed. Geoffrey A. Oddie (Richmond: Curzon, 1997). Among Blavatsky and Olcott's academic contacts were many scholars, including M. M. Kunte, K. R. Cama, Ram Misra Shastri, Bala Shastri, and Adityaram Bhattacharya. Olcott, *Old Diary Leaves Second Series*, 23, 30, 287, 126, 273, 287.

[7] Ibid., 13, 22.

[8] Ibid., 78.

[9] Mitra was one of the earliest members of the Society in India, joining on 9 November 1877. Olcott had corresponded with him since 5 July 1877. See Blavatsky, *Letters*, 587. See also Godwin, *Theosophical Enlightenment*, 327 and Mriganka Mukhopadhyay, 'A Short History of the Theosophical Movement in Bengal', in *Paralok-Tattwa* by Makhanlal Roychowdhury (Kolkata: Bengal Theosophical Society, 2016), 106–113.

business manager of the publications department responsible for issuing *The Theosophist* and considered himself a disciple of Koot Hoomi.[10]

These were just a few of the people with whom Blavatsky had a 'rapidly widening correspondence' in India.[11] According to Olcott, every evening after their arrival, they 'held an impromptu durbar' in which 'the knottiest problems of philosophy, metaphysics, and science were discussed'.[12]

> Visitors kept on crowding our bungalow, and stopping until late every evening to discuss religious questions [. . .] thus did we come, so early in our connection with the Hindus, to know the difference between Western and Eastern ideals of life. [. . .] The Soul was the burning topic of debate and then, for the first time, H. P. B. and I became absorbed in the problems of its cyclic progressions and reincarnations.[13]

As we have already established, having previously taught metempsychosis onto higher spheres after death, it was around 1881 or 1882 that Blavatsky started teaching the normative karmic return of the human spirit to life on earth. That being so, and bearing in mind the date of Blavatsky's arrival in India, it seems reasonable to assume, as Helmut Zander did, that India had some influence on Blavatsky's adoption of reincarnation as a doctrine. Zander reasoned that although Blavatsky was already acquainted with European doctrines of reincarnation when she arrived, she took them seriously only via the 'midwifery' of Asia.[14] Even if this is not the whole story, it is a plausible part of it.

The reincarnation theory Blavatsky would eventually embrace was framed in the terminology of *Vedanta*, a type of philosophy that

---

[10] Sven Eek, *Dâmodar and the Pioneers of the Theosophical Movement* (Adyar: Theosophical Publishing House, 1978), 2–5. On Damodar taking *pansil*, see Olcott, *Old Diary Leaves Second Series*, 292. Damodar disappeared on a journey to Tibet. On Damodar's disappearance, see Henry Steel Olcott, *Old Diary Leaves Third Series 1883–1887* (Adyar: Theosophical Publishing Company, 1929), 259–268.

[11] Olcott, *Old Diary Leaves Second Series*, 38.

[12] Ibid., 21.

[13] Ibid., 25.

[14] Zander, *Seelenwanderung*, 478–481.

developed the monistic and non-monistic currents of the *Upanishads,* a collection of Indian philosophical and religious texts probably dating back to around 800–500 BCE.[15] The eighth-century CE Keralan Brahmin, Shankara, wrote commentaries on the *Upanishads,* developing the monistic strand of *Upanishadic* thought into a non-dualistic form of *Vedanta* known as *Advaita.*[16] According to his interpretation, the fundamental essence of the universe was *Brahman,* of which *atman* was considered an individualised form, that is, *Brahman* refracted through limiting conditions into the appearance of a self. Identical with the divine, the self was not truly the self of everyday consciousness, although ignorance (*avidya*) led to failure to apprehend this, resulting in entrapment in the cycle of rebirth. Knowledge of non-duality (*advaita*) was said to be the path to liberation.

In Blavatsky's account of the development of the cosmos, at the beginning of a period called a *manvantara, parabrahman* emitted *mulaprakriti* (matter), thereafter emanating the 'first' or 'un-manifested' logos, followed by a second logos.[17] There followed the universal soul, the source of immortal, reincarnating monads.[18] For Blavatsky, *atma* was the seventh human principle and was 'identical with the universal Spirit'.[19]

---

[15] The beginnings of *Vedanta* are ascribed to Badarayana, who is said to have compiled the *Vedanta Sutras* around the second century CE as a commentary on the *Upanishads.* The tradition was maintained and developed by a series of priests, of whom the most famous were Yamuna, Madhva, and Shankara, each associated with a different school. See Fred W. Clothey, *Religion in India: A Historical Introduction* (Abingdon: Routledge, 2006), 103. Blavatsky was aware of the three different schools of *Vedanta* but was particularly interested in Shankara's *Advaita,* which she described as the only 'absolutely pantheistical' school. H. P. Blavatsky, 'Neo-Buddhism', in *Blavatsky Collected Writings,* ed. Boris de Zirkoff, vol. 12, 344. Rama Misra Shastri's article on *Vedanta* in the first volume of *The Theosophist* lists the different schools. Rama Misra Shastri, 'The Vedant Darsana', *The Theosophist* 1, no. 6 (March 1880), 158.

[16] The traditional dates for Shankara are 788–820. Advaita Vedanta was one of three kinds. The other two were the *Visishtadvaita* of Ramanuja (c. 1017–1137 CE), which represented a qualified non-dualism and was based on the theistic strands of *Upanishadic* thought, and the *Dvaita Vedanta* of Madhva (*c.* 1197–1276 CE), which was dualistic. See Ninian Smart, 'Indian Philosophy', in *The Encyclopedia of Philosophy,* ed. Paul Edwards (New York and London: Macmillan, 1967), 156 and Ninian Smart, *World Philosophies* (London and New York: Routledge, 2008), 23.

[17] Blavatsky, *Secret Doctrine I,* 380.

[18] Ibid., 16–17.

[19] Blavatsky, *Key to Theosophy,* 76.

At the end of the *manvantara,* monads would re-absorbed after completing their journey through matter. She referred to Shankara when discussing the monad's reincarnationary journey:

> The monad, then, can be traced through the course of its pilgrimage and its changes of transitory vehicles only from the incipient stage of the manifested Universe. In Pralaya, or the intermediate period between two manvantaras, it loses its name, as it loses it when the real ONE self of man merges into Brahm in cases of high Samadhi (the *Turiya* state) or final Nirvana; 'when the disciple' in the words of Shankara, 'having attained that primeval consciousness, absolute bliss, of which the nature is truth, which is without form and action, abandons this illusive body that has been assumed by the *atma* just as an actor (abandons) the dress (put on).'[20]

In spite of the reference to Shankara and the Sanskrit terminology, Blavatsky's vision had a neo-Platonic basis that resonated strongly with Plotinus' scheme of the transcendent unknowable 'One' emanating the Divine Mind (*nous*) followed by the upper and lower parts of the Universal Soul. According to Fritz Staal, because of certain resonances between the two systems, this neo-Platonic framing was a virtually unavoidable outcome of Blavatsky's Western heritage. 'Western philosophy,' wrote Staal, 'reacts in a characteristic way to the problems of Advaita.'[21] 'We look through Neoplatonic eyes at Advaita, and the attitude of Western thought with regard to Neoplatonism predetermines our attitude to Advaita.'[22]

---

[20] Blavatsky, *Secret Doctrine II,* 570, 244.

[21] J. F. Staal, *Advaita and Neoplatonism: A Study in Comparative Philosophy* (Madras: University of Madras 1961), vii.

[22] Ibid., 27. The parallels and differences that can be discerned between neo-Platonism and Advaita are beyond the scope of this chapter. Some of them are outlined in Ibid., 161 f. Staal summarises one aspect: 'The main Neoplatonic theme is that there is a hierarchy of being, at the summit of which is the One, the most perfect and highly evaluated entity. In Plotinus there is also a tendency which stresses the perfection of the One to such a degree that the rest of the universe is nothing in comparison with it. In Advaita, on the other hand, the main tendency is to absolutely and uncompromisingly deny the reality of anything apart from the absolute Brahman.' Ibid., 231.

Blavatsky had already presented a version of her emanationary scheme in her first major work, *Isis Unveiled*, and associated it with Plato.[23] She had also referred to a Hindu version of the teaching, using terms like *bhagavant* and Brahma.[24] In *The Secret Doctrine*, she expanded the Sanskrit vocabulary and also assimilated the Buddhist notion of *Adi Buddha*—which she equated with *parabrahman*—as part of a modernising trope that identified 'true' Buddhism with 'true' Hinduism. Blavatsky contrasted this 'correct' understanding with the 'misunderstandings' of contemporary academic Orientalists. She bolstered her interpretations with selections from scholarship on Hindu topics,[25] academic studies of Buddhist thought,[26] and the work of amateur scholars of a heterodox inclination.[27]

[23] 'With Plato, the primal being is an emanation of the Demiurgic Mind (*Nous*), which contains from the eternity the "*idea*" of the "to be created world" within itself, and which idea he produces out of himself. The laws of nature are the established relations of this *idea* to the forms of its manifestations.' Blavatsky, *Isis I*, 55–56.

[24] 'The Hindu Bhagavant does not create; he enters the egg of the world, and emanates from it as Brahm. [. . .] Brahma dissolves himself into the Visible Universe, every atom of which is himself. When this is done, the not-manifested, indivisible, and indefinite Monas retires into the undisturbed and majestic solitude of its unity. The manifested deity, a duad at first, now becomes a triad; its triune quality emanates incessantly spiritual powers, who become immortal gods (souls). Each of these souls must be united in its turn with a human being, and from the moment of its consciousness it commences a series of births and deaths.' Ibid., 347–348. For more of Blavatsky's cross-cultural comparisons see Blavatsky, *Isis II*, 173.

[25] Sources Blavatsky quoted include John Dowson, *A Classical Dictionary of Hindu Mythology and Religion, Geography, History, and Literature* (London: Trübner and Co., 1888)—see Blavatsky, *The Secret Doctrine I*, 80, 89, and 116—Martin Haug, *Aitareya Brahmanam of the Rig Veda* (Bombay: Government Central Book Depot, 1863)—Blavatsky, *The Secret Doctrine I*, 101—and Edward Moor, *The Hindu Pantheon* (London: K. Johnson, 1810)—Blavatsky, *Isis II*, 86, 427, 512–423, Blavatsky, *Secret Doctrine II*, 548, 560.

[26] Among her Buddhist sources were Emil Schlagintweit, *Buddhism in Tibet* (Leipzig: F. A. Brockhaus, 1863); Henry Alabaster, *The Wheel of the Law: Buddhism Illustrated by Siamese Sources* (London: Trübner and Co., 1871); T. W. Rhys Davids, *Buddhism* (Non-Christian Religious Systems; London: Society for Promoting Christian Knowledge, [1877]); and W. Woodville Rockhill, *The Life of the Buddha* (London: Trübner and Co., 1884)

[27] For example, An Indian Missionary [Hargrave Jennings], *The Indian Religions: Or Results of the Mysterious Buddhism* (London: Thomas Cautley Newby, 1858) and *Curious Things of the Outside World. Last Fire* (London: T. and W. Boone, 1861).

In addition to these sources, Indian Theosophists also provided Blavatsky with the terminology and concepts necessary to her depictions of reincarnation. In this chapter, we will explore the roles of two of them, namely, Mohini M. Chatterji and Tallapragada Subba Row. Blavatsky offered the resulting Orientalist-heterodox-Vedantic synthesis as an alternative to materialist monism of Ernst Haeckel explored in the previous chapter. Hence, quoting Alexander Pope (whose 'God' she replaced with '*Parabrahm*') she concluded, 'Thus runs *their* philosophy of evolution, differing as we see, from that of Hæckel:—"All are but parts of one stupendous whole, Whose body Nature is, and (Parabrahm) the soul." '[28]

Orientalism

Many studies have discussed the 'Orientalism' of Theosophy. Some have emphasised Theosophy's Western character.[29] For example, Joscelyn Godwin argued that although the Theosophists 'introduced into the vernacular such concepts as karma and reincarnation, meditation, and the spiritual path', their efforts were 'characteristically Western'.[30] Similarly, Wouter Hanegraaff maintained Blavatsky's later assimilation of a doctrine of karma took place

> Within an already-existing western framework of spiritual progress. This has implications for the question of her 'orientalism'. It is not the case that she moved from an occidental to an oriental perspective

---

[28] Blavatsky, *Secret Doctrine II*, 189.

[29] For an overview of Theosophy and it relation to Oriental sources, see Nicholas Goodrick-Clarke, 'The Theosophical Society, Orientalism, and the "Mystic East": Western Esotericism and Eastern Religion in Theosophy', *Theosophical History* 13 (2007) and Christopher Partridge, 'Lost Horizon: H. P. Blavatsky and Theosophical Orientalism', in *Handbook of the Theosophical Current*, ed. Hammer and Rothstein. Studies that explore the Orientalist aspects of Theosophy include Mark Bevir, 'The West Turns Eastward: Madame Blavatsky and the Transformation of the Occult Tradition', *Journal of the American Academy of Religion* 62, no. 3 (1994); Prothero, 'Protestant Buddhism' and *The White Buddhist*; Andrew Dawson, 'East Is East, Except When It's West', *Journal of Religion and Society* 8 (2006); and Isaac Lubelsky, *Celestial India: Madame Blavatsky and the Birth of Indian Nationalism* (Oakville: Equinox, 2012).

[30] Godwin, *Theosophical Enlightenment*, 378

and abandoned western beliefs in favour of oriental ones. Her fundamental belief system was an occultist version of romantic evolutionism from beginning to end.[31]

Godwin and Hanegraaff's arguments correctly went beyond Theosophy's prima facie Indian appearance to reveal Western philosophical concerns, and they have been of import in correcting Theosophy's widespread initial and straightforward association with Buddhism and Hinduism.[32] Blavatsky had encouraged such identifications, telling Olcott, for example, that her masters in reincarnation theory were Patanjali, Kapila, Kanada, and the systems of *Aryavarta*.[33] As Godwin and Hanegraaff's work indicated, we would be right to be suspicious of such statements.

More recently, Hanegraaff expanded his argument, stating that although the Theosophical Society had begun as a 'Western esoteric current' dominated by the Orientalist imagination of nineteenth-century European scholarship and popular literature, it became 'entangled' with Hindu thought after Blavatsky and Olcott arrived in Bombay in 1879.[34] It was not that Theosophists moved from a Western vision of

[31] Hanegraaff, *New Age Religion*, 471.
[32] For example, writing in 1895, Merwin Marie Snell stated Theosophy was 'Hinduism'. Snell continued, 'The facts that it accepts the authority of the Vedas, and even speaks of Buddha as an incarnation of Vishnu, would alone be sufficient to determine this decision; but nearly all the elements of its religio-philosophical system are distinctly Hindu, and it resembles only those forms of Buddhism which have certainly been Hinduized.' Merwin-Marie Snell, 'Modern Theosophy in Its Relation to Hinduism and Buddhism II', *The Biblical World* 5 (1895), 264. Similarly, a 'Brahman Theosophist' writing in *The Theosophist* in 1884 argued Theosophical teachings were 'familiar to a great many Hindus' and that Hindu sacred writings 'from the *Vedas* to the *Puranas*, contain almost all the spiritual truths that the [Theosophical] Mahatmas have revealed'. A Brahman Theosophist, 'Esoteric Buddhism and Hinduism', *The Theosophist* 5, no. 9 (June 1884), 224–225. Blavatsky identified as a Buddhist. See 'Interview in *The New York World*', 23 January 1877, in *Letters of H. P. Blavatsky*, ed. Barker, 291. Letter to W. H. Burr, 19 November 1877 and Letter to N. de Fadeyev, 11 December 1877, in ibid., 383.
[33] Olcott, *Old Diary Leaves First Series*, 283–284. Patanjali was the author of the *Yoga Sutras*. Kapila was associated with *Sankhya* philosophy. Kanada was the founder of *Vaishesika* philosophy, and *Aryavarta* indicated northern and central India.
[34] For discussion of the notion of 'Western esotericism' see Granholm, 'Locating the West' and Hanegraaff, 'The Globalisation of Esotericism', *Correspondences* 3 (2015).

the Orient towards an 'authentic' Asian one, but that they came to be involved in 'extremely complicated historical processes of imaginal construction and reconstruction that [took] place in a variety of specific local contexts'. This resulted in 'a mutual fertilisation of Indian religions and Western esotericism that would finally transform both almost beyond recognition'.[35]

Indeed, the most persuasive studies have drawn on the insights of post-colonial studies to go beyond Edward Said's by now well-known notion of Orientalism as a master-narrative of Western imperialism that constructs and controls its subjugated 'Other'.[36] They have demonstrated that Theosophy's Orientalism was not solely a form of Western identity formation; it was also appropriated by colonised people for their own purposes.[37] As Karl Baier recently contended,

It is not simply an encounter between Western Theosophy and South Asian tradition that we are looking at here, but a complex reciprocal process of transculturation within the Theosophical Society itself. [. . .] Members of both groups were not representatives of more-or-less well-defined traditions, but rather, protagonists of cultures-in-the-making, who had undergone serious deculturation. This brought a specific dynamic to the intercultural exchanges. On the one hand, there were anglicized high-caste Indians (mostly young male Brahmins) who tried to construct and renew their cultural heritage under the conditions of the Raj. Theosophy offered them a convenient space in which to mark out this trajectory. On the other hand, there were indophile theosophists who departed from their European and North American mainstream culture to create a

---

[35] Wouter Hanegraaff, 'Western Esotericism and the Orient'.

[36] Edward W. Said, *Orientalism* (London: Penguin, 2003), 3. See J. J. Clarke, *Oriental Enlightenment: The Encounter between Asian and Western Thought* (London: Routledge, 1997), 8. Said has been criticised on a number of fronts, but his analysis remains influential. See Gyan Prakash, 'Orientalism Now', *History and Theory* 34, no. 3 (October 1995). Said responded to his challengers in Edward W. Said, 'Orientalism Reconsidered', *Cultural Critique* 1 (Autumn 1985).

[37] Karl Baier, 'Theosophical Orientalism and the Structures of Intercultural Transfer: Annotations on the Appropriation of the *cakras* in early Theosophy', in *Theosophical Appropriations*, ed. Chajes and Huss, 318–319.

defiant movement that blended elements from various sources such as Freemasonry, Rosicrucianism, liberal Protestantism, Spiritism, Mesmerism, and modern magic.[38]

In a similar vein, Michael Bergunder convincingly argued that European history was not separate from that of the colonies; processes of European identity formation were entangled with those of the colonised. Theosophy was especially indebted to the perspectives of nineteenth-century English-speaking Hindu elites, among whom it played a decisive role in the dissemination of Orientalist knowledge.[39] In such contexts, concepts like 'religion' and 'Hinduism' emerged in the nineteenth century as part of this global religious history and were the result of multidirectional and interrelated discourses.[40] The following will consider some of these interactions, and how they contributed to the form Blavatsky's reincarnation theory came to take.

The Invention of Hinduism and Buddhism

The birth of Theosophy in 1875 followed around a hundred years of focused European academic interest in the Orient. In the context of the British colonisation of Bengal beginning in 1765, William Jones (1746–1794) and Charles Wilkins (1750–1836) had launched the Asiatic Society of Bengal in 1784.[41] The following year, Wilkins published his English translation of the *Bhagavad Gita*, and European readers were introduced to it for the first time as a central Hindu text. The number of scholarly publications thereafter increased, with the late nineteenth century marking a watershed in what Raymond Schwab termed the 'Oriental Renaissance'.[42] Significant events included the foundation of

---

[38] Baier, 'Theosophical Orientalism', 310.

[39] Bergunder, 'Experiments with Theosophical Truth', 404 and 407.

[40] Ibid., 401. For further discussion of these issues in the context of the Theosophists' Buddhism, see Julie Chajes, 'Orientalist Aggregates: Theosophical Buddhism between Innovation and Tradition', in *Festschrift for Nicholas Goodrick-Clarke*, ed. Tim Rudbøg and Jo Hedesan, forthcoming.

[41] Raymond Schwab, *Oriental Renaissance: Europe's Rediscovery of India and the East, 1680–1880* (New York: Columbia University Press, 1984), 4, 7, 33, 51.

[42] Ibid., 4, 11, 16.

the Ecole des Hautes Etudes in Paris in 1868 to include Indic studies on
the curriculum for the first time, and the publication of the fifty-volume
series *Sacred Books of the East* (from 1879), edited by the German-born
Oxford-based Orientalist Friedrich Max Müller (1823–1900).

It was during the nineteenth century that the category 'Hinduism'
first came into vogue. It was a modern construct, and emerged under
specific historical conditions.[43] A word without a precise correlate in
any Indian language (in which terms such as *dharma* had tradition-
ally been used to describe beliefs and practices), 'Hinduism' came
to be adopted both by academic Orientalists and Indian people to
designate a unified religion. This was problematic, however, since
there was no distinct entity that could be labelled in this way without
glossing over the substantial differences—and sometimes contradictions—between different Indian philosophical and religious systems. Despite this, the category was widely adopted and came to
play a fundamental role in scholarship as well as in Indian religious
and political life. It was a process influenced by the theorisations of
European Orientalists, but the Indian public contributed to its development and popularisation too.[44]

During the nineteenth century, 'Hinduism' was commonly cast in
both a positive and a negative light. On the one hand, Hindu practices
were widely condemned, for example because of their 'idolatry' and the
sexual connotations of Shiva *lingams* (phalluses). Then there were the
perceived inequalities of the Hindu caste system, the self-immolation of
widows on their husband's funeral pyres (*suttee*), and child marriages.[45]
Under the influence of the Bengal Renaissance beginning around 1830,
reformers such as Rammohan Roy (1772–1833) criticised such elements

[43] The term 'Hindu' (the Sanskrit word originally meant 'Indian') came into use among
Europeans in the eighteenth century. Previously, Indian religions had been described
by Christians as 'Heathenism'. Richard King, *Orientalism and Religion: Postcolonial
Theory, India, and 'The Mystic East'* (London and New York: Routledge, 2001), 99.
David Chidester, 'Colonialism', in *Guide to the Study of Religion*, ed. W. Braun and
R. T. McCutcheon (New York: Cassell, 2000), 427. Peter Harrison cited in King,
Orientalism and Religion, 35.
[44] Richard Hughes Seager, *The World's Parliament of Religions: The East/West Encounter,
Chicago, 1893* (Bloomington and Indianapolis: Indiana University Press, 1995), 96.
[45] Godwin, *Theosophical Enlightenment*, 311.

of Hindu life.[46] In 1828, Roy established the Brahmo Samaj, an influential monotheistic Hindu reform movement based on theistic principles drawn from the Vedas, the Koran, and Enlightenment thought. Roy and other reformers aimed to eliminate undesirable elements with the goal of revealing 'true Hinduism'. The latter was identified with *Vedanta*, the *Upanishads*, and the *Bhagavad Gita*. Under the influence of Roy and others, a modernising version of Vedanta that drew particularly on Advaita emerged as an ideological movement and as part of the wider emergence of neo-Hinduism.[47] This neo–*Advaita Vedanta* became so popular that it became virtually synonymous with *Vedanta*, and even with Hinduism more generally.[48]

Coexisting with other more traditional forms, the result of these reforms was a neo-Hinduism that represented a significant rupture with the past and in which much from the classical traditions was left out or simplified.[49] In such modernising interpretations, Hinduism was often portrayed as a 'mystical', 'Eastern' religion. Some argued it had the potential to rescue the 'West' from its growing materialism. Neo-Hinduism was commonly framed by a universalist and perennialist agenda that taught all religions expressed the same truth at a fundamental level.[50] It was a perspective that had much in common with that of Theosophy.

Just as Hinduism is a convenient, misleading, and historically contingent label, so too is Buddhism an intellectual abstraction that is used to cover numerous divergent systems. As Philip Almond persuasively argued, as a category, Buddhism was 'discovered' and 'imaginatively

---

[46] On Roy, see Seager, *The World's Parliament of Religions*, 112. The Bengal Renaissance was an intellectual, religious, and cultural movement that took place in Bengal during the period of British rule. It began around 1830, with Roy, who is considered the father of the Bengal Renaissance, and continued into the twentieth century. See David Kopf, *British Orientalism and the Bengal Renaissance: The Dynamics of Indian Modernization, 1773–1835* (Berkeley and Los Angeles: University of California Press, 1969).

[47] De Michelis, *Modern Yoga*, 39.

[48] King, *Orientalism and Religion*, 128. Niranjan Dhar has argued that Henry Thomas Colebrook was the first to identify *Vedanta* as 'the religion of the Hindus'. Ibid., 130.

[49] Elizabeth De Michelis, *A History of Modern Yoga: Patañjali and Western Esotericism* (London: Continuum, 2008), 52 and 73.

[50] King, *Orientalism and Religion*, 120.

created' in Europe and America during the first half of the nineteenth century, where it was 'determined by the Victorian culture in which it emerged as an object of discourse'.[51] Like Hinduism, Buddhism was subject to positive and negative interpretations. Initially, it was even harder for Europeans to digest, with prominent Orientalists such as Max Müller, Eugène Burnouf (1801–1852), and Jules Barthélemy Saint-Hilaire (1805–1895), portraying it as a gloomy religion of negation, or as a sort of collective madness.[52] The Theravada tradition was portrayed as nihilistic and atheistic, and the Mahayana and Tantrayana as full of repulsive 'idols'. Nevertheless, the popularity of Buddhism increased throughout the early decades of the century and by the 1850s, its influence could be felt among the middle and upper classes.[53] Reasons for its eventual popularity included its perceived dissimilarity (or similarity) to Christianity, the supposed justice of the concept of karma, and the apparent compatibility between Buddhism and science. *The Light of Asia* (1879) by Edwin Arnold (1832–1904) was particularly influential in bringing a more positive image of the Buddha to the West.[54]

The emergence of 'Buddhism' as a category contributed to the development of what David McMahan has termed Buddhist modernism, a modern hybrid tradition with roots in the Enlightenment, Romanticism, American Transcendentalism, and colonialism. McMahan asserted Buddhist modernism constituted a new type of Buddhism that was the result of processes of 'modernization, westernization, reinterpretation, image-making, re-vitalization, and reform'. These processes took place in Asian countries as well as the West, where Buddhist modernism was fashioned both by Asian and Western actors in response to the challenges of modernity. These included growing epistemic uncertainty, religious pluralism, the threat of nihilism, and perceived conflicts between science and religion.[55] Modernising interpreters of Buddhism, both Asian and Western, often shared certain viewpoints

---

[51] Philip C. Almond, *The British Discovery of Buddhism* (Cambridge: Cambridge University Press, 1988), 4.
[52] Godwin, *Theosophical Enlightenment*, 266, 324.
[53] Almond, *The British Discovery of Buddhism*, 2–3.
[54] Edwin Arnold, *The Light of Asia* (London: Routledge & Kegan Paul, 1964).
[55] McMahan, *Buddhist Modernism*, 5.

and these had resonances with the approaches of neo-Hindu thinkers. Seeking to purify Buddhism of mythological or superstitious elements as well as 'popular accretions', they tended to distinguish between the Buddhism of the philosophical elite and the Buddhism of the masses with the goal of arriving at the original essence of Buddhism.[56] Often, this was identified with Theravada Buddhism—which was historically prior to Mahayana—but it was not unheard of for Mahayana too to be portrayed as a repository of unsullied ancient Buddhist truths. As in neo-Hinduism, in modernising interpretations, Buddhism was often depicted in perennialist or universalist terms.[57]

Blavatsky's definitions of Buddhism and Hinduism had modernising characteristics. She argued for the existence of a perennial esoteric doctrine lying at the heart of both traditions whose closest representatives were *Advaita Vedanta* and *Yogacara*, a fourth-century CE school associated with Mahayana Buddhism.[58] Criticising both 'Brahmanism' and 'orthodox Buddhism', she summed up her position as follows:

> Brahmanism and Buddhism, both viewed from their orthodox aspects, are as inimical and as irreconcilable as water and oil. Each of these great bodies, however, has a vulnerable place in its constitution.

---

[56] On the 'demythologisation' of Buddhism, see Robert Sharf, 'The Zen of Japanese Nationalism', *History of Religions* 33, no. 1 (1993), 1–43 and 'Whose Zen? Zen Nationalism Revisited', in *Awakenings: Zen, the Kyoto School, and the Question of Nationalism*, ed. James W. Heisig and John Maraldo Rude (Honolulu: University of Hawai'i Press, 1995), 44–45.

[57] On modernising interpretations of Buddhism, see McMahan, *Buddhist Modernism* and 'Modernity and the Discourse of Scientific Buddhism', *Journal of the American Academy of Religion* 72, no. 4 (2004); Richard Gombrich and Gananath Obeyesekere, *Buddhism Transformed: Religious Change in Sri Lanka* (Princeton. NJ: Princeton University Press, 1988); and Donald Lopez, ed., *A Modern Buddhist Bible: Essential Readings from East and West* (Boston: Beacon Press, 2002). On intersections between Theosophy and modernising interpretations of Buddhism see Prothero, *White Buddhist* and Sin'ichi Yoshinaga, 'Theosophy and Buddhist Reformers in the Middle of the Meiji Period: An Introduction', *Japanese Religions* 34, no. 2 (2009) and 'Three Boys on a Great Vehicle: "Mahayana Buddhism" and a Trans-National Network', *Contemporary Buddhism: An Interdisciplinary Journal* 14, no. 1 (2013).

[58] Blavatsky, *Secret Doctrine I*, 46. On Yogacara, see Paul Williams with Anthony Tribe, *Buddhist Thought* (London and New York: Routledge, 2000), 152–160 and Paul Williams, *Mahāyāna Buddhism* (New York: Routledge, 2009), 84–102.

While even in their esoteric interpretation both can agree but to dis-
agree, once that their respective vulnerable points are confronted,
every disagreement must fall, for the two will find themselves on
common ground. The 'heel of Achilles' of orthodox Brahmanism
is the Adwaita philosophy, whose followers are called by the pious
'Buddhists in disguise'; as that of orthodox Buddhism is Northern
mysticism, as represented by the disciples of the philosophies of
Aryâsanga (the Yogâchârya School) and Mahâyâna, who are twitted
in their turn by their coreligionists as 'Vedantins in disguise'. The
esoteric philosophy of both these can be but one if carefully ana-
lysed and compared, as Gautama Buddha and Sankarachârya are
most closely connected, if one believes tradition and certain esoteric
teachings. Thus every difference between the two will be found one
of form rather than of substance.[59]

On Blavatsky's view, then, true Buddhism and Hinduism (both ultimately identical with Theosophy) were to be uncovered by re-
moving popular accretions as well as countering 'orthodox' Brahmanic,
Buddhist, and scholarly misrepresentations. Esoteric Buddhism, argued
Blavatsky, was identical 'with the Secret Wisdom taught by Krishna'
(i.e., with the *Bhagavad Gita*) and with that of Shankara (of Vedantic
fame).[60] In other words, true Buddhism was identified with the texts
and traditions typically valued by neo-Hindu thinkers. As for the objections of an academic Orientalist such as Thomas Rhys Davids, said
Blavatsky, he knew nothing of 'true esoteric teachings'. Consequently,
one could only 'heartily laugh at him'.[61]

[59] Blavatsky, *Secret Doctrine II*, 637.
[60] Blavatsky argued this esoteric Buddhism (which was identical with the Theosophical
secret doctrine) could be found within Theravada and Mahayana Buddhism, though it
was distinct from, and antedated both. Tibet had received the secret doctrine from India
a long time before Buddhism had arrived there, so that early Buddhists reaching Tibet
recognised the religion of the Tibetans. Thus, even though Tibet received Buddhism
relatively late, its scriptures still contained esoteric Buddhism. H. P. Blavatsky, 'Tibetan
Teachings', *Lucifer* 15, nos. 85 and 86 (September and October 1894).
[61] For example, see Blavatsky, *Secret Doctrine I*, 539.

Mohini Mohun Chatterji

On the other hand, there were those who did understand esoteric traditions, in Blavatsky's opinion, and some of them were among the Indian members of her society. A major source in Blavatsky's understanding of *Vedanta* seems to have been a serialised translation of Shankara's *Viveka Chudamani* published in *The Theosophist* between 1885 and 1886 under the title 'The Crest Jewel of Wisdom'.[62] The translator was Mohini Mohun Chatterji (1858–1936), a Brahmin and member of the Western-educated professional bourgeoisie that was typically interested in Theosophy. Chatterji had the added honour of being descended from Rammohan Roy's family and he was also a member of the Brahmo Samaj.[63] Such prestigious members as Chatterji considerably strengthened the standing of the Society in India, especially in Bengal.[64] Mohini was a graduate of Calcutta University, where he studied modern European languages, Western philosophy, and law, which eventually became his profession. He joined the Society in 1882 and was elected assistant secretary of the Bengal branch that had been established in Calcutta the same year. After having received personal letters from Maser Koot Hoomi, he accompanied Blavatsky and Olcott to Paris and then London in 1884.[65] Mohini was, therefore, a member of Blavatsky's closest circle. In 1887, he resigned from the Society.[66]

[62] There were five instalments: Mohini M. Chatterji, 'The Crest-Jewel of Wisdom', *The Theosophist* 7, no. 73 (October 1885); *The Theosophist* 7, no. 76 (January 1886); *The Theosophist* 7, no. 78 (March 1886); *The Theosophist* 7, no. 82 (July 1886); and *The Theosophist* 7, no. 83 (August 1886).

[63] For a biographical sketch, see Mriganka Mukhopadhyay, 'Mohini: A Case Study of a Transnational Spiritual Space in the History of the Theosophical Society', forthcoming.

[64] Mriganka Mukhopadhyay, 'The Occult and the Orient: The Theosophical Society and the Socio-Religious Space in Colonial India', *Presidency Historical Review* 1, no. 2, (December 2015). See also Mukhopadhyay, 'A Short History of the Theosophical Movement in Bengal'.

[65] Diane Sasson, *Yearning for the New Age* (Bloomington and Indianapolis: Indiana University Press, 2012), 76–82. Sasson gives an excellent analysis of the Theosophists' Orientalist expectations of Mohini. For an analysis of Mohini's insistence that he was a disciple of Koot Hoomi (and not Blavatsky), see Scott, 'Miracle Publics', 181–182. Mohini left the Society in 1887, following a scandal.

[66] See Mukhopadhyay, *Mohini*, for a discussion of his reasons for leaving the Society and his life in India afterwards. Mohini apparently became disillusioned with

Mohini's translation referred to the Sanskrit names of the seven human principles used by Blavatsky in *The Secret Doctrine*. It detailed Vedantic ideas about reincarnation and escape from the cycle of incarnations through apprehension of the *atman*'s true nature. Reincarnation was supposed to be the result of the incorrect attribution (by the human principle of *manas*) of the *atman*'s qualities to 'that which is not *atman*'.[67] *Vedanta* was said to provide the means by which to overcome this error. 'By a proper comprehension of the purport of the *Vedanta* is produced the excellent knowledge; by that the great mystery of birth and rebirth is terminated.'[68] The result would be 'liberation', achieved 'by the direct perception of the identity of the individual with the universal self'.[69] More specifically, this perception was to involve 'the knowledge that *Brahm* (the supreme spirit) and *atma* are one and the same'.[70] Thus, the individual would 'not return to conditioned existence', that is, they would cease to reincarnate.[71]

In the context of a discussion of 'modern exact science's (limited) grasp of the origins of existence, Blavatsky explicitly referred to Mohini's translation in *The Secret Doctrine*, explaining that 'a European who would undertake to solve the problem of existence by the articles of faith of the true Vedantin' should 'read and study the sublime teachings on the subject of Soul and Spirit, of Sankarâchârya (*Viveka Chudâmani*)'. In the footnote she indicated that this work had been translated for the *Theosophist*, by Mohini M. Chatterji under the title of 'Crest Jewel of Wisdom'.[72]

Theosophy. He also apparently had a series of affairs, leading to his being branded a 'failed *chela*' by Blavatsky.

[67] Chatterji, *Crest IV*, 664.
[68] Chatterji, *Crest I*, 68.
[69] Chatterji, *Crest II*, 254.
[70] Chatterji, *Crest V*, 725
[71] Ibid., 726.
[72] Blavatsky, *Secret Doctrine I*, 569–70.

Tallapragada Subba Row

Another Indian Theosophist to make an important contribution to Blavatsky's understanding of *Vedanta* was Tallapragada Subba Row (1856–1890). Subba Row came from a Telugu-speaking Brahmin family, had benefitted from a Western education, and worked as a lawyer in Madras.[73] He was highly esteemed by Blavatsky, and Olcott even gave his presence in Madras as one of the reasons for their choice of that location for the Society's headquarters. Blavatsky referred to Subba Row as a 'true Vedantic Adwaitee of the genuine, esoteric Brahman faith and an occultist'.[74] He had initially corresponded with Blavatsky and with Damodar K. Mavalankar, thereafter requesting a private audience with Olcott and joining the Society in 1882.[75] Eventually, he became president of the Madras Branch.[76] He even acted as editor of *The Theosophist* during Blavatsky's absence.[77] Reflecting on the events of 1886, Olcott wrote that they 'saw a good deal of T. Subba Row at Headquarters [. . .] and enjoyed many opportunities to profit by his instructive occult teachings'.[78] Row resigned from the Society in 1888 following disagreements with Blavatsky and, according to Olcott, with his 'anglo-Indian backers'.[79]

Some of Blavatsky's references to reincarnation in her later writings were direct quotations from Subba Row. For example, in *The Theosophical Glossary* (1892), Blavatsky defined the Sanskrit term *sutratman* as 'the thread of spirit', 'the immortal Ego, the Individuality which incarnates in men one life after the other, and upon which are strung, like beads on a string, his countless Personalities'.[80] This was

---

[73] N. C. Ramanujachary, *A Lonely Disciple: Monograph on T. Subba Row 1856–90* (Adyar: Theosophical Publishing House, 1993), ix.

[74] For a full list of quotations from Blavatsky, praising Row, see Henk J. Spierenburg, ed., *T. Subba Row, Collected Writings*, 2 vols. (San Diego: Point Loma Publications 2001), vol. 1, xxiii–xxiv. Olcott also praised him. See Olcott, *Old Diary Leaves Second Series*, 362.

[75] Ibid., 343.

[76] H. S. Olcott, 'Death of T. Subba Row, B. A., B. L.', *The Theosophist* 11, no. 130 (July 1890). On choice of Adyar, see Olcott, *Old Diary Leaves Second Series*, 362.

[77] Note (No title or author), *The Theosophist* 5, no. 6 (March 1884), 154.

[78] Olcott, *Old Diary Leaves Third Series*, 382.

[79] Spierenburg, ed., *Subba Row Collected Writings Vol. 1*, xx.

[80] Blavatsky, *Theosophical Glossary*, 291.

highly reminiscent of Subba Row's description of *sūtrātmā* as the plane of existence on which the *kārana sharīra* operates. He wrote: it 'is called *sūtrātmā*, because, like so many beads strung on a thread, successive personalities are strung on this *kārana sharīra*, as the individual passes through incarnation after incarnation'.[81]

Blavatsky also quoted Subba Row when discussing reincarnation in *The Secret Doctrine*, claiming *kundalini sakti* was

> the power which brings about that 'continuous adjustment of *internal relations to external relations*' which is the essence of life according to Herbert Spencer, and that '*continuous adjustment of external relations to internal relations*' which is the basis of transmigration of souls, *punar janman* (re-birth) in the doctrines of the ancient Hindu philosophers. A Yogi must thoroughly subjugate this power before he can attain Moksham [moksha—freedom from the rebirth cycle].[82]

Blavatsky seems to have taken this virtually verbatim from Subba Row, who, in his first Theosophical article, 'The Twelve Signs of the Zodiac', wrote that *Kundalinisakti* indicated

> The power or force which brings about that 'continuous adjustment of *external relations to internal relations*' which is the essence of life according to Herbert Spencer [and which is] the basis of transmigration of souls or punarjanma (re-birth) according to the doctrines of the ancient Hindu philosophers.[83]

Herbert Spencer

Subba Row and Blavatsky both acknowledged a debt to the ideas of the social Darwinist Herbert Spencer, who, in his influential work *First Principles of a New System of Philosophy* (1862), had defined life as 'the

---

[81] T. Subba Row, *Philosophy of the Bhagavad Gita*, 34
[82] Blavatsky, *Secret Doctrine I*, 293.
[83] T. Subba Row, 'The Twelve Signs of the Zodiac', *The Theosophist* 3, no. 2 (Nov 1881).

continuous adjustment of internal relations to external relations'.[84] Spencer had stated this in the context of an argument for the relativity of knowledge and for the existence of a Divine Absolute that he maintained was at the root of all religions. Spencer argued evolution and dissolution were continually occurring throughout creation. These two processes were always in antagonism and tension with one another. 'Evolution,' Spencer explained, 'under its simplest and most general aspect is the integration of matter and concomitant dissipation of motion; while Dissolution is the absorption of motion and concomitant disintegration of matter.'[85] Spencer maintained that evolution could be a lot more besides, such as a chance from the homogenous to the heterogeneous, the indefinite to the definite, the simple to the complex, or from confusion to order.[86] He applied these ideas to the development of life and biological organisms as well as to societies.

Blavatsky was aware of Spencer's ideas, apparently directly as well as through Subba Row, since she quoted Spencer's *First Principles* in *The Secret Doctrine*. She was impressed, but, unsurprisingly, didn't believe Spencer had apprehended the truth in its entirety.

> It is curious to notice how, in the evolutionary cycles of ideas, ancient thought seems to be reflected in modern speculation. Had Mr. Herbert Spencer read and studied ancient Hindu philosophers when he wrote a certain passage in his 'First Principles' (p. 482), or is it an independent flash of inner perception that made him say half correctly, half incorrectly, '[there is] an immeasurable period during which the attracting forces predominating, cause universal concentration, and then an immeasurable period, during which the repulsive forces predominating, cause universal diffusion—alternate eras of Evolution and dissolution.'[87]

---

[84] Herbert Spencer, *First Principles of a New System of Philosophy* (London: Williams and Norgate, 1870), 84.
[85] Ibid., 285.
[86] Ibid., 362.
[87] Blavatsky, *Secret Doctrine I*, 12.

The *Vishnu Purana*

Blavatsky felt she understood the periods of evolution and dissolution better than did Spencer, and this was because she had access to Hindu sources. Her occasionally antagonistic attitude to the translator notwithstanding, an important source for her was a translation of the *Vishnu Purana* (1840) made by Horace Hayman Wilson (1786–1860).[88] Among many other things, the *Vishnu Purana* described the four *yugas* or ages of the world: the *Krita Yuga, Treta Yuga, Dwapara Yuga,* and *Kali Yuga.*[89] Each of these ages was said to be preceded by a period called its *sandhya* (or twilight), and was followed by another period of equal length called *sandhyansa* (a portion of twilight). The total of the four *yugas* gave one *manvantara*, which represented the reign of a *manu*, one of the mythical progenitors of mankind. There were said to be fourteen such *manus* in total, with seven future *manus* and *manvantaras.*[90] Two thousand *manvantaras* were said to comprise a *kalpa*, or a night and a day of Brahma. At the beginning of each *kalpa*, Brahma was said to create the world.[91]

In *The Secret Doctrine,* Blavatsky summarised her understanding of the ideas Wilson had presented in his translation.[92] She explained that after a day of Brahmâ comes 'Pralaya, when all the Souls rest in Nirvana'.[93] She described the many different types of *pralaya*, quoting Wilson: 'The first kind [of *pralaya*] happens in between Brahma's days. The second occurs after an age, or life of Brahma and the third is individual *pralaya*, or nirvana "after having reached which, there is no more future existence possible, no rebirth till after the *Maha Pralaya*"'.[94] But perhaps most importantly, Wilson's translation proposed a correspondence between cosmic cycles and individual ones. 'In this way [. . .] this whole world, although in essence imperishable and eternal, appears and disappears, as if it were subject to birth and death.'[95] In other words,

[88] Blavatsky, *Secret Doctrine I*, 19, 46, 50; Blavatsky, *Secret Doctrine II*, 48, 155, 162.
[89] H. H. Wilson, *Vishnu Purana* (London: John Murray, 1840), 23–24.
[90] Ibid., 266–271.
[91] Ibid., 43.
[92] Blavatsky, *Secret Doctrine II*, 368.
[93] Ibid., 245.
[94] Ibid., 370.
[95] Wilson, *Vishnu Purana*, 157.

both the cosmos and the individual underwent reincarnation, an idea that is at the centre of Blavatsky's theory of reincarnation.

Adi Buddha

In *The Secret Doctrine*, Blavatsky was particularly heavily indebted to Subba Row's 'Notes on the Bhagavad Gita', claiming they were the source of 'The best metaphysical definition of primeval theogony in the spirit of the Vedantins'.[96] Published in *The Theosophist*, these 'Notes' were based on lectures Subba Row had delivered in 1885 and 1886. In those lectures, he gave an allegorical interpretation in which the character of Arjuna from the *Bhagavad Gita* represented the monad and Krishna the Logos.[97] In *The Secret Doctrine*, Blavatsky explicitly drew on Subba Row's description of *Parabrahman*, stating it was 'the unknown and the incognisable' and equating it with the (neo-Platonic) One.[98] Quoting Subba Row directly, she described the process of emanation that took place at the birth of the cosmos, in which the 'One' emanated the first logos, or *Eswara*. This metaphysical tenet, Blavatsky maintained, could hardly have been better described than by Mr. Subba Row.[99] She also equated *Parabrahman* with the Buddhist concept of *Adi Buddha*, describing the process of emanation as follows, using the Platonic term *logos*:

> In the esoteric, and even exoteric Buddhism of the North, Adi Buddha, the One unknown, without beginning or end, [is] identical with Parabrahm. [. . . It] emits a bright ray from its darkness. This is the *Logos* (the first), or Vajradhara, the Supreme Buddha. As the Lord of all Mysteries he cannot manifest, but sends into the world of manifestation his heart—the 'diamond heart', Vajrasattva. This is the second *logos* of creation.[100]

[96] Blavatsky, *Secret Doctrine I*, 428.
[97] J. Barton Scott, *Spiritual Despots: Modern Hinduism and the Genealogies of Self-Rule* (Chicago: University of Chicago Press, 2016), 196.
[98] Blavatsky, *Secret Doctrine I*, 428.
[99] Ibid., 130.
[100] Ibid., 571.

The notion of *Adi Buddha* originates in the Buddhist theory of the *trikaya*, the idea that a Buddha has three bodies, one of which is subtle and is known as a *sambhoga-kaya* (enjoyment body). This subtle body is said to be located on another plane of reality.[101] Thomas Rhys Davids's *Buddhism* (1877) was an influential source for Blavatsky on this topic. Rhys Davids explained that in the tenth century, a new infinite, self-existent, and omniscient being was invented—*Adi Buddha*, the primordial Buddha.[102] In a letter to A. P. Sinnett, Blavatsky wrote that this late date was an error of Davids's, because *Adi Buddha* was mentioned in the oldest Sanskrit works.[103] Accordingly, she spoke of *Adi Buddha* as 'the One unknown, without beginning or end, identical with Parabrahm and Ain-Soph'.[104]

Blavatsky probably found further support for her equation of *parabrahman* and *Adi Buddha* in *Essays on the Languages, Literature, and Religion of Nepal and Tibet* (1874) by the British naturalist and scholar of Tibetan Buddhism, Brian Hodgson (1801–1894).[105] Hodgson argued for the equivalence of Buddhism and Brahmanism in a similar way to Blavatsky:

> In regard to the destiny of the soul, I can find no moral difference between [Buddhists] and the Brahmanical sages. By all, metempsychosis and absorption are accepted. But absorbed into what? into BRAHME, say the *Brahmans*,—into *Sunyata*, or *Svabhava*, or *Pranja*, or *Adi Buddha*, say the various sects of the *Bauddhas*.[106]

---

[101] According to this theory, the body that appears as a human being is not the real Buddha but a body of magical creation, a *nirmana-kaya*. The body closest to the real body of a Buddha is the *dharma-kaya*, or dharma body, the sum of perfected good qualities that constitute a Buddha. The *dharma-kaya* may also refer to the body of teachings and texts left behind by a Buddha. Williams, *Buddhist Thought*, 172–176; Rupert Gethin, *The Foundations of Buddhism* (Oxford: Oxford University Press, 1998), 233.

[102] Rhys Davids, *Buddhism*, 206–207.

[103] Letter to A. Sinnett in Henk Spierenburg, *The Buddhism of H. P. Blavatsky* (San Diego: Point Loma, 1991), 3.

[104] Blavatsky, *Secret Doctrine I*, 571.

[105] Brian Hodgson, *Essays on the Languages, Literature, and Religion of Nepal and Tibet* (London: Trübner and co, 1874).

[106] Ibid., 26.

Conclusions

Blavatsky's doctrine of reincarnation, with its notions of the emission and absorption of souls into *Parabrahman/Adi Buddha*, exemplifies an entanglement of several elements, including the modernising constructions/interpretations of Hinduism and Buddhism that were proposed by Western-educated Indian elites, academic Orientalism, Western philosophy and science, and occultism. For example, as we have seen, Herbert Spencer's attempt to reconcile science and religion was applied to *Vedanta* by a Western-educated Brahmin Theosophist alongside Platonic perspectives. This was then adopted by Blavatsky as part of a response to Ernst Haeckel's materialist monism.

Despite the undeniable influence of Western theories of rebirth on Blavatsky's perspectives, it seems plausible that conversations between Blavatsky, Dayananda, and other Indian and Ceylonese contacts contributed, at least in part, to her shift from metempsychosis to reincarnation around 1882. Echoing statements found in Wilson's translation of the *Vishnu Purana,* it was a reincarnationary model that was fractal and cyclic, and in which the life, death, and rebirth patterns of the individual mirrored those of the universe. In the aftermath of the Bengal Renaissance and in the context of a burgeoning neo-Hinduism, Western-educated Theosophists such as Mohini Chatterji and Subba Row provided Blavatsky with information about *Advaita Vedanta,* furnishing her with the terminology necessary to elaborate reincarnation in Vedantic terms. Blavatsky could not escape her neo-Platonic heritage, however. Her esotericising interpretations of Plato and his followers had already been present in *Isis Unveiled* and they persisted in *The Secret Doctrine,* sometimes explicitly and sometimes as a subtext. Blavatsky drew on contemporary scholarship of Buddhism to append the concept of *Adi Buddha* to her emanationary, reincarnationist cosmology in a modernising interpretation that identified Buddhism and Hinduism (in their supposedly true, esoteric interpretations) with Theosophy. This multifaceted entanglement was a crucial aspect of the emergence of Blavatsky's reincarnationism as a modern and global phenomenon, a characteristic perhaps because of which it achieved considerable traction in the decades to follow.

8

Conclusions

AS IS WELL ESTABLISHED in the scholarly literature, Theosophy represented an attempt to provide unity in the face of the growing pluralism of the modern world.[1] Blavatsky compared this aspect of Theosophy with the notion of *sutratman*, which, as we saw in the previous chapter, she had originally elaborated as part of her reincarnation doctrine.

> SOME years ago we remarked that 'the Esoteric Doctrine may well be called the "thread-doctrine", since, like *Sutrâtman*, in the Vedanta philosophy, it passes through and strings together all the ancient philosophical religious systems, and reconciles and explains them all.' We say now it does more. It not only reconciles the various and apparently conflicting systems, but it checks the discoveries of modern exact science, and shows some of them to be necessarily correct, since they are found corroborated in the ancient records. All this will, no doubt, be regarded as terribly impertinent and disrespectful, a veritable crime of *lèse-Science*; nevertheless, it is a fact.[2]

For Blavatsky, like the thread on which lives were hung, Theosophy was the thread on which all philosophies and religions were hung, reconciling them and revealing their contradictions as merely apparent ones.

---

[1] Washington, *Blavatsky's Baboon*, 9; McMahen, 'Scientific Buddhism', 920; Bevir, 'West Turns Eastward', 758.
[2] *Secret Doctrine I*, 610

Blavatsky was an admirer of Ralph Waldo Emerson, whose embrace of Asian thought alongside neo-Platonism prefigured her own. Lawrence Buell argued that part of Emerson's appeal was the suggestive character of his writings; in a context in which the rational had been to some extent discredited, Emerson focused on moral uplift and inspiration rather than specific facts.[3] The opposite can be said of Blavatsky, whose writings (no matter how imperfectly they achieved this) were concerned with connecting the dots of historical and doctrinal particularities as concretely as possible. Theosophy certainly represented—as Stephen Prothero put it so well—an elite attempt to 'uplift' Spiritualism from its perceived philosophical vulgarities, but Blavatsky achieved this by 'pinning things down', stringing together, for example, components of Spiritualist rebirth theories with the minutiae of ancient histories and etymologies she derived from her extensive reading.

On more than one occasion, colleagues have suggested that Blavatsky's writings resist easy exegesis. This is certainly true, they do resist *easy* exegesis. They certainly do not resist *any* exegesis, however. Her methods may seem unorthodox, unsystematic, and perhaps even unethical (to those who would cast her as a plagiarist), but this does not mean there is no unity or profundity of thought to be discerned in her books, articles, and letters. Inconsistencies and contradictions notwithstanding, there is a clear coherence, and although one of the central theses of this book has been that Blavatsky changed her mind about rebirth, tried to cover up the change, and failed, I have also shown that there was continuity in her thinking. Indeed, it would be a mistake to ignore either the continuities or the discontinuities at the expense of each other; both are there. She may have changed her mind about the form rebirth took, but she displayed similar tendencies of thought throughout her life. Rebirth always had some sort of cyclic element, it was always progressive, and it was always about the conservation of life as if it were a form of energy that could not disappear but only change form. These fundamentals remained even as Blavatsky's perspectives

---

[3] Lawrence I. Buell, 'Reading Emerson for the Structures: The Coherence of the Essays', in *Emerson's Essays*, ed. Harold Bloom (New York: Chelsea House, 2006), 51.

developed through the assimilation of more and more information and experience.

It is precisely Blavatsky's tendency towards incessant quotation, allusion, and name-dropping that makes her so useful to the historian. Our close readings of Blavatsky's theories of metempsychosis and reincarnation have uncovered diverse underling textual sources, including those Blavatsky believed confirmed her ideas and those whose theories she believed she had disproved. Her doctrine of metempsychosis had derived, largely, from one specific current of Anglo-American Spiritualism, and had been underpinned by a Romantic, progressivist evolutionism. Blavatsky brought this together with the American neo-Platonism of Alexander Wilder and the natural philosophy of Stewart and Tait's *The Unseen Universe*. This conglomerate doctrine then metamorphosed into the fractal macrocosmic reincarnationism of Blavatsky's *Secret Doctrine* period, in conversation with the neo-*Vedanta* of upper-caste Western-educated Theosophists in India and the reincarnation theory of Anna Bonus Kingsford. These stood side by side in Blavatsky's discussions of reincarnation with a variety of scientific theories, especially those associated with the 'eclipse of Darwinism' during the 1880s.

The four final chapters of this study set these adaptations of Blavatsky's in relief against signal late nineteenth-century cultural trends such as the Spiritualist craze, the growth of science and debates surrounding its relationship with metaphysics, widespread interest in the Classical world, nineteenth-century Orientalism, and the emergence of the modernising interpretations of Hinduism and Buddhism of Asian and Western spokespersons. The discussion revealed the various elements of Blavatsky rebirth doctrines to be inseparable from the nineteenth-century discourses among which they arose, lending support to Michael Bergunder's claim that the rise of categories such as 'esotericism', 'science', 'Hinduism', and 'Buddhism' in the late nineteenth century had closely related, entangled, and global histories.[4] Indeed, Blavatsky's theories demonstrate that it is impossible to understand any one of her constructions without reference to the others; her definitions of Hinduism,

[4] Michael Bergunder, ' "Religion" and "Science" within a Global Religious History', *Aries* 16 (86–141).

Buddhism, and science, as well as Platonism and Spiritualism, were all interdependent. They were also built in opposition to Blavatsky's 'Others': scientists deemed materialists, Orientalist scholars who had misunderstood their texts, orthodox Brahmins and Buddhists, French Spiritists, and all the other authorities Blavatsky admonished. Because it arose in response to such diverse stimuli and in such varied contexts, Blavatsky's reincarnation doctrine could be said to be many things at once: an alternative to Darwinian natural selection, a critique of contemporary Spiritualism, part of an esoteric history of religion, and a response to colonialism. Through the prism of historical analysis, therefore, one doctrine—reincarnation—can be refracted into many colours to reveal aspects of the intellectual and cultural world of nineteenth century Europe, America, and India in a spectrum of new and interconnected lights.

What might the attraction of such a doctrine have been to Blavatsky (and her readers)? Presumably, she eventually came to find the later doctrine of reincarnation more appealing than the metempsychosis of her earlier period, which she had re-modelled. If *Isis Unveiled* was to be believed, no matter how talented they were, Spiritualist mediums were incapable of contacting dead loved ones at séances because only the empy astral shells of the deceased were available. The departed would probably have been annihilated, since only very few achieved immortality and transmigrated to the next sphere. Metempsychosis wasn't an especially democratic doctrine, or indeed a comforting one.

This wasn't as much the case with reincarnation. In the theory Blavatsky presented in *The Secret Doctrine* and other later writings, one might still not have expected to converse with the dead at séances, but one might have been comforted by the idea of them enjoying some good karma in *devachan*. They would eventually return to Earth to continue their evolution, progressing through multiple lives on Earth and in due course continuing to higher globes. However, although reincarnation could be perceived as a more consoling and democratic doctrine than metempsychosis, it still placed a greater distance between the living and the dead than did Theosophy's main rival in the reincarnationist turf wars: French Spiritism. Clearly, there were going to those who preferred the idea that séance spirits were more that clattering astral trash.

Blavatsky was quite disdainful of such a perspective. She insisted on at least a thousand years between each rebirth and that even if you reincarnated at around the same time as your deceased loved one, neither of you would be "yourselves" anymore. New babies could never be the reincarnations of recently deceased friends and relatives. Even though it was perhaps easier to digest than metempsychosis had been, Blavatsky's reincarnation theory could still be perceived as less consoling than Kardec's. It was rather impersonal in nature, emphasising grand, cosmic evolutionary schemes over and above the emotional needs of grieving individuals. The one need Blavatsky was compelled to address was the necessity to explain the apparent injustices of life. Karma solved this problem nicely, at least for the present moment, in which karma was operative. What it meant for the aeons before human egos existed and karma emerged, Blavatsky never explained.

For Blavatsky, reincarnation was about the significance of the current moment in time and humanity's power to grasp it by aligning itself with the cosmos' inherent evolutionary drive. Like many commentators of the fin de siècle, she felt (and quite rightly) that she was living in a pivotal historical moment. Unlike the better-known authors, however, Blavatsky's interpretation was an occultist one: the critical juncture was incarnation as a human of the fifth root race of the fourth round of the Earth Chain. This was the point of exact equilibrium between spirit and matter, and humanity was responsible for assisting in the upward turn towards (re-)spiritualisation. Was it all about the impersonal 'tides' of the cosmos, the great 'inbreaths' and 'outbreaths' of Brahma to which Blavatsky referred, or was humanity capable of affecting the progress of evolution with its choices? It wasn't always clear. Karma had a supporting (but perhaps not starring) role in the drama of evolution while sitting at the core of Blavatsky's theodicy. Absorption in the Divine, nirvana, could only be achieved through 'aeons of suffering' and through knowing evil, as well as good, (i.e. through karma).[5] This tension between the progressive orthogenesis of the cosmos on the one hand and the emphasis on human power, choice, and karma on the other was never really resolved. Both were important elements of Blavatsky's thought.

---

[5] Blavatsky, *Secret Doctrine II*, 81.

In short, Blavatsky's reincarnation doctrine could be appealing as a solution to the great problems of life, suffering, and death for modern, liberal, and scientifically minded individuals. Those who embraced it were usually middle class and well educated, and probably yearned for an all-encompassing spirituality that was unsentimental yet to some degree consoling. Drawing on many of the trends of the day (Classicism, Orientalism, Spiritualism) it was a fashionably dressed theory that responded to the most current concerns. As a supposed revival of ancient wisdom, reincarnationism nodded towards a widespread nineteenth-century nostalgia for times gone by while simultaneously committed to the future as part of a universal scientific religion that was supposed to resolve the conflict between materialism and theology and unite mankind.

It was this historically and culturally contingent amalgamation that provided the foundations of the reincarnationism of subsequent Theosophical literature and the myriad of Theosophically influenced movements within New Age and alternative spirituality today. Those who developed Blavatsky's reincarnation theory included the influential later Theosophist Charles Leadbeater (1854–1934); the founder of Anthroposophy, Rudolf Steiner (1861–1925); the trance medium Edgar Cayce (1877–1945); and the well-known author on Theosophical themes, Alice Bailey, as well as the numerous thinkers indebted to them.[6] Largely due to the influence of Theosophy and such offshoots, it is no longer unusual for those in the West today who describe themselves as Christians to believe in reincarnation as a form of spiritual progress.[7] Henry Steel Olcott would have been pleased. Until the previous decade, he reminisced, reincarnation had 'been almost unthinkable by the average Western'. This was no longer the case. Multitudes who still rejected it as unproved had 'learned to recognise its value as a hypothesis explaining many of the mysteries of human life'.[8] Olcott had played a minor role in bringing this about but his dear friend and colleague, Blavatsky, had played a major one. That being the case, she was among the principal architects of religion in modern times.

---

[6] Hammer, *Claiming Knowledge*, 469.
[7] Schmidt-Leukel, *Transformation by Integration*, 68.
[8] Olcott, *Old Diary Leaves 5*, 243.

BIBLIOGRAPHY

PRIMARY SOURCES

[No title or author]. *The Theosophist* 5, no. 6 (March 1884), 154.

[No author]. 'Dr Sexton at Cavendish Rooms'. *Medium and Daybreak* 6, no. 275 (9 July 1875), 439.

[No author]. 'Metempsychosis: Mrs. Tappan's Oration at Cavendish Rooms'. *Medium and Daybreak* 6, no. 256 (26 February 1875), 137–139.

[No author]. 'Metempsychosis and Reincarnation'. *Medium and Daybreak* 6, no. 264 (23 April 1875), 266–267.

[No author]. 'The Vedanta Philosophy Expounded by the Society of Benares Pandits and Translated for *the Theosophist* by Pandit Surya Narayen Sec'y'. *The Theosophist* 1, no. 8 (May 1880), 201–202.

[No author]. 'Blavatsky Still Lives'. *The New York Times* (6 January 1889), 10.

Alabaster, Henry. *The Wheel of the Law. Buddhism Illustrated by Siamese Sources.* London: Trübner and Co., 1871.

Anthon, Charles. *A Classical Dictionary.* New York: Harper and Brothers, 1841.

Aristotle. *De Anima*, trans. R. D. Hicks. Amherst: Prometheus Books, 1991.

Arnold, Edwin. *The Light of Asia*. London: Routledge & Kegan Paul, 1964.

Barker, A. Trevor, ed. *The Mahatma Letters to A. P. Sinnett*. London: Unwin, 1923.

Besant, Annie. 'On the Watch Tower'. *Lucifer* 10, no. 57 (May 1892), 177–184.

Blackwell, Anna. *The Philosophy of Existence: The Testimony of the Ages.* London: J. Burns, 1871.

Blavatsky, H. P. 'The Magical Evocation of Apollonius of Tyana: A Chapter from Eliphas Levi'. *Spiritual Scientist* 3, no. 9 (4 November 1875), 104–105.

Blavatsky, H. P. *Isis Unveiled: A Master-Key to the Mysteries of Ancient and Modern Science and Theology*. New York: J. W. Bouton, 1877.

———. 'Fragments from Madame Blavatsky'. In *Blavatsky Collected Writings*, ed. Boris de Zirkoff, vol. 1, 365–368. Wheaton, IL: Theosophical Publishing House, 1950–1991. [Translation from the French, originally published in *La Revue Spirite* (April 1878).]

———. 'The Popular Idea of Soul Survival'. *The Theosophist* 1, no. 3 (Dec 1879), 60–62.

———. 'What Is Theosophy?' In *Blavatsky Collected Writings*, ed. Boris de Zirkoff, vol. 2, 500–507. Wheaton, IL: Theosophical Publishing House, 1950–1991. [Originally published in *La Revue Spirite* (November 1880).]

———. 'Kabalah and Kabalists at the Close of the Nineteenth Century'. *Lucifer* 10, no. 57 (May 1882), 185–196.

———. 'The Adept Brothers'. 'Editor's Note'. *The Theosophist* 3, no. 9 (June 1882), 225–226.

———. ' "Isis Unveiled" and the "Theosophist" on Reincarnation'. *The Theosophist* 3, no. 11 (August 1882), 288–289.

———. 'Theosophy and Spiritism'. In *Blavatsky Collected Writings*, ed. Boris de Zirkoff, vol. 5, 36–65. Wheaton, IL: Theosophical Publishing House, 1950–1991. [Originally published in the *Bulletin Mensuel de la Société Scientifique d'Études Psychologiques* (15 July 1883), 129–151.]

———. 'The Teachings of Allan Kardec'. *The Theosophist* 4, no. 11 (August 1883), 281.

———. 'Nirvana'. *The Theosophist* 5, no. 10 (July 1884), 246.

———. 'Theories about Reincarnation and Spirits'. *The Path* 1, no. 8 (November 1886), 232–245.

———. *The Secret Doctrine: The Synthesis of Science, Religion, and Philosophy*. London: The Theosophical Publishing Company, 1888.

———. 'Force of Prejudice'. *Lucifer* 4, no. 23 (July 1889), 353–360.

———. 'My Books'. *Lucifer* 8, no. 45 (15 May 1891), 241–247.

———. 'Tibetan Teachings'. *Lucifer* 15, nos. 85 and 86 (September and October 1894), 9–17 and 97–104.

———. *The Key to Theosophy*. London and New York: The Theosophical Publishing Company, 1889.

———. *Theosophical Glossary*. Krotona: Theosophical Publishing House, 1918.

———. 'Letter of H. P. B. to Adelberth de Bourbon'. *The Theosophist* 73 (December 1951), 153–158.

———. 'Esoteric Instruction Number Three'. In *Blavatsky Collected Writings*, ed. Boris de Zirkoff, vol. 12, 581–652. Wheaton, IL: Theosophical Publishing House, 1950–1991.

———. 'Esoteric Instruction Number Five'. In *Blavatsky Collected Writings*, ed. Boris de Zirkoff, vol. 12, 691–712. Wheaton, IL: Theosophical Publishing House, 1950–1991.

————. 'Mr Arthur Lillie'. In *Blavatsky Collected Writings*, ed. Boris de Zirkoff, vol. 6, 288–294. Wheaton, IL: Theosophical Publishing House, 1950–1991.

————. 'On Hibernation, the Ârya Samâj, etc'. In *Blavatsky Collected Writings*, ed. Boris de Zirkoff, vol. 6, 313–315. Wheaton, IL: Theosophical Publishing House, 1950–1991.

————. 'Neo-Buddhism'. In *Blavatsky Collected Writings*, ed. Boris de Zirkoff, vol. 12, 334–349. Wheaton, IL: Theosophical Publishing House, 1991.

————. *The Letters of H. P. Blavatsky 1861–1879*, ed. John Algeo. Wheaton, IL, and Chennai: Quest Books, Theosophical Publishing House, 2003.

Bluck, R. S. 'The Phaedrus and Reincarnation'. *American Journal of Philology* 79, no. 2 (1958), 156–164.

A Brahman Theosophist, 'Esoteric Buddhism and Hinduism'. *The Theosophist* 5, no. 9 (June 1884), 223–225.

Britten, Emma Hardinge. *Modern American Spiritualism*. New York: Published by the author, 1870.

————. 'The Doctrine of Re-Incarnation'. *The Spiritual Scientist* 2, no. 11 (20 May 1875), 128–129; and 2, no. 12 (27 May 1875), 140–141.

————. *Art Magic*. New York: Published by the author, 1876.

————, trans. and ed. *Ghost Land; Or Researches into the Mysteries of Occultism*. Boston: Published for the editor, 1876.

Bunsen, C. C. J. *Egypt's Place in Universal History*. London: Longmans, Green, and Co., 1867.

Caithness, Countess of. *Old Truths in a New Light, or, An Earnest Endeavour to Reconcile Material Science with Spiritual Science, and with Scripture*. London: Chapman and Hall, 1876.

Chatterji, Mohini M. 'The Crest-Jewel of Wisdom I'. *The Theosophist* 7, no. 73 (October 1885), 65–68.

————. 'The Crest-Jewel of Wisdom II'. *The Theosophist* 7, no. 76 (January 1886), 253–258.

————. 'The Crest-Jewel of Wisdom III'. *The Theosophist* 7, no. 78 (March 1886), 386–390.

————. 'The Crest-Jewel of Wisdom IV'. *The Theosophist* 7, no. 82 (July 1886), 661–665.

————. 'The Crest-Jewel of Wisdom V'. *The Theosophist* 7, no. 83 (August 1886), 724–732.

Coleman, William Emmette. 'The Sources of Madame Blavatsky's Writings'. In *A Modern Priestess of Isis*, ed. Vsevolod Solovyoff, 353–366. London: Longmans, Green and Co., 1895.

Crookes, William. *Researches in the Phenomena of Spiritualism*. Manchester: Two Worlds, 1926.

Davids, T. W. Rhys. *Buddhism*. London: SPCK, [1877].

Davis, Andrew Jackson. *The Harmonial Philosophy: A Compendium of the Works of Andrew Jackson Davis, edited by A Doctor of Hermetic Science*. London: William Rider, 1923.

Denton, William, and Elizabeth Denton. *The Soul of Things*. Wellesley,
    MA: Denton Publishing Company, 1888.

Dharmadasa, K. N. O. *Language, Religion, and Ethnic Assertiveness: The Growth
    of Sinhalese Nationalism in Sri Lanka*. Ann Arbor: University of Michigan
    Press, 1992.

Dowson, John. *A Classical Dictionary of Hindu Mythology and Religion,
    Geography, History, and Literature*. London: Trübner and Co., 1888.

Dunlap, S. F. *Vestiges of the Spirit-History of Man*. New York: D. Appleton and
    Company, 1858.

Dunlap, S. F. *Sōd: The Mysteries of Adoni*. London: Williams and Norgate, 1861.

———. *Sōd: The Son of The Man*. London and Edinburgh: Williams and
    Norgate, 1861.

Ennemoser, Joseph. *The History of Magic*, trans. William Howitt.
    London: George Bell and Sons, 1893.

Franck, Adolphe. *La Kabbale ou la philosophie religieuse des Hébreux*.
    Paris: Librairie de L. Hachette, 1843.

Gadgil, Rao Bahadar Janardhan Sakharam. 'Hindu Ideas about Communion
    with the Dead'. *The Theosophist* 1, no. 3 (Dec 1879), 68–69.

Gasparin, Agénor de. *Science vs. Spiritualism: A Treatise on Turning Tables, the
    Supernatural in General and Spirits*, trans. E. W. Robert. New York: Kiggins
    and Kellogg, 1857.

Ginsburg, David. *The Kabbalah: Its Doctrines, Development, and Literature. An
    Essay*. London: Longmans, Green, Reader, and Dyer, 1865.

Gunanande, Mohottivatte. 'The Law of the Lord Sakhya Muni'. *The Theosophist*
    1, no. 2 (November 1879), 43–44.

Harris, Thomas Lake. *An Epic of the Starry Heaven*. New York: Partridge and
    Brittan, 1855.

Haug, Martin. *Aitareya Brahmanam of the Rig Veda*. Bombay: Government
    Central Book Depot, 1863.

Hegel, Georg Wilhelm Friedrich. *The Philosophy of History*.
    New York: Dover, 1956.

Higgins, Godfrey. *Anacalypsis: An Attempt to Draw Aside the Veil of the Saitic Isis*.
    London: Longman, Rees, Brown, Green and Longman, 1836.

Hoomi, Koot. 'Letter 9, from Koot Hoomi to A. P. Sinnett, received 8 July
    1881'. In *The Mahatma Letters to A. P. Sinnett*, ed. A. Trevor Barker, 38–51.
    London: Unwin, 1923.

Howitt, William. *The History of the Supernatural*, 2 vols. London: Longman,
    Green, Longman, Roberts and Green, 1863.

[Hume, A. O.]. 'Fragments of Occult Truth'. *The Theosophist* 3, no. 25 (October
    1881), 17–22; *The Theosophist* 3, no. 30 (March 1882), 157–160; *The Theosophist*
    3, no. 36 (September 1882), 307–314.

[Jennings, Hargrave]. *The Indian Religions: Or Results of the Mysterious Buddhism*.
    Thomas Cautley Newby, 1858.

Jennings, Hargrave. *Curious Things of the Outside World. Last Fire.*
London: T. and W. Boone, 1861.

Kaplan, Aryeh, trans. *The Bahir: An Ancient Kabbalistic Text Attributed to Rabbi
Nehuniah ben HaKana.* New York: Samuel Wesier, 1979.

Kardec, Allan. *Le livre des esprits.* Paris: E. Dentu, 1857.

———. *Le livre des médiums.* Paris: Didier et cie, 1861.

———. *The Book on Mediums Or; Guide for Mediums and Invocators*, trans.
Emma Wood. Boston: Colby and Rich, 1874.

———. *The Spirits Book*, trans Anna Blackwell. Boston: Colby and Rich, 1875.

King, C. W. *The Gnostics and Their Remains, Ancient and Medieval.*
London: David Nutt, 1887.

Kingsford, Anna Bonus, and Edward Maitland. *The Perfect Way; or, The Finding
of Christ.* London: Field and Tuer, 1882.

———. 'The Perfect Way'. *The Theosophist* 3, no. 12 (September 1882), 295–296.

Kircher, Athanasius. *Oedipus Aegyptiacus.* Rome: 1652–1654.

Knorr von Rosenroth, Christian. *Kabbala Denudata.* Hildesheim and
New York: George Olms Verlag, 1974.

Laing, Samuel. *Modern Science and Modern Thought.* London: Chapman and
Hall, 1885.

Lempriere [*sic*], J. *A Classical Dictionary.* London: T. Cadell and W. Davies, 1820.

Lévi, Eliphas. *La clef des grandes mystères.* Paris: Germer Baillière, 1861.

Lévi, Eliphas. *The History of Magic*, trans. A. E. Waite. London: Rider and
Co., 1974.

MacGregor Mathers, Samuel Liddell. *The Kabbalah Unveiled.* London: George
Redway, 1887.

Maitland, Edward. *Anna Kingsford: Her Life, Letters, Diary, and Work.*
London: George Redway, 1896.

Maitland, Edward. *The Story of Anna Kingsford and Edward Maitland and of the
New Gospel of Interpretation.* Birmingham: Ruskin Press, 1905.

Massey, Charles Carlton. ' "Isis Unveiled" and the "Theosophist" on
Reincarnation'. *Light* 79, no. 2 (8 July 1882), 323.

Matt, Daniel, et al., trans. *The Zohar: Pritzker Edition*, 12 vols. Stanford: Stanford
University Press, 2003–2017.

Mead, George Robert Stowe. 'A Proposed Enquiry Concerning "Reincarnation
in the Church Fathers" '. *The Theosophical Review* 37 (December 1905),
329–330.

———. 'Origen on Reincarnation'. *The Theosophical Review* 37 (February 1906),
513–527.

———. 'Irenaeus on Reincarnation'. *The Theosophical Review* 38 (March
1906), 38–48.

———. 'Justin Martyr on Reincarnation'. *The Theosophical Review* 38 (April
1906), 129–136.

———. 'Reincarnation in the Christian Tradition'. *The Theosophical Review* 38
(April 1906), 253–259.

————, ed. 'The Pistis Sophia'. With additional notes by Helena Petrovna Blavatsky. *Lucifer* 8, no. 45 (15 May 1891), 201–204.

Moor, Edward. *The Hindu Pantheon*. London: K. Johnson, 1810.

Mosheim, Johann Lorenz. *Institutionum historiae ecclesiasticae antiquioris et recentioris libri IV*. Helmstedt: 1726–1755.

Murdock, James. *Mosheim's Institutes of Ecclesiastical History, Ancient and Modern*. London: William Tegg, 1867.

Myer, Isaac. *Qabbalah*. Philadelphia: Published by the author, 1888.

Olcott, Henry Steel. 'Death of T. Subba Row, B. A., B. L'. *The Theosophist* 11, no. 130 (July 1890), 576–578.

————. *Old Diary Leaves First Series*. New York and London: G. P. Putnam's Sons, 1895.

————. *Old Diary Leaves Second Series 1878–83*. Adyar: The Theosophical Publishing House, 1974.

————. *Old Diary Leaves Third Series 1883–87*. Adyar: Theosophical Publishing House, 1929.

Payne-Knight, Richard. *The Symbolical Language of Ancient Art and Mythology*. New York: J. W. Bouton, 1876.

Plato. *Complete Works*, ed. John M.Cooper. Indianapolis: Hackett, 1997.

Plotinus. *The Enneads*, trans. Stephen MacKenna. London: Penguin, 1991.

Podmore, Frank. *Studies in Psychical Research*. London: Kegan Paul, Trench, Trübner & Co., 1887.

Quatrefages, A. De. *The Human Species*. New York: D. Appleton, 1890.

Randolph, Paschal Beverly. *After Death; or; Disembodied Man*. Boston: Printed for the author, 1868.

[Randolph, Paschal Beverly]. *Dealings with the Dead; The Human Soul, Its Migrations and Transmigrations*. Utica: M. J. Randolph, 1861–1862.

Rockhill, W. Woodville. *The Life of the Buddha*. London: Trübner and Co., 1884.

Sankhadar, Babu Jwala Prasad. 'Aeen-I-Hoshang'. *The Theosophist* 3, no. 8 (May 1882), 210–211.

Schlagintweit, Emil. *Buddhism in Tibet*. Leipzig: F. A. Brockhaus, 1863.

Schmidt, Oscar. *The Doctrine of Descent and Darwinism*. London: Henry S. King and Co., 1875.

Shastri, Rama Misra. 'The Vedant Darsana'. *The Theosophist* 1, no. 6 (March 1880), 158–159.

Sinnett, Alfred Percy. *The Occult World*. London: Trübner and Co., 1881.

————. 'Review of The Perfect Way'. *The Theosophist* 3, no. 9 (June 1882), 232–235.

————. *Esoteric Buddhism*. London: Trübner and Co., 1883.

————. *Incidents in the Life of Madame Blavatsky*. New York: J. W. Bouton, 1886.

Snell, Merwin-Marie. 'Modern Theosophy in Its Relation to Hinduism and Buddhism II'. *The Biblical World* 5 (1895), 258–265.

Solovyoff, Vsevolod, ed. *A Modern Priestess of Isis*. London: Longmans, Green and Co., 1895.

Spencer, Herbert. *First Principles of a New System of Philosophy*. London: Williams and Norgate, 1870.

Stallo, J. B. *Concepts and Theories of Modern Physics*. London: Kegan and Paul, Trench and Co., 1882.

Stewart, Balfour, and Peter Guthrie Tait. *The Unseen Universe, or, Physical Speculations on a Future State*. New York: Macmillan, 1875.

Sumangala, H. 'The Nature and Office of Buddha's Religion I', *The Theosophist* 1, no. 2 (November 1879), 43.

———. 'The Nature and Office of Buddha's Religion II'. *The Theosophist* 1, no. 5 (February 1880), 122.

———. 'The Buddhist Idea about Soul'. *The Theosophist* 1, no. 6 (March 1880), 144.

Walker, E. D. *Reincarnation: A Study in Forgotten Truth*. New York: John W. Lovell, 1888.

Wilder, Alexander. 'How "Isis Unveiled" Was Written'. *The Word* 7 (April–September 1908), 78–87.

———. *The Later Platonists and Other Miscellaneous Writings of Alexander Wilder*. Henry County, Ohio: Kitchen Press, 2009.

Wilson, H. H. *Vishnu Purana*. London: John Murray, 1840.

Winchell, Alexander. *World Life*. Chicago: S. C. Griggs and Company, 1883.

Zeller, Eduard. *Plato and the Older Academy*, trans. Sarah Frances Alleyne and Alfred Goodwin. London: Longmans, Green and Co., 1876.

SECONDARY SOURCES

Abrams, M. H. *Natural Supernaturalism: Tradition and Revolution in Romantic Literature*. New York and London: W. W. Norton 1973.

Albanese, Catherine L. *A Republic of Mind and Spirit: A Cultural History of American Metaphysical Religion*. New Haven: Yale University Press, 2007.

Almond, Philip C. *The British Discovery of Buddhism*. Cambridge: Cambridge University Press, 1988.

Anderson, Paul. *Platonism in the Midwest*. New York: Columbia University Press.

Ashcraft, W. Michael. *The Dawn of the New Cycle: Point Loma Theosophists and American Culture*. Knoxville: University of Tennessee Press, 2002.

Asprem, Egil. 'Theosophical Attitudes towards Science: Past and Present'. In *Handbook of the Theosophical Current*, ed. Olav Hammer and Michael Rothstein, 405–428. Leiden and Boston: Brill, 2013.

———. 'Science and the Occult'. In *The Occult World*, ed. Christopher Partridge, 710–719. Abingdon: Routledge, 2015.

Baier, Karl. *Meditation und Moderne: Zur Genese eines Kernbereichs moderner Spiritualität in der Wechselwirkung zwischen Westeuropa, Nordamerika, und Asien*. Würzburg: Königshausen & Neumann Verlag, 2009.

————. 'Theosophical Orientalism and the Structures of Intercultural
     Transfer: Annotations on the Appropriation of the *cakras* in early Theosophy'.
     In *Theosophical Appropriations: Esotericism, Kabbalah, and the Transformation
     of Traditions*, ed. Julie Chajes and Boaz Huss, 318–319. Beer Sheva: Ben-
     Gurion University Press, 2016.
Barton, Ruth. 'John Tyndall, Pantheist: A Rereading of the Belfast Address'.
     Osiris 2, no. 3 (1987), 111–134.
Bauduin, Tessel. 'The Occult and the Visual Arts'. In *The Occult World*, ed.
     Christopher Partridge, 429–445. Abingdon: Routledge, 2015.
Bender, Courtney. 'American Reincarnations: What the Many Lives of Past
     Lives Tell Us about Contemporary Spiritual Practice'. *Journal of the American
     Academy of Religion* 75, no. 3 (September 2007), 589–614.
Benz, Ernst. *Emanuel Swedenborg*. West Chester, PA: Swedenborg
     Foundation, 2002.
Bergunder, Michael. 'What Is Esotericism? Cultural Studies Approaches and the
     Problems of Definition in Religious Studies'. *Method and Theory in the Study
     of Religions* 22, no. 1 (2010), 9–36.
————. 'Experiments with Theosophical Truth: Gandhi, Esotericism, and
     Global Religious History'. *Journal of the American Academy of Religion* 82, no.
     2 (1 June 2014), 398–426.
————. '"Religion" and "Science" Within a Global Religious History'. *Aries* 16,
     no. 1 (2016), 86–141.
Bevir, Mark. 'The West Turns Eastward: Madame Blavatsky and the
     Transformation of the Occult Tradition'. *Journal of the American Academy of
     Religion* 62, no. 3 (1994), 747–767.
Blumenthal, H. J. *Plotinus' Psychology: His Doctrines of the Embodied Soul*. The
     Hague: Martinus Nijhoff, 1971.
Bogdan, Henrik, and Gordan Djurdjevic, eds. *Occultism in a Global Perspective*.
     Durham: Acumen, 2013.
Bowler, Peter J. 'Holding Your Head Up High: Degeneration and Orthogenesis
     in Theories of Human Evolution'. In *History, Humanity, and Evolution: Essays
     for John C. Greene*, ed. James R. Moore, 329–353. Cambridge: Cambridge
     University Press, 1989.
Bowler, Peter J. *The Eclipse of Darwinism*. Baltimore and London: Johns
     Hopkins University Press, 1992.
Braude, Anne. *Radical Spirits: Spiritualism and Women's Rights in Nineteenth-
     Century America*. Boston: Beacon Press, 1989.
Bremmer, Jan. *The Rise and Fall of the Afterlife*. London: Routledge, 2002.
Brock, William Hodson. *William Crookes (1832–1919) and the Commercialization
     of Science*. Aldershot: Ashgate, 2008.
Burkert, Walter. *Lore and Science in Ancient Pythagoreanism*, trans. Edwin L.
     Minar Jr. Cambridge, MA: Harvard University Press, 1972.

Burkhardt, Frederick, Samantha Evans, and Alison M. Pearn,
   eds. *Evolution: Selected Letters of Charles Darwin 1860–1870*.
   Cambridge: Cambridge University Press, 2008.
Campbell, Bruce F. *Ancient Wisdom Revived: A History of the Theosophical
   Movement*. Berkeley: University of California Press, 1980.
Carlson, Maria. *No Religion Higher Than the Truth*. Princeton, NJ: Princeton
   University Press, 1993.
Chajes, Julie (née Hall). 'The Saptaparna: The Meaning and Origins of the
   Theosophical Septenary Constitution of Man'. *Theosophical History* 13, no. 4
   (October 2007), 5–38.
———. 'Metempsychosis and Reincarnation in *Isis Unveiled*'. *Theosophical
   History* 16, nos. 3 & 4 (July–October 2012), 128–150.
———. 'Blavatsky and Monotheism: Towards the Historicisation of a Critical
   Category'. *Journal of Religion in Europe* 9 (2016): 247–275.
———. 'Construction through Appropriation: Kabbalah in Blavatsky's Early
   Works'. In *Theosophical Appropriations: Esotericism, Kabbalah, and the
   Transformation of Traditions*, ed. Julie Chajes and Boaz Huss, 33–72. Beer
   Sheva: Ben-Gurion University Press, 2016.
———. 'Reincarnation in H. P. Blavatsky's *The Secret Doctrine*'. *Correspondences*
   5 (2017), 65–93.
———. 'Blavatsky and the Lives Sciences', *Aries* 18 (2018), 258–286.
———. 'Orientalist Aggregates: Theosophical Buddhism between Innovation
   and Tradition'. In *Festschrift for Nicholas Goodrick-Clarke*, ed. Tim Rudbøg
   and Jo Hedesan. Forthcoming.
Chajes, Julie, and Boaz Huss, eds. *Theosophical Appropriations: Esotericism,
   Kabbalah, and the Transformation of Traditions*. Beer Sheva: Ben-Gurion
   University Press, 2016.
Chidester, David. 'Colonialism'. In *Guide to the Study of Religion*, ed. W. Braun
   and R. T. McCutcheon, 423–437. New York: Cassell, 2000.
Chrysiddes, George D. 'Defining the New Age'. In *Handbook of the New Age*, ed.
   Daren Kemp and James R. Lewis. Leiden: Brill, 2007, 5–24.
Clarke, Bruce. *Dora Marsden and Early Modernism: Gender, Individualism,
   Science*. Ann Arbor: University of Michigan, 1996.
———. *Energy Forms: Allegory and Science in the Era of Classical
   Thermodynamics*. Ann Arbor: University of Michigan Press, 2001.
Clarke, J. J. *Oriental Enlightenment: The Encounter between Asian and Western
   Thought*. London: Routledge, 1997.
Clothey, Fred W. *Religion in India: A Historical Introduction*.
   Abingdon: Routledge, 2006.
Cohen, Daniel J. *Equations from God: Pure Mathematics and Victorian Faith*.
   Baltimore: Johns Hopkins University Press, 2007.
Cohen, Lara Langer. *The Fabrication of American Literature*.
   Philadelphia: University of Pennsylvania Press, 2012.

Cooter, Roger, and Stephen Pumfrey. 'Separate Spheres and Public
    Places: Reflections on the History of Science Popularization and Science in
    Popular Culture'. *History of Science* 32 (1994), 237–267.
Cranston, Sylvia. *H. P. B. The Extraordinary Life and Influence of Helena
    Blavatsky, Founder of the Theosophical Movement.* New York: G. P. Putnam's
    Sons, 1993.
Curl, James Stevens. *The Egyptian Revival: Ancient Egypt as the Inspiration for
    Design Motifs in the West.* London and New York: Routledge, 2005.
Dan, Joseph. *The Christian Kabbalah: Jewish Mystical Books & Their Christian
    Interpreters: A Symposium.* Cambridge, MA: Harvard College Library, 1997.
Dawson, Andrew. 'East Is East, Except When It's West'. *Journal of Religion and
    Society* 8 (2006), 1–13.
De Michelis, Elizabeth. *A History of Modern Yoga: Patañjali and Western
    Esotericism.* London: Continuum, 2008.
Deveney, John Patrick. *Paschal Beverly Randolph: A Nineteenth-Century Black
    American Spiritualist, Rosicrucian, and Sex Magician.* Albany: State University
    of New York Press, 1997.
Deveney, John Patrick. 'Astral Projection or Liberation of the Double and the
    Work of the Early Theosophical Society'. *Theosophical History Occasional
    Papers* 6 (1997).
———. 'Sauce for the Goose: William Emmette Coleman's Defence to a
    Charge of Plagiarism'. *Theosophical History* 8, no. 10 (October 2002), 272–273.
———. 'D. E. de Lara, John Storer Cobb, and The New Era'. *Theosophical
    History* 15, no. 4 (2011), 27–33.
———. 'The Two Theosophical Societies: Prolonged Life, Conditional
    Immortality, and the Individualized Immortal Monad'. In *Theosophical
    Appropriations: Esotericism, Kabbalah, and the Transformation of Traditions,*
    ed. Julie Chajes and Boaz Huss, 93–114. Beer Sheva: Ben-Gurion University
    Press, 2016.
Dixon, Joy. *Divine Feminine: Theosophy and Feminism in England.* Baltimore and
    London: Johns Hopkins University Press, 2001.
Dodin, Thierry, and Heinz Räther, eds. *Imagining Tibet.* Boston: Wisdom
    Publications, 2001.
Eek, Sven. *Dâmodar and the Pioneers of the Theosophical Movement.*
    Adyar: Theosophical Publishing House, 1978.
Ellwood, Robert S. 'The American Theosophical Synthesis'. In *The Occult in
    America: New Historical Perspectives,* ed. Howard Kerr and Charles L. Crow,
    111–134. Urbana and Chicago: University of Illinois Press, 1986.
Evangelista, Stefano. *British Aestheticism and Ancient Greece: Hellenism, Reception,
    Gods in Exile.* Basingstoke, Hampshire: Palgrave Macmillan, 2009.
Faivre, Antoine. 'Egyptomany'. In *Dictionary of Gnosis and Western Esotericism,*
    ed. Wouter Hanegraaff, in collaboration with Antoine Faivre, Roelof van den
    Broek, and Jean-Pierre Brach, 328–330. Leiden and Boston: Brill, 2006.

Faivre, Antoine. *Western Esotericism*. Albany: State University of New York Press, 2010.

Ferentinou, Victoria. 'Light from Within or Light from Above? Theosophical Appropriations in Early Twentieth-Century Greek Culture'. In *Theosophical Appropriations: Esotericism, Kabbalah, and the Transformation of Traditions*, ed. Julie Chajes and Boaz Huss, 273–307. Beer Sheva: Ben-Gurion University Press, 2016.

Ferguson, Christine. 'Recent Studies in Nineteenth-Century Spiritualism'. *Literature Compass* 9, no. 6 (2012), 431–440.

Fideler, David. 'Introduction'. In *The Pythagorean Sourcebook and Library: An Anthology of Ancient Writings Which Relate to Pythagoras and Pythagorean Philosophy*, ed. Kenneth Sylvan Guthrie and David Fideler, 19–54. Grand Rapids: Phanes Press, 1988.

Finkelstein, Gabriel. *Emil Du Bois Reymond: Neuroscience, Self, and Society in Nineteenth-Century Germany*. Cambridge and London: MIT Press, 2013.

Forshaw, Peter J. 'Kabbalah'. In *The Occult World*, ed. Christopher Partridge, 541–551. Abingdon: Routledge, 2015.

French, Brendan. 'Blavatsky, Dostoevski, and Occult *Starchestvo*'. *Aries* 7, no. 2 (2007), 161–184.

Fuller, Robert C. *Mesmerism and the American Cure of Souls*. Philadelphia: University of Pennsylvania Press, 1982.

———. *Spiritual, but Not Religious: Understanding Unchurched America*. Oxford: Oxford University Press, 2011.

Gange, David. *Dialogues with the Dead: Egyptology in British Culture and Religion, 1822–1922*. Oxford: Oxford University Press, 2013.

Gauld, Alan. *A History of Hypnotism*. Cambridge: Cambridge University Press, 1992.

Gethin, Rupert. *The Foundations of Buddhism*. Oxford: Oxford University Press, 1998.

Gilbert, Robert. *The Great Chain of Unreason: The Publication and Distribution of the Literature of Rejected Knowledge in England During the Victorian Era*. Unpublished PhD Thesis, University of London, 2009.

Godwin, Joscelyn. *The Beginnings of Theosophy in France*. London: Theosophical History, 1989.

———. *The Theosophical Enlightenment*. Albany: State University of New York Press, 1994.

———. 'Lady Caithness and Her Connection with Theosophy'. *Theosophical History* 8, no. 4 (October 2000), 127–146.

Godwin, Joscelyn, Christian Chanel, and John Patrick Deveney. *The Hermetic Brotherhood of Luxor: Initiatic and Historical Documents of an Order of Practical Occultism*. York Beach: Samuel Weiser, 1995.

Goldhill, Simon. *Victorian Culture and Classical Antiquity: Art, Opera, Fiction, and the Proclamation of Modernity*. Princeton, NJ: Princeton University Press, 2011.

Gombrich, Richard, and Gananath Obeyesekere. *Buddhism Transformed: Religious Change in Sri Lanka*. Princeton, NJ: Princeton University Press, 1988.

Gomes, Michael. *Theosophy in the Nineteenth Century: An Annotated Bibliography*. New York and London: Garland Publishing, 1994.

Goodrick-Clarke, Clare, and Nicholas Goodrick-Clarke, eds. *G. R. S. Mead and the Gnostic Quest*. Berkeley, CA: North Atlantic Books, 2005.

Goodrick-Clarke, Nicholas. *Helena Blavatsky*. Berkeley, CA: North Atlantic Books, 2004.

———. 'The Theosophical Society, Orientalism, and the "Mystic East": Western Esotericism and Eastern Religion in Theosophy'. *Theosophical History* 13 (2007), 3–28.

———. 'Western Esoteric Traditions and Theosophy'. In *Handbook of the Theosophical Current*, ed. Olav Hammer and Michael Rothstein, 261–307. Leiden and Boston: Brill, 2013.

Granholm, Kennet. 'Locating the West: Problematizing the *Western* in Western Esotericism and Occultism'. In *Occultism in a Global Perspective*, ed. Henrik Bogdan and Gordan Djurdjevic, 17–26. Durham: Acumen, 2013.

Gregory, Frederick. *Scientific Materialism in Nineteenth-Century Germany*. Dordrecht and Boston: D. Reidel Publishing Company, 1977.

Gutierrez, Cathy. *Plato's Ghost*. Oxford: Oxford University Press, 2009.

———. 'Spiritualism: Communication with the Dead'. *Religion Compass* 4, no. 12 (2010), 737–745.

Hammer, Olav. *Claiming Knowledge: Strategies of Epistemology from Theosophy to the New Age*. Leiden: Brill, 2004.

———. 'Jewish Mysticism Meets the Age of Aquarius: Elizabeth Clare Prophet on the Kabbalah'. In *Theosophical Appropriations*, ed. Julie Chajes and Boaz Huss, 223–242. Beer Sheva: Ben Gurion University Press, 2016.

Hammer, Olav, and Michael Rothstein, eds. *Handbook of the Theosophical Current*. Leiden and Boston: Brill, 2013.

Hanegraaff, Wouter J. *New Age Religion and Western Culture: Western Esotericism in the Mirror of Secular Thought*. Leiden: Brill, 1996.

———. 'Esotericism'. In *Dictionary of Gnosis and Western Esotericism*, ed. Wouter Hanegraaff, in collaboration with Antoine Faivre, Roelof van den Broek, and Jean-Pierre Brach, 336–340. Leiden: Brill, 2006.

———. 'The New Age Movement and Western Esotericism'. In *Handbook of the New Age*, ed. Daren Kemp and James R. Lewis, 25–50. Leiden: Brill, 2007.

———. 'The Globalisation of Esotericism.' *Correspondences* 3 (2015), 55–91.

———. 'The Theosophical Imagination'. *Correspondences* 5 (2017), 3–39.

———. 'Western Esotericism and the Orient in the First Theosophical Society'. In *Theosophy across Boundaries*, ed. Hans-Martin Krämer and Julian Strube. Forthcoming.

————, ed., in collaboration with Antoine Faivre, Roelof van den Broek, and Jean-Pierre Brach. *Dictionary of Gnosis and Western Esotericism*. Leiden and Boston: Brill 2006.

Hanes, W. Travis. 'On the Origins of the Indian National Congress: A Case Study of Cross-Cultural Synthesis'. *Journal of World History* 4, no. 1 (Spring 1993), 69–98.

Harper, George Mills. *The Neoplatonism of William Blake*. Chapel Hill: University of North Carolina Press, 1961.

Harrington, Melissa. 'Paganism and the New Age'. In *Handbook of the New Age*, ed. Daren Kemp and James R. Lewis, 435–452. Leiden: Brill, 2007.

Heelas, Paul. *The New Age Movement: The Celebration of the Self and the Sacralization of Modernity*. Oxford: Blackwell, 1996.

Heimann, P. M. 'The "Unseen Universe": Physics and the Philosophy of Nature in Victorian Britain'. *The British Journal for the History of Science* 6, no. 1 (June 1972), 73–79.

Huss, Boaz. 'The New Age of Kabbalah'. *Journal of Modern Jewish Studies* 6, no. 2 (2007), 107–125.

————. 'Spirituality: The Emergence of a New Cultural Category and Its Challenge to the Religious and the Secular'. *Journal of Contemporary Religion* 29, no. 1 (2014), 47–60.

————. 'Qabbalah, the Theos-Sophia of the Jews: Jewish Theosophists and Their Perceptions of Kabbalah'. In *Theosophical Appropriations: Esotericism, Kabbalah, and the Transformation of Traditions*, ed. Julie Chajes and Boaz Huss, 137–166. Beer Sheva: Ben-Gurion University Press, 2016.

Hutch, Richard A. 'Helena Blavatsky Unveiled'. *The Journal of Religious History* 11, no. 2 (December 1980), 320–341.

Hutton, Ronald. *Triumph of the Moon: A History of Modern Pagan Witchcraft*. Oxford: Oxford University Press, 1999.

Idel, Moshe. 'Kabbalah, Platonism, and Prisca Theologia: The Case of R. Menasseh ben Israel'. In *Menasseh ben Israel and His World*, ed. Y. Kaplan, H. Méchoulan, et al., 207–219. Leiden: Brill, 1989.

Introvigne, Massimo. 'Lawren Harris and the Theosophical Appropriation of Canadian Nationalism'. In *Theosophical Appropriations: Esotericism, Kabbalah, and the Transformation of Traditions*, ed. Julie Chajes and Boaz Huss, 355–386. Beer Sheva: Ben-Gurion University Press, 2016.

Irwin, Lee. *Reincarnation in America: An Esoteric History*. Lanham, MD, and London: Lexington Books, 2017.

Irwin, Lee. 'Reincarnation in America: A Brief Historical Overview'. *Religions* 8, no. 10 (2017), 222.

Jackson, Carl T. *The Oriental Religions and American Thought: Nineteenth-Century Explorations*. Westport, CT, and London: Greenwood Press, 1981.

Jenkins, Richard. *The Victorians and Ancient Greece*. Oxford: John Wiley and Sons, 1981.

Johnson, K. Paul. *In Search of the Masters*. South Boston: Self-published, 1990.

————. *The Masters Revealed: Madame Blavatsky and the Myth of the Great White Lodge*. Albany: State University of New York Press, 1994.

Kaplan, Y., H. Méchoulan, and Richard H. Popkin, eds. *Menasseh ben Israel and His World*. Leiden: Brill, 1989.

Karuanatilake, H. N. S. 'The Local and Foreign Impact of the Pânadurâ Vadaya'. *Journal of the Royal Asiatic Society of Sri Lanka*, New Series, 49 (2004), 67–86.

Kemp, Daren. 'Christians and New Age'. In *Handbook of the New Age*, ed. Daren Kemp and James R. Lewis, 453–472. Leiden: Brill, 2007.

Kemp, Daren, and James R. Lewis, eds. *Handbook of the New Age*. Leiden: Brill, 2007.

Kerr, Howard, and Charles L. Crow, eds. *The Occult in America: New Historical Perspectives*. Urbana and Chicago: University of Illinois Press, 1986.

King, Richard. *Orientalism and Religion: Postcolonial Theory, India, and 'The Mystic East'*. London and New York: Routledge, 2001.

Kohler, George. 'Judaism Buried or Revitalised? *Wissenschaft des Judentums* in Nineteenth-Century Germany—Impact, Actuality, and Applicability Today'. In *Jewish Thought and Jewish Belief*, ed. D. J. Lasker, 27–63. Beer Sheva: Ben-Gurion University Press, 2012.

Kontou, Tatiana, and Sarah Wilburn. *Ashgate Research Companion to Nineteenth-Century Spiritualism and the Occult*. Farnham and Burlington: Ashgate, 2012.

Kopf, David. *British Orientalism and the Bengal Renaissance: The Dynamics of Indian Modernization, 1773–1835*. Berkeley and Los Angeles: University of California Press, 1969.

Kuzmin, Eugene. 'Maksimilian Voloshin and the Kabbalah'. In *Theosophical Appropriations: Esotericism, Kabbalah, and the Transformation of Traditions*, ed. Julie Chajes and Boaz Huss, 167–195. Beer Sheva: Ben-Gurion University Press, 2016.

Lachman, Gary. *Madame Blavatsky: The Mother of Modern Spirituality*. New York: Penguin, 2012.

Larsen, Timothy. *Crisis of Doubt: Honest Faith in Nineteenth-Century England*. Oxford: Oxford University Press, 2006.

Lasker, Daniel J., ed. *Jewish Thought and Jewish Belief*. Beer Sheva: Ben-Gurion University Press, 2012.

Lavoie, Jeffrey D. *The Theosophical Society: The History of a Spiritualist Movement*. Boca Raton, FL: Brown Walker Press, 2012.

Leijenhorst, Cees. 'Neoplatonism III: Since the Renaissance'. In *Dictionary of Gnosis and Western Esotericism*, ed. Wouter Hanegraaff, in collaboration with Antoine Faivre, Roelof van den Broek, and Jean-Pierre Brach, 841–846. Leiden and Boston: Brill, 2006.

Lenoir, Timothy. *The Strategy of Life: Teleology and Mechanics in Nineteenth-Century German Biology*. Dordrecht and London: D. Reidel, 1982.

Lev, Shimon. 'Gandhi and His Jewish Theosophist Supporters in South Africa'. In *Theosophical Appropriations: Esotericism, Kabbalah, and the Transformation of Traditions*, ed. Julie Chajes and Boaz Huss, 245–271. Beer Sheva: Ben-Gurion University Press, 2016.

Lewis, James R. 'Science and the New Age'. In *Handbook of the New Age*, ed. Daren Kemp and James R. Lewis, 207–229. Leiden: Brill, 2007.

Lightman, Bernard. *Victorian Popularizers of Science: Designing Nature for New Audiences*. Chicago and London: University of Chicago Press, 2007.

Long, Herbert Strainge. *A Study of the Doctrine of Metempsychosis in Greece from Pythagoras to Plato*. Princeton, NJ: Privately printed, 1948.

Lopez, Donald, ed. *A Modern Buddhist Bible: Essential Readings from East and West*. Boston: Beacon Press, 2002.

Lovejoy, Arthur O. *The Great Chain of Being*. Cambridge, MA, and London: Harvard University Press, 2001.

Lubelsky, Isaac. *Celestial India: Madame Blavatsky and the Birth of Indian Nationalism*. Oakville: Equinox, 2012.

Macfarlane, Robert. *Original Copy: Plagiarism and Originality in Nineteenth-Century Literature*. Oxford: Oxford University Press, 2007.

Mathiesen, Robert. *The Unseen Worlds of Emma Hardinge Britten: Some Chapters in the History of Western Occultism*. Fullerton: Theosophical History, 2001.

McCalla, Arthur. '*Palingenesie philosophique* to *Palingenesie sociale*: From a Scientific Ideology to a Historical Ideology'. *Journal of the History of Ideas* 55, no. 3 (July 1994), 421–439.

McMahan, David. 'Modernity and the Discourse of Scientific Buddhism'. *Journal of the American Academy of Religion* 72, no. 4 (2004), 897–933.

———. *The Making of Buddhist Modernism*. Oxford: Oxford University Press, 2009.

Mead, Marion. *Madame Blavatsky: The Woman Behind the Myth*. New York: G. P. Putnam's Sons, 1980.

Merchant, Carolyn. 'The Vitalism of Anne Conway: Its Impact on Leibniz's Concept of the Monad'. *Journal of the History of Philosophy* 17, no. 3 (July 1979), 255–269.

———. 'The Vitalism of Francis Mercury van Helmont: Its Influence on Leibniz'. *Ambix* 26, no. 3 (1979), 170–183.

Monroe, John Warne. 'Crossing Over: Allan Kardec and the Transnationalism of Modern Spiritualism'. In *Handbook of Spiritualism and Channeling*, ed. Cathy Gutierrez, 248–274. Leiden: Brill, 2015.

Moore, James R. *The Post-Darwinian Controversies*. Cambridge: Cambridge University Press, 1979.

———. 'The Crisis of Faith: Reformation vs Revolution'. In *Religion in Victorian Britain*, ed. Gerald Parsons and James R. Moore. Manchester: Manchester University Press, 1988. *Volume 2: Controversies*, 220–237.

———. 'Religion and Science'. In *The Cambridge History of Science: Volume 6, the Modern Biological and Earth Sciences*, ed. Peter J. Bowler and John V. Pickstone, 541–562. Cambridge: Cambridge University Press, 2009.

Morrisson, Mark S. *Modern Alchemy: Occultism and the Emergence of Atomic Theory.* Oxford: Oxford University Press, 2007.

———. 'The Periodical Culture of the Occult Revival: Esoteric Wisdom, Modernity, and Counter-Public Spheres'. *Journal of Modern Literature* 31, no. 2 (2008), 1–22.

Moulton, Edward C. 'The Beginnings of the Theosophical Movement in India, 1879–1885'. In *Religious Conversion Movements in South Asia,* ed. Geoffrey A. Oddie, 106–167. Richmond: Curzon, 1997.

Mukhopadhyay, Mriganka. 'The Occult and the Orient: The Theosophical Society and the Socio-Religious Space in Colonial India'. *Presidency Historical Review* 1, no. 2 (December 2015), 9–37.

———. 'A Short History of the Theosophical Movement in Bengal'. In *Paralok-Tattwa,* by Makhanlal Roychowdhury, 103–132. Kolkata: Bengal Theosophical Society, 2016.

———. 'Mohini: A Case Study of a Transnational Spiritual Space in the History of the Theosophical Society'. Forthcoming.

Myerson, Joel, ed. *A Historical Guide to Ralph Waldo Emerson.* Oxford: Oxford University Press, 2000.

Neff, Mary K., ed. *Personal Memoires of H. P. Blavatsky.* London: Rider, 1937. Kessinger photographic reprint.

Noakes, Richard. 'Spiritualism, Science, and the Supernatural in mid-Victorian Britain'. In *The Victorian Supernatural,* ed. Carolyn Burdett Nicola Bown and Pamela Thurschwell, 23–43. Cambridge: Cambridge University Press, 2004.

———. 'The Historiography of Psychical Research: Lessons from Histories of the Sciences'. *Journal of the Society for Psychical Research* 72, no. 2 (April 2008), 68–85.

Oppenheim, Janet. *The Other World: Spiritualism and Psychical Research in England, 1850–1914.* Cambridge: Cambridge University Press, 1985.

Owen, Alex. *The Darkened Room: Women, Power, and Spiritualism in Late Victorian England.* London: Virago Press, 1989.

Pasi, Marco. 'Exégèse et Sexualité: L'occultisme oublié de Lady Caithness'. *Politica Hermetica* 20 (2006), 73–89.

Pasi, Marco. *Kabbalah and Modernity: Interpretations, Transformations, Adaptations,* ed. B. Huss, M. Pasi, and Kocku von Stuckrad. Leiden and Boston: Brill, 2010.

Partridge, Christopher. 'Lost Horizon: H. P. Blavatsky and Theosophical Orientalism'. In *Handbook of the Theosophical Current,* ed. Olav Hammer and Michael Rothstein, 309–333. Leiden and Boston: Brill, 2013.

———, ed. *The Occult World.* Abingdon: Routledge, 2015.

Pedersen, Paul. 'Tibet, Theosophy, and the Psychologization of Buddhism'. In *Imagining Tibet,* ed. Thierry Dodin and Heinz Räther, 151–166. Boston: Wisdom Publications, 2001.

Poller, Jake. 'Under a Glamour: Annie Besant, Charles Leadbeater and Neo-Theosophy'. In *The Occult Imagination in Britain, 1875–1947*, ed. Christine Ferguson and Andrew Radford, 77–93. London: Routledge, 2018.

Pontiac, Ronnie. 'The Eclectic Life of Alexander Wilder: Alchemical Generals, Isis Unveiled, and Early American Holistic Medicine.' *Newtopia Magazine*, 15 Feb 2013. https://newtopiamagazine.wordpress.com/2013/02/15/the-eclectic-life-of-alexander-wilder-alchemical-generals-isis-unveiled-and-early-american-holistic-medicine/.

Prakash, Gyan. 'Orientalism Now'. *History and Theory* 34, no. 3 (October 1995), 199–212.

Prothero, Stephen. 'From Spiritualism to Theosophy: "Uplifting" a Democratic Tradition'. *Religion and American Culture* 3, no. 2 (Summer 1993), 197–216.

———. 'Henry Steel Olcott and "Protestant Buddhism"'. *Journal of the American Academy of Religion* 63, no. 2 (Summer 1995), 281–302.

———. *The White Buddhist: The Asian Odyssey of Henry Steel Olcott.* Bloomington: Indiana University Press, 1996.

Ramanujachary, N. C. *A Lonely Disciple: Monograph on T. Subba Row 1856–90.* Adyar: Theosophical Publishing House, 1993.

Ramstedt, Martin. 'New Age and Business'. In *Handbook of the New Age*, ed. Daren Kemp and James R. Lewis, 185–206. Leiden: Brill, 2007.

Ransom, Josephine. *A Short History of the Theosophical Society.* Adyar: Theosophical Publishing House, 1938.

Richards, Robert J. *The Meaning of Evolution: The Morphological and Ideological Reconstruction of Darwin's Theory.* Chicago and London: University of Chicago Press, 1992.

Rupke, Nicolaas. *Richard Owen: Biology without Darwin.* Chicago and London: University of Chicago Press, 1994.

Ruse, Michael. *Monad to Man: The Concept of Progress in Evolutionary Biology.* Cambridge, MA: Harvard University Press, 1996.

Ryan, Charles J. *H. P. Blavatsky and the Theosophical Movement.* Pasadena, CA: Theosophical University Press, 1975.

Said, Edward W. 'Orientalism Reconsidered'. *Cultural Critique* 1 (Autumn 1985), 89–107.

———. *Orientalism.* London: Penguin, 2003.

Santucci, James A. 'Blavatsky, Helena Petrovna'. In *Dictionary of Gnosis and Western Esotericism*, ed. Wouter Hanegraaff, in collaboration with Antoine Faivre, Roelof van den Broek, and Jean-Pierre Brach, 177–185. Leiden and Boston: Brill, 2006.

Sasson, Diane. *Yearning for the New Age.* Bloomington and Indianapolis: Indiana University Press, 2012.

Schlossberg, Herbert. *Conflict and Crisis in the Religious Life of Late Victorian England.* New Brunswick, NJ: Transaction Publishers, 2009.

Schmidt, Charles. 'Perennial Philosophy from Agostino Steuco to Leibniz'. *Journal of the History of Ideas* 27 (1966), 505–532.

Schmidt-Biggemann, Wilhelm. *Geschichte der christlichen Kabbala*. Stuttgart-Bad Cannstatt: Frommann Holzboog, 2015.

Schmidt-Leukel, Perry. *Transformation by Integration: How Inter-Faith Encounter Changes Christianity*. London: SCM Press, 2009.

Scholem, Gershom. *On the Mystical Shape of the Godhead*. New York: Schocken, 1991.

Schwab, Raymond. *Oriental Renaissance: Europe's Rediscovery of India and the East, 1680–1880*. New York: Columbia University Press, 1984.

Scott, J. Barton. 'Miracle Publics: Theosophy, Christianity, and the Coulomb Affair'. *History of Religions* 49, no. 2 (November 2009), 172–196.

Scott, J. Barton. *Spiritual Despots: Modern Hinduism and the Genealogies of Self-Rule*. Chicago: University of Chicago Press, 2016.

Seager, Richard Hughes. *The World's Parliament of Religions: The East/West Encounter, Chicago, 1893*. Bloomington and Indianapolis: Indiana University Press, 1995.

Sharf, Robert. 'The Zen of Japanese Nationalism'. *History of Religions* 33, no. 1 (August 1993), 1–43.

———. 'Whose Zen? Zen Nationalism Revisited'. In *Awakenings: Zen, the Kyoto School, and the Question of Nationalism*, ed. James W. Heisig and John Maraldo Rude, 40–51. Honolulu: University of Hawai'i Press, 1995.

Sharp, Lynn L. *Secular Spirituality: Reincarnation and Spiritism in Nineteenth-Century France*. Lanham, MD: Lexington Books, 2006.

Siémons, Jean-Louis. *Ammonius Saccas and His 'Eclectic Philosophy' as presented by Alexander Wilder*. Fullerton: Theosophical History, 1994.

Smart, Ninian. 'Indian Philosophy'. In *The Encyclopedia of Philosophy*, ed. Paul Edwards, 155–169. New York and London: Macmillan, 1967.

———. *World Philosophies*. London and New York: Routledge, 2008.

Spierenburg, Henk J. *The Buddhism of H. P. Blavatsky*. San Diego: Point Loma, 1991.

———, ed. *T. Subba Row, Collected Writings*. San Diego: Point Loma Publications, 2001.

Staal, J. F. *Advaita and Neoplatonism: A Study in Comparative Philosophy*. Madras: University of Madras, 1961.

Stuckrad, Kocku von. *The Scientification of Religion: A Historical Study of Discursive Change 1800–2000*. Boston and Berlin: De Gruyter, 2014.

Subba Row, T. 'The Twelve Signs of the Zodiac'. *The Theosophist* 3, no. 2 (Nov 1881), 41–44.

Sutcliffe, Steven, and Marion Bowman, eds. *Beyond New Age: Exploring Alternative Spirituality*. Edinburgh: Edinburgh University Press, 2000.

Tingay, Kevin. 'Madame Blavatsky's Children: Theosophy and Its Heirs'. In *Beyond New Age: Exploring Alternative Spirituality*, ed. by Steven Sutcliffe and Marion Bowman, 37–50. Edinburgh: Edinburgh University Press, 2000.

Tollenaere, Hermann A. O. de. *The Politics of Divine Wisdom: Theosophy and Labour, National, and Women's Movements in Indonesia and South Asia 1875–1947*. Leiden: Uitgeverij Katholiek Universiteit Nijmegen, 1996.

Trompf, Gary. 'Imagining Macrohistory? Madame Blavatsky from *Isis Unveiled* (1877) to *The Secret Doctrine* (1888)'. *Literature and Aesthetics* 21, no. 1 (June 2011), 43–71.

Turner, Franck M. *The Greek Heritage in Victorian Britain*. New Haven and London: Yale University Press, 1981.

———. *Contesting Cultural Authority: Essays in Victorian Intellectual Life*. Cambridge: Cambridge University Press, 1993.

Tyson, Joseph Howard. *Madame Blavatsky Revisited*. Lincoln, iUniverse, 2007.

Versluis, Arthur. *American Transcendentalism and Asian Religions*. New York: Oxford University Press, 1993.

———. *The Esoteric Origins of the American Renaissance*. Oxford: Oxford University Press, 2001.

Viswanathan, Gauri. 'Monism and Suffering: A Theosophical Perspective'. In *Monism: Science, Philosophy, Religion, and the History of a Worldview*, ed. Todd H. Weir, 91–106. New York: Palgrave Macmillan, 2012.

Vucinich, Alexander. *Darwin in Russian Thought*. Berkeley and Los Angeles: University of California Press, 1988.

Walter, Tony, and Helen Waterhouse. 'Lives-Long Learning: The Effects of Reincarnation Belief on Everyday Life in England.' *Nova Religio* 5, no. 1 (October 2001) 85–101.

Washington, Peter. *Madame Blavatsky's Baboon*. New York: Schocken Books, 1995.

Webster, Stephen. *Thinking about Biology*. Cambridge: Cambridge University Press, 2003.

Weir, Todd H. 'The Riddles of Monism: An Introductory Essay'. In *Monism: Science, Philosophy, Religion, and the History of a Worldview*, ed. Todd H. Weir, 1–44. New York: Palgrave Macmillan, 2012.

Whitehead, Alfred North. *Process and Reality: An Essay in Cosmology*. New York: Free Press, 1979.

Williams, Paul. *Mahāyāna Buddhism*. New York: Routledge, 2009.

Williams, Paul, with Anthony Tribe. *Buddhist Thought*. London and New York: Routledge, 2000.

Winchester, Jake B. 'Roots of the Oriental Gnosis: W. E. Coleman, H. P. Blavatsky, S. F. Dunlap'. Unpublished M.A. Thesis, University of Amsterdam, 2015.

Wortham, John David. *British Egyptology: 1549–1906*. Newton Abbot: David and Charles, 1971.

Yates, Frances. *The Rosicrucian Enlightenment*. London and New York: Ark Paperbacks, 1986.

Yoshinaga, Sin'ichi. 'Theosophy and Buddhist Reformers in the Middle of the Meiji Period: An Introduction'. *Japanese Religions* 34, no. 2 (2009), 119–131.

———. 'Three Boys on a Great Vehicle: "Mahayana Buddhism" and a Trans-National Network'. *Contemporary Buddhism: An Interdisciplinary Journal* 14, no. 1 (2013), 52–65.

Young, Robert M. 'The Impact of Darwin on Conventional Thought'. In *The Victorian Crisis of Faith*, ed. Anthony Symondson, 13–35. London: SPCK, 1970.

Zander, Helmut. *Geschichte der Seelenwanderung in Europa: Alternative religiöse Traditionen von der Antike bis Heute*. Darmstadt: Wissenschaftliche Buchgesellschaft, 1999.

Zander, Helmut. *Anthroposophie in Deutschland. Theosophische Milieus und gesellschaftliche Praxis, 1884 bis 1945*. Göttingen: Vandenhoeck and Ruprecht, 2007.

Zander, Helmut. 'Transformations of Anthroposophy from the Death of Rudolf Steiner to the Present Day'. In *Theosophical Appropriations: Esotericism, Kabbalah, and the Transformation of Traditions*, ed. Julie Chajes and Boaz Huss, 387–410. Beer Sheva: Ben-Gurion University Press, 2016.

Zirkoff, Boris de. *Blavatsky Collected Writings*. Wheaton, IL: Theosophical Publishing House, 1950–1991.

———. 'Dr. Alexander Wilder'. In *The Later Platonists and Other Miscellaneous Writings of Alexander Wilder*. Henry County, Ohio: Kitchen Press, 2009.

INDEX